GCSE
RELIGIOUS STUDIES

Catherine Lane
Lecturer in Religious Education
La Sainte Union College, Southampton

Letts
EDUCATIONAL

Every effort has been made to trace copyright holders and to obtain their permission for the use of copyright material. The authors and publishers will gladly receive information enabling them to rectify any error or omission in subsequent editions.

First published 1995

Letts Educational
Aldine House
Aldine Place
London W12 8AW
0181 743 7514

Text: © Catherine Lane 1995
Design and illustrations: © BPP (Letts Educational) Ltd 1995

All our Rights Reserved. No part of this publication may be reproduced, stored in a retrieval system, or transmitted, in any form or by any means, electronic, mechanical, photocopying, recording or otherwise, without the prior permission of Letts Educational.

British Library Cataloguing in Publication Data
A CIP record for this book is available from the British Library.

ISBN 1 85758 332 9

Printed in Great Britain by
WM Print Limited, Walsall, West Midlands WS2 9NE

Letts Educational is the trading name of BPP (Letts Educational) Ltd

Preface

This book will help you to prepare and revise for GCSE and Standard Grade Religious Studies exams for all of the exam syllabuses based on Christianity, Islam and Judaism and the complementary papers based on these religions' teachings on social, moral and ethical issues.

I have identified the key areas from all syllabuses and included charts so that you can check what you need to know for your course. This book is designed to help you – I have included advice on how you might revise for each topic, plus large bodies of information which you must know and show that you understand. There is no substitute for learning, as you must have the relevant information with which to answer questions. Furthermore, it is not enough to talk in general terms, you must also support what you say when you are giving an opinion. To help you do this you will find a scripture quotation or a church teaching alongside many explanations in the text. You should take the trouble to learn these – they are short so this should not be too difficult.

Read the chapters, act on the practical advice and continually test yourself using the quick tests and, as you near the exams, make use of the practice questions.

Thanks are accorded to the following Examining Groups for permission to reproduce questions from recent examinations and sample assessment material:

Midland Examining Group (MEG)
Northern Examinations and Assessment Board (NEAB)
Scottish Examination Board (SEB)
Southern Examining Group (SEG)
University of London Examinations and Assessment Council (ULEAC)

The answers given are my suggestions based on my knowledge as a teacher and examiner and are in no way the responsibility of the Examining Groups.

I wish to express my personal gratitude to Peter Lane, sounding board and mentor; to my wonderful colleagues of every persuasion in the Department of Theology at Queen Elizabeth's School, Wimborne who have been great encouragers; to my family – Marianne and Joseph who were tolerant of a busy mother – Elspeth who arrived in the middle – and Chris who took them all away when necessary. Finally thanks to everyone at Letts Educational for their guidance and support.

Photographs
These have been reproduced by kind permission of the following: Andes Press Agency p19, p29, p137, p139, p147. Keith Ellis Collection p138. Mary Evans Picture Library p22, p45, p79. Sonia Halliday Photographs p111, p118. Popperfoto p91. Peter Sanders Photography p64, p124, p125, p149. Topham Picturepoint p71, p99.

Illustrations on p62 and p147 are reproduced by kind permission of the Jewish National Fund.

Contents

Introduction	1
How to use this book	1
Religious studies at GCSE	2
Assessment objectives at GCSE	2
Assessment objectives at Standard Grade	3
Tiers of entry: Standard Grade	3
Syllabus analysis	4
Coursework	13
Examination Boards: addresses	14

SECTION 1 CHRISTIANITY

1	Christian beliefs	15
1.1	Jesus and His commandments	16
1.2	The Trinity	16
1.3	Jesus the Incarnation	16
1.4	The Resurrection	16
1.5	The Communion of Saints and forgiveness of sins	17
	Summary	17
	Quick questions	17

2	Christian sources of authority	18
2.1	The Bible	18
2.2	Authority gained by personal experience	19
	Summary	19
	Quick questions	20

3	Christian organisation	21
3.1	The Roman Catholic tradition	21
3.2	The Orthodox church	21
3.3	The Protestant churches	22
3.4	Ecumenism	23
3.5	Christians working together	23
3.6	The nature of the Church	24
	Summary	24
	Quick questions	25

4	Christian practices	26
4.1	Worship	26
4.2	Rites of passage	28
4.3	Festivals and feasts	30
4.4	Pilgrimage	32
4.5	Places of worship	33
	Summary	35
	Quick questions	36

5	Jesus and the Gospels	37
5.1	Using this chapter	37
5.2	The person of Jesus	37
5.3	The importance of the Gospels	38
5.4	Mark's Gospel	39
5.5	Luke's Gospel	47
5.6	Matthew's Gospel	53
5.7	The miracles of Jesus	56
	Summary	57
	Quick questions	58

SECTION 2 CONTEMPORARY ISSUES

6	Personal and social relationships	59
6.1	Christian approaches	59
6.2	Focus on Judaism	61
6.3	Focus on Islam	63
	Summary	64
	Quick questions	65

7	Personal and social issues	66
7.1	Christian approaches	66
7.2	Focus on Judaism	68
7.3	Focus on Islam	68
	Summary	69
	Quick questions	69

8	Prejudice and discrimination	70
8.1	Prejudice	70
8.2	Discrimination	73
8.3	Freedom of religious practice	74
8.4	Prejudice within the religions	74
8.5	The Holocaust	74
8.6	Religious teachings	75
	Summary	75
	Quick questions	76

9	Peace and conflict	77
9.1	Christian approaches	77
9.2	Focus on Judaism	81
9.3	Focus on Islam	81
	Summary	82
	Quick questions	82

10	Law and order in society	83
10.1	State responsibilities and Christian teaching	83
10.2	Focus on Judaism	85
10.3	Focus on Islam	85
	Summary	86
	Quick questions	87

11	Poverty and environmental issues	88
11.1	Causes of poverty	88
11.2	Christian responses to world poverty	89
11.3	Focus on Judaism	90
11.4	Focus on Islam	91
	Summary	92
	Quick questions	92

12	Work and leisure	93
12.1	Christian approaches	93
12.2	Focus on Judaism	95
12.3	Focus on Islam	95
	Summary	96
	Quick questions	96

13	Religion and the State	97	16.7	Kashrut (food laws)	117
13.1	Christianity in England	97	16.8	The synagogue	118
13.2	Focus on Judaism	100		Summary	119
13.3	Focus on Islam	100		Quick questions	119
	Summary	101			
	Quick questions	102	SECTION 4 ISLAM		

Contemporary issues in society
(table of passages) 103

SECTION 3 JUDAISM

14	Jewish beliefs	105
14.1	The Torah	105
14.2	Covenant with Abraham	105
14.3	Jacob called Israel	105
14.4	A 'Kingdom of priests, a holy nation' (Exod. 19:1–15)	105
14.5	The Messianic Age	106
	Summary	107
	Quick questions	107

15	Sources of authority in Judaism	108
15.1	The Tenakh	108
15.2	The Torah	108
15.3	The Noahide code	108
15.4	Nevi'im – books of the prophets	109
15.5	Ketubim (writings)	109
15.6	The Talmud	109
15.7	The Mishnah	109
15.8	Maimonides	110
15.9	Midrash	110
15.10	Authority from people	110
	Summary	111
	Quick questions	112

16	Practice and organisation in Judaism	113
16.1	Different traditions	113
16.2	Differing cultures	113
16.3	Worship	114
16.4	Festivals	115
16.5	Rites of passage	117
16.6	Pilgrimage	117

17	Islamic beliefs	121
17.1	Tawhid	121
17.2	Rusulullah	121
17.3	Akhirah	122
	Summary	122
	Quick questions	122

18	Sources of authority in Islam	123
18.1	The Qur'an	123
18.2	The Prophet Mohammed	124
	Summary	125
	Quick questions	126

19	Islamic practices	127
19.1	The five pillars	127
19.2	Festivals	130
19.3	Rites of passage	131
	Summary	132
	Quick questions	132

20	Organisation in Islam	133
20.1	The caliphs	133
20.2	The Shari'ah	134
20.3	Alternative ways	134
	Summary	134
	Quick questions	135

Appendix: Picture stimulus 136

Examination questions 143

Examination answers 154

Glossaries 166
Christian glossary 166
Judaism glossary 169
Islam glossary 171

Index 174

Introduction

How to use this book

This book has been written to help you prepare for GCSE and Standard Grade Religious Studies Examinations. It provides:

- Hints on how best to use the book during your preparation and revision for the exam.

- Information about GCSE in England, Wales and Northern Ireland, and Standard Grade in Scotland.

- Tables explaining what your syllabus requires in the *Syllabus Analysis* section (pages 4–13). Advice on how to use these tables is given below. This book covers all GCSE and Standard Grade syllabuses on Christianity, Islam and Judaism. It has special sections to cover the information needed for papers on Roman Catholic Christianity set by ULEAC, NEAB, SEG and WJEC. It also gives the Roman Catholic teaching and perspective on contemporary social issues alongside the general Christian attitudes and the teachings in Islam and Judaism.

- A table showing the appropriate Scripture passages you should be familiar with for the relevant areas of your syllabus (pages 103–4).

- Twenty chapters of text designed to cover as much as possible of the information you may need to use in your examination and coursework.

- A special chapter (Chapter 5) covering the life of Jesus and showing specific Gospel references and their applications.

- A summary at the end of each chapter picking out key facts and ideas which act as starting points for deeper study of each theme.

- A quick test at the end of each chapter to help you memorise key points so that you can include the correct information in your examination answers.

- Longer questions from examination papers and sample material.

- Examples of essay questions requiring answers in extended prose.

- Suggested answer structures for exam questions.

- Clear guidance on how to write an extended essay answer.

- A glossary of religious words with the spelling used by SCAA and any alternative spellings you may have been given plus a definition of the word. Other important words or terms are fully explained in the text.

- Indications of coursework requirements and information which can be used for coursework assignments.

Using the tables

1. Find the table which gives the syllabus you are following.
2. Make sure you understand what you are expected to do.
3. Look at the table showing Scripture passages and highlight the ones you need to be familiar with.

Using the chapters, quick tests and longer questions

Revision must be an active exercise. No matter how many times you read something, until you test yourself, you won't know what you have learnt. This is the way to proceed:

1. When you have identified the chapters you need, read one carefully.
2. Look at the quick questions and re-read the chapter.
3. Using the chapter, answer the questions.
4. Check your answers.
5. Answer the questions again without looking at the chapter.
6. Check your answers again.
7. Look up any you couldn't do, and then re-test.
8. Keep re-testing until you can answer all the questions without hesitation.

Note: The answers to all the quick questions are immediately available in the relevant summary of the chapter

Religious studies at GCSE

Religious Studies is not a National Curriculum subject but every student has to study Religious Education. If you are sitting GCSE you may have chosen it as an option; or you may attend a school where it is compulsory for all students to enter GCSE in Religious Studies. You will not find National Curriculum levels of attainment applied in Religious Studies but SCAA has set out clear rules about how the subject should be examined and the kind of things syllabuses should contain. GCSE Religious Studies is therefore at the same level of attainment as all other GCSE subjects.

When studying, remember that your examiner will be assessing how far you have reached the ASSESSMENT OBJECTIVES, which are the purpose of your studying the subject.

Assessment objectives at GCSE

RS 1   To demonstrate *knowledge* and *understanding* of the key elements of (a given religion) including *beliefs, practices, sources of authority* and *organisation*.

RS 2   To demonstrate *knowledge* and *understanding* of the effect of (a given religion) on individual or corporate *moral behaviour, attitudes, social practices and lifestyles*.

RS 3   To produce *evidence* and *arguments* to support and evaluate points.

The examination tables on pages 4–13 will tell you what balance in the assessment objectives is tested in each element of the course.

Assessment objectives at Standard Grade

Performance is assessed by demonstration of:

1. *Knowledge and understanding.* Pupils should be able to demonstrate knowledge and understanding of specified sources and current practice in Christianity and one other world religion, and also in specified issues of belief and morality in relation to religion and contemporary society.
2. *Evaluating.* Pupils should be able to consider the implications of religious concepts, practices and viewpoints for the individual and society today. They should be able to express and justify an opinion on religious and moral issues.
3. *Investigating.* Pupils should be able to plan the investigation; conduct the investigation; and present a report with conclusions.

Tiers of entry: Standard Grade

Standard grade is offered at Foundation, General and Credit levels and your final award will be given according to an average score that you attain across the assessment objectives. You should decide with your teacher which level/levels to attempt, from:

- Foundation only
- Foundation and General
- General and Credit

Syllabus analysis

University of London Examinations and Assessment Council (ULEAC)

Band A: Core studies

Unit 1 Christianity
Unit 2 Christianity (RC)
Unit 3 Islam
Unit 4 Judaism

Band B: Extension (Issues and texts)

Unit 5 Christianity – Contemporary Issues arising from Mark's Gospel
Unit 6 Islam
Unit 7 Judaism

Candidates will study their chosen religion in A and B (no mixing of faiths)

ULEAC 1477

Examination	
Paper numbers	1
Time	2 hours
% of total	80
Types of question	
Short answer	
Structured extended prose	✓
Extended essay	
Picture/stimulus	

Coursework	
Number of assignments	4
% of total	20
Length of assignments	1,000

Band B units concern contemporary issues with special reference to Mark's Gospel (Unit 5), the Qur'an (Unit 6) and Tanakh Siddur (Unit 7). The written paper includes all seven units. Candidates must answer questions on each of the two units they have studied, *either* two Christian units from Band A or Unit 5 + 1 or 2, Unit 6 + 3 or Unit 7 + 4.

Northern Examinations and Assessment Board (NEAB)

Syllabus A – Multi-faith

Candidates study two of:

- Christianity;
- Buddhism;
- Hinduism;
- Islam;
- Judaism;
- Sikhism.

Each part contains a combination of three objectives.

NEAB Syllabus A

Examination	
Paper numbers	2 of 1–6
Times	$1\frac{3}{4}$ h each
% of total	40 + 40
Types of question	
Short answer	✓
Structured extended prose	✓
Extended essay	
Picture/stimulus	✓
% of assessment objective	RS 1 32 RS 2 28 RS 3 20

Coursework	
Number of assignments	2
% of total	20
Length of assignments	
% of assessment objective	RS 1 83 RS 2 7 RS 3 5

Introduction

Syllabus B

Paper 1

One from:
1a Christianity
1b Christian belief and practice (RC tradition)
1c The Christian Life and the Gospel of Mark

Paper 2

One from:
2a Effects of Christianity on behaviour, attitudes and lifestyles
2b Effects of RC tradition on BAL

NEAB Syllabus B
Christian belief and practice

Candidates study for 2 written papers

Forbidden combination: 1A and 2B

Examination	
Paper numbers	1 + 2
Times	$1\frac{3}{4}$ h each
% of total	40 + 40
Types of question	
Short answer	✓
Structured extended prose	✓
Extended essay	
Picture/stimulus	✓
% of assessment objective	RS 1 32 RS 2 28 RS 3 8 + 12

Coursework	
Number of assignments	2
% of total	20
Length of assignments	Not specified
% of assessment objective	RS 1 8 RS 2 7 RS 3 2 + 3

Syllabus C – Christian belief and practice (modular)

A balance of modules encompassing different aspects of Christian belief and effects thereof. Candidates sit different modules depending on tier.

NEAB Syllabus C
Christian belief and practice (modular)

Candidates study:

One core module –
Section 1A (Tier R)
Section 1B (Tier P or Q)

Section 1A – The human condition
Section 1B – The liturgical year

Section 2 (all tiers) – Jesus Christ

Section 3 (all tiers) – New principles of Christian living

Optional modules:

1 = Christian Mission
2 = Christian Spiritual Life
3 = Christian Vocation
4 = Topics from history of the Church
P 1 of 1, 2, 3
Q 2 of 1, 2, 3
R 3 of 1, 2, 4

Tiers available	P	Q	R
Paper numbers (by tier)	P × 1	Q × 1	R × 1
Times	1½ h	2 h	2 h
% of total	50	50	50
Types of question			
Short answer	✓	✓	
Structured extended prose	✓	✓	✓
Extended essay			
Picture/stimulus	✓	✓	✓
% of assessment objective		RS 1 22 RS 2 17 RS 3 11	
Coursework			
Number of assignments	2	2	2
% of total	10 + 10	10 + 10	10 + 10
Length of assignments	Not specified	Not specified	Not specified
% of assessment objective		RS 1 6 RS 2 6 RS 3 8	
Modular test no.	1	2	3
Time	1 × 45 min	2 × 45 min	3 × 45 min
% of total	30	15 + 15	10 + 10 + 10
% of assessment objective		RS 1 12 RS 2 12 RS 3 6	

Midland Examining Group (MEG)

1 Christianity through a study of Luke and Acts
2 Christian perspectives on personal, social and world issues
3 Christianity
4 Hinduism
5 Islam
6 Judaism
7 Sikhism

Candidates submit two papers: any combination except 1 & 3

MEG Syllabus 1730

Examination	
Paper numbers	2 of 1–7
Times	$1\frac{1}{2}$ h
% of total	40 + 40
Types of question	
Short answer	
Structured extended prose	✓
Extended essay	
Picture/stimulus	✓
% of assessment objective	RS 1 16 + 16 RS 2 14 + 14 RS 3 10 + 10

Coursework	
Number of assignments	2
% of total	10 + 10
Length of assignments	1,500
% of assessment objective	RS 1 4 + 4 RS 2 3.5 + 3.5 RS 3 2.5 + 2.5

Southern Examining Group (SEG)

Syllabus A

Candidates study two from:
1 The Christian Church
2 Christian perspectives on contemporary issues
3 Christianity through the life and teaching of Jesus, as demonstrated in the synoptic Gospels.

Syllabus B – Inter-faith studies and ethics

Section A

A study of any two from:

- Buddhism,
- Christianity,
- Hinduism,
- Islam,
- Judaism,
- Sikhism.

Section B
A study of the ethical teachings of any two of named world faiths through themes:
Marriage and family
Peace and conflict
Humankind and nature

SEG Syllabuses A and B

Examination	
Paper numbers	1
Times	2 h
% of total	80
Types of question	
Short answer	✓
Structured extended prose	✓
Extended essay	✓
Picture/stimulus	✓
% of assessment objective	RS 1 32 RS 2 28 RS 3 20

Coursework	
Number of assignments	2
% of total	20
Length of assignments	1,500–2,000
% of assessment objective	RS 1 8 RS 2 7 RS 3 5

Syllabus C – Christianity according to the Roman Catholic tradition

1 Jesus Christ
2 Passion and Resurrection of Jesus (common to both papers)
3 Either St Luke's Gospel (public ministry) or Issues in Christian living
4 The Church
5 Life, marriage and the family

Candidates study 5 units for 2 exam papers

SEG Syllabus C

Examination	
Paper numbers	2
Times	1 h 15 min × 2
% of total	80
Types of question	
Short answer	✓
Structured extended prose	✓
Extended essay	
Picture/stimulus	
% of assessment objective	RS 1 18 + 18 RS 2 14 + 14 RS 3 8 + 8

Coursework assignments related to Unit 4 The Church or Unit 5 Life, marriage and family	
Number of assignments	2
% of total	20
Length of assignments	1,500–2,000
% of assessment objective	RS 1 4 RS 2 7 RS 3 9

Welsh Joint Education Committee (WJEC)

Group 1
- Christianity
- Christianity in the RC tradition

Group 2
- Further aspects of Christianity
- Christianity through the Gospels

Group 3
- Judaism
- Islam
- Hinduism
- Buddhism and Sikhism subject to demand

Candidates study one option from each of any two groups.

WJEC

Examination	
Paper numbers	2 options
Times	2 h
% of total	80
Types of question	
Short answer	✓
Structured extended prose	✓
Extended essay	
Picture/stimulus	✓
% of assessment objective	RS 1 40 RS 2 35 RS 3 25

Coursework	
Number of assignments	2
% of total	20
Length of assignments	500–750
% of assessment objective	RS 1 8 RS 2 7 RS 3 5

Northern Ireland Council for the Curriculum Examinations and Assessment (NICCEA)

Syllabus A (Paper 1A)

A Focus on Jesus through law, prophets, promise and community (40%)
and
B The Church in the modern world; its life and practice (15%)
and
Either marriage, home and family; Christian perspectives and response (15%)
Or service for others: Who is my neighbour? (15%)

Syllabus B (Paper 1B)

A Focus on Jesus through law, prophets, promise and community (40%)
and
B Another pattern of religious belief (30%), one of either Hinduism, Judaism or Islam. (Extension Paper Syllabus A and B to differentiate candidates with questions of greater depth and detail.)

Syllabus C

A Aspects of life and ministry of Jesus in the Synoptic Gospels (40%)
and
B The Church in the modern world; its life and practice (15%)
and
Either marriage, home and family; Christian perspectives and response. (15%)
Or service for others; Who is my neighbour? (15%)

NB In all cases Section A is 40% and Section B 30% of total mark.

NICCEA
Syllabus A, B, C

Tiers available	Common Paper	Extension
Grades	C–G	A–G
Paper numbers	1	1
Times	2½ h	1½ h
% of total	70	For differentiation
Types of question		
Short answer	✓	
Structured extended prose		✓
Extended essay		
Picture/stimulus	✓	
% of assessment objective	K 40 U 20 E 10	K 35 U 40 E 25
Coursework		
Number of assignments	6	
% of total	30	
Length of assignments	500–1000	
% of assessment objective	K 5 U 15 E 10	

Scottish Examination Board (SEB)

Candidates study:

Unit 1 Christianity
Unit 2 Judaism or Islam or Hinduism
Unit 3 Issues of belief
Unit 4 Issues of morality

Investigation relating to belief or morality

SEB Standard Grade

Tiers available	**Credit**	**General**	**Foundation**
Paper numbers	Credit	General	Foundation
Times	$1\frac{1}{4}$ h	$1\frac{1}{4}$ h	$1\frac{1}{4}$ h
Types of question			
Short answer			
Structured extended prose	✓	✓	✓
Extended essay			
Picture/stimulus	✓	✓	✓
Assessable elements	\multicolumn{3}{c}{K + U 33 / E 33}		
Investigation			
Number and length of assignments	1 × 500–1,000 words	1 × 500–1,000 words	1 × 500–1,000 words
% of assessment objective	\multicolumn{3}{c}{Investigating 33}		
% of total	\multicolumn{3}{c}{3 assessable elements have equal worth – grade reflects mean of 3 marks given for each element}		

Candidates may sit:
foundation only   Grades 7, 6, 5
F + G   Grades 3, 4, 5, 6
G + C   Grades 1, 2, 3, 4

Coursework

You can see from the tables for your syllabus how many coursework assignments (and their lengths) you are required to produce.

The titles will be set by your teacher and approved by the Exam Board. After that it is your responsibility to make sure you understand which assessment objectives, in which proportion, are being examined in which assignments – and work to those.

If at any point you are not sure, ask your teacher.

Many of the points which apply for the exam apply for coursework also. Always support what you say by using the appropriate teaching from the church, from Scripture or from your own experience.

Aim to produce the recommended amount and try to be original in your presentation.

Use any help you can, including your school and local libraries; the local minister and the congregation; friends; family and parents. If necessary, plan ahead and write to agencies for assistance. Addresses for these are available through the library service.

Examination Boards: addresses

To obtain syllabuses, past examination papers and further details, write to your Examining Group.

MEG **Midland Examining Group**
1 Hills Road
Cambridge
CB1 2EU

Tel: 01223 553311

NEAB **Northern Examinations and Assessment Board**
12 Harter Street
Manchester
M1 6HL

Tel: 0161 953 1180

NICCEA **Northern Ireland Council for the Curriculum Examinations and Assessment**
Beechill House
42 Beechill Road
Belfast
BT8 4RS

Tel: 01232 704666

SEB **Scottish Examination Board**
Ironmills Road
Dalkeith
Midlothian
EH22 1LE

Tel: 0131 663 6601

SEG **Southern Examining Group**
Stag Hill House
Guildford
GU2 5XJ

Tel: 01483 506506

ULEAC **University of London Examinations and Assessment Council**
Stewart House
32 Russell Square
London
WC1B 5DN

Tel: 0171 331 4000

WJEC **Welsh Joint Education Committee**
245 Western Avenue
Cardiff
CF5 2YX

Tel: 01222 265000

Chapter 1
Christian beliefs

Christians are people who believe in Jesus Christ and accept Him as their personal Lord and saviour, the guide and focus of their lives. They try to follow the way that Jesus showed in His life on earth and through His teaching. Over the centuries followers have developed different ways of explaining their beliefs about Jesus and formed different Christian denominations.

The beliefs of all Christians are set out in the Apostles' Creed.

I believe in God, the Father Almighty, maker of heaven and earth.
I believe in Jesus Christ, His only Son, Our Lord.
He was conceived by the Holy Spirit and born of the Virgin Mary.
He suffered under Pontius Pilate, was crucified, died, and was buried.
He descended to the dead.
On the third day he rose again from the dead.
He ascended into heaven, and he sits at the right hand of the Father Almighty.
He will come again to judge the living and the dead.
I believe in the Holy Spirit,
the holy catholic church,
the communion of saints,
the forgiveness of sins,
the resurrection of the body,
and the life everlasting.

The Nicene Creed

We believe in one God,
the Father, the almighty,
maker of heaven and earth,
of all that is, seen and unseen

We believe in One Lord, Jesus Christ,
the only Son Of God,
eternally begotten of the Father,
God from God, Light from Light,
true God from true God,
begotten not made,
of one being with the Father.
Through Him all things were made.
For us men and for our salvation
he came down from heaven;
by the power of the Holy Spirit
he became incarnate of the Virgin Mary and was made man.
For our sake he was crucified under Pontius Pilate;
he suffered death and was buried.

On the third day he rose again
in accordance with the Scriptures;
he ascended into heaven
and is seated at the right hand of the Father.
He will come again in glory
to judge the living and the dead,
and his kingdom will have no end.

We believe in the Holy Spirit,
the Lord, the giver of life,
who proceeds from the Father and the Son.
With the Father and the Son he is worshipped and glorified.
He has spoken through the prophets.

We believe in one holy catholic and apostolic Church.
We acknowledge one baptism for the forgiveness of sins.
We look for the resurrection of the dead,
and the life of the world to come. Amen.

These are the fundamental beliefs on which all Christians base their faith in Jesus Christ.

Chapter 1 Christian beliefs

1.1 Jesus and His commandments

The most important commandments that Jesus gave to His followers were:

- 'You must love the Lord your God with all your heart, with all your soul, with all your mind and with all your strength,' and
- 'You must love your neighbour as yourself.'

Jesus taught that there was no other commandment greater than these and they underline Christian belief.

Seemingly the words of the creed stand clearly on their own as a statement of beliefs. However, depending on the Christian denominations to which they belong, different people might understand the words to have slightly different meanings.

1.2 The Trinity

Christians believe in the trinitarian nature of God. It is a mystery of faith that there can be three persons in one God. These are the Father, Son and Spirit and each one is the same yet different.

God the Father

The Father is the creator of all things and is all powerful, all knowing and all loving. He is also the 'Daddy', often called *Abba*. He loves unconditionally and is Father of all.

God the Son

The Son is the incarnation of the Father, the promised Messiah, accepted by Christians as Saviour and Lord. Jesus is uniquely, fully God and fully man, human and divine.

God the Spirit

The Spirit is the giver of life and lives in all Christians as they try to do the work of God. He brings strength and courage.

1.3 Jesus the Incarnation

Jesus was conceived of the Holy Spirit and born of the Virgin Mary. He was crucified under Pontius Pilate. It had been prophesied in the Old Testament that the Messiah would have to suffer and die. Christians believe that when the Son of God was crucified it was to atone for the sins of all mankind. By his death he saved all mankind and showed them the way to eternal life through dedication to the will of God.

1.4 The Resurrection

The resurrection is the hope for all Christians. Different people may believe in the resurrection in slightly different ways but in essence it means life after death. Jesus rose from the tomb and was to be found really among the living. He then went up to heaven where He awaits the time of final judgement, when He will return. The Apostles' Creed professes belief in the resurrection of the body. Some Christians see this as meaning they will be recognisable in the same physical body after death but others see it as more an affirmation that the spirit of a person lives forever.

The holy catholic church refers to the universal Christian church of all followers of Jesus.

1.5 The Communion of Saints and forgiveness of sins

The Communion of Saints is all those who have died and gone before into heaven and are believed by many Christians to be in a position to intercede for others. Christians believe that their sins can be forgiven provided they repent and show firm purpose of amendment. In the Roman Catholic tradition it is also important to make an act of penance, which may be prayers or an act of self denial.

During the Roman Catholic Mass and Church of England communion services believers recite the Nicene Creed which contains the same beliefs spoken in a way which is more elaborate and in the nature of praise appropriate to worship.

Summary

1. Christian beliefs are expressed in the Nicene Creed and Apostles' Creed. Christians regularly recite both.
2. God is the all-powerful creator and Father of all mankind.
3. Jesus Christ is the incarnation of God, fully human and fully divine.
4. Jesus Christ is the Son of God and saviour of all mankind.
5. Jesus Christ was crucified, died and rose from the dead to ascend to heaven.
6. The Holy Spirit is manifest in the lives of individuals and in their actions.
7. The holy catholic church is the universal Christian church.
8. The Communion of saints are the faithful who have died and whom Christians believe to be with God.
9. Christians believe in forgiveness of sins and the resurrection of the body.
10. The most important commandments for all Christians are the two great commandments to love God and love your neighbour.
11. Christians believe in the trinitarian nature of God: the Father, Son and Spirit are all part of God.

Quick questions

1. In which prayers do Christians profess their faith?
2. What do Christians believe about God?
3. What do Christians believe about Jesus?
4. What do Christians believe about the Holy Spirit?
5. What do Christians understand by the Trinity?
6. How was salvation assured for all Christians?
7. What do Christians understand by the final judgement?
8. What is the basic Christian belief about life after death?
9. What are the two great commandments that a Christian should keep?

Chapter 2
Christian sources of authority

2.1 The Bible

The first and primary source of authority in Christianity is the Bible. The Bible is a 'library' of books comprising many different categories of writing including history; biography; legend; poetry; letters and psalms. The Old Testament is made up of 39 books of Jewish Scriptures and forms the roots out of which Christianity grew. It is therefore an essential part of Christian understanding and used widely in worship and prayer. The New Testament tells the story of Jesus and outlines the growth of the early Christian church.

The four Gospels are the most important part of the Bible for Christians. Gospel means 'good news' and these tell the good news about Jesus from the perspective of the writers. The Gospels of Matthew, Mark and Luke are all similar to one another and probably based on that of Mark which was written first in about AD 60. Because of their similarities these Gospels are known as the synoptic Gospels.

The New Testament also contains:

- The Acts of the Apostles, which tells of the growth of Christianity and the lives of the early martyrs.

- The thirteen letters of Paul to different communities telling them his thoughts about the life and teachings of Jesus. This was the interpretation on which the early church was based.

- Eight other letters by early Christian leaders.

- The 'Revelation of John', which was written to give inspiration to Christians facing persecution from Nero.

Different Christian denominations use the Bible in different ways in their corporate worship. Generally the Bible is revered and a service will contain Old and New Testament readings and a psalm. The Bible is not treated as sacred in the way the Jewish Torah or the Adi Granth (Sikh holy book) are regarded as sacred. This is because the person of Jesus is the most important aspect of Christianity.

In the Roman Catholic Mass there is usually a New and Old Testament reading, and a psalm, but part of one of the Gospels is read by the priest and for the reading the congregation stands as a mark of respect and recognition that they are hearing the Word of God.

Increasingly across all Denominations the idea that is found at the beginning of St John's Gospel – 'In the beginning there was God and the word was with God and God was the word' – has caused Christians to use the Gospel more as a vehicle of prayer, and the words are not only discussed and taught but they are prayed and meditated on.

As well as using the Scriptures in corporate worship Christians use them as part of communal worship: they join in communities to read, study and pray, using the Bible as a vehicle and an inspiration. The Bible can also be used for private prayer according to the needs of the individual. A pattern of prayer set out in a guide book can be followed, or people can follow readings which dwell upon appropriate themes answering particular needs or worries. Some Christians like to work their way methodically through the whole Bible, meditating on each part.

2.2 Authority gained by personal experience

Authority in religious terms does not always mean *people in charge* and *rules handed down*. Authority can imply a personal sense of belief. Thus the ways in which people come to religious belief become part of the authority. For the most part, religious belief can be regarded as completely intangible, but it is still convincing and powerful to millions.

People can come to religious belief by, for example, witnessing the faith of others, seeing or participating in worship or experiencing personal faith in times of great trouble. Belief can grow through revelation of what they perceive to be God working in their life or the lives of others – or in their friendships and personal relationships. Examples of the latter could be:

1. ways in which believers practise their faith by working with those in need;
2. ways in which believers allow their belief to guide their lives in work, relationships, child-rearing and decision-making;
3. witnessing the contentment that a believer might experience in trying to follow a way through life which he or she feels to be Christ-centred.
4. witnessing the strength and peace a believer finds in faith at times of enormous personal suffering.

A Bible meeting

Summary

1. The Bible is the Christian Holy Book and source of authority.
2. The Bible is a collection of books of different types of writing.

3 Christians regard the Old Testament as the story of the Jews' understanding of their history and the basis for Christian teaching.
4 The New Testament is the Good News about Jesus and the story of early Christianity.
5 The Bible is used in all forms of Christian corporate worship and readings are taken from all parts.
6 Christians use the Bible for private and group study and for prayer and reflection.
7 People recognise personal experience as a source of religious authority. How people live because of their professed belief is cited as a reason for following certain teachings.

Quick questions

1 How do Christians regard the Old Testament?
2 How do Christians use the Bible in corporate worship?
3 How would a Christian use the Bible for private prayer?
4 What does the word 'Gospel' mean?
5 Which are the synoptic Gospels?
6 Why are those Gospels synoptic?
7 How would people use personal experience as a source of authority in Christianity?

Chapter 3
Christian organisation

While the primary source of authority in the Christian church must always be what Christians accept as the teachings of Jesus Christ, inevitably as Christianity has grown and denominations have developed authority within the organisations has been accorded to some members of the Christian Church.

3.1 The Roman Catholic tradition

The head of the Roman Catholic church throughout the world is the Pope. Roman Catholicism is the single largest denomination, accounting for 61% of all Christians. The Pope is the bishop of Rome and is leader of the church as the recognised successor of the first Bishop of Rome, St Peter. Every pope gains this position by what is known as the Apostolic succession.

Authority in the Roman Catholic church is vested in the bishops. There is a hierarchical structure. Most countries have a cardinal who is the figurehead. Areas are then divided into dioceses, each one organised by a bishop. It is the role of the bishop to interpret the authoritative teaching of the church for his priests who will then disseminate it to the people.

This structure still exists yet since the Second Vatican Council (Vatican II, 1962–1965) the lay people have been consulted more widely about their views and have been part of policy-making processes, through groups such as parish councils.

Within the Roman Catholic tradition church members and leaders can refer to many written documents as sources of authority. There are Vatican documents on all subjects. There is a strict code of law, known as canon law, which relates to all church matters and is interpreted by trained and appointed canon lawyers.

3.2 The Orthodox church

The Orthodox church split from the Roman Catholic church in 1054 when the Pope's representative went to Constantinople and excommunicated the patriarch and the patriarch retaliated by excommunicating the Pope. Constantinople was the centre of the Eastern Church and over the years differences had grown between the Eastern and Western churches. The main one centred on the authority of the Pope, who believed himself to have authority over all bishops whereas the Orthodox bishops regarded all bishops as equal and responsible for key decisions. They also had disagreements about the wording of the creed, the use of different types of bread (the West used unleavened and the East ordinary bread), and the status of priests. In the Eastern church married men were able to become local priests.

The leaders of the Orthodox church are the patriarchs; there is one for each country, the senior one being the Patriarch of Constantinople. He does not have supreme authority but leads the others on important issues. Bishops and priests preside over the liturgy, which is when bread and wine is believed to be transformed into the body and blood of Christ.

The bishops have charge over a number of churches. They have been priests and are not married. In the Orthodox church a man should be 30 years old before he becomes a priest, and while a local priest may be married he will not go on to be a bishop. Once a man is a priest, he cannot get married; if he is married *before* becoming a priest and his wife dies while he is a priest, he may not marry again.

3.3 The Protestant churches

The Protestant churches arose out of protest against Roman Catholicism. Martin Luther posed 95 points for discussion about the corruption in the church, especially the practice of buying 'indulgences'. An 'indulgence' was believed to be granted through doing penance and brought about the forgiveness of sin. Catholics had been allowed to 'buy' them with bribes, thus doing away with the need to do Penance. Penances had been quite severe, especially in the middle ages when people might literally wear sack cloth and pour ashes on their heads and walk miles to pray for forgiveness at a shrine such as Walsingham. Luther was excommunicated for arguing that forgiveness could be obtained through individual prayer and that the Bible, not the church, was the source of authority for Christians. He had many followers and by his death in 1546 much of Germany, Denmark and Sweden were following a form of Christianity called Lutheran.

Martin Luther: burning the Papal Bull (1520)

Luther's ideas about the authority of the Bible were taken up by John Calvin in Switzerland and John Knox in Scotland. Because the ministers in Calvin's church were called presbyters, Knox's form of protestantism became known as Presbyterian.

These Protestant churches removed themselves from papacy and Roman tradition. They had no images in church. The Protestant Church of England was formed because

Henry VIII wanted to divorce Catherine of Aragon and marry Anne Boleyn. The Pope refused to allow this so Henry declared himself head of the Church in England.

Under Elizabeth I a prayer book was devised combining Protestant and Catholic ideas and the church became the Church of England or Anglican Church. Some Anglicans prefer the term Anglo-Catholic and are very close to Roman Catholicism in their belief and worship.

A group of puritans who rejected the Church of England as too Catholic formed free churches which were nonconformist, and from this group other denominations grew. The idea of a free church is that it is not connected to the state or any established state religion. These are the non-episcopal churches and, as with the Presbyterian churches, they have no bishops in authority. The lay people preach and read and lead services. A council of lay people makes decisions and forms policy about church organisation. Among the free churches are:

- *Congregationalists*, who formed a congregation with their own elected leaders and limited membership to committed Christians. (The Congregationalist and the Presbyterian churches joined together in 1960 to form the United Reformed Church.)
- *Baptists*, who believe that only those old enough to have made a conscious commitment to Christ should be baptised.
- *The Society of Friends or Quakers*, who believe religion means to follow personal conviction. They are absolute pacifists.
- *Methodists*, who were founded and led by John and Charles Wesley in the eighteenth century. Methodists began by joining together to study and pray methodically.
- *The Salvation Army*, begun by William Booth in 1865 to take Christ's message out to the poor in a healing and helping ministry.
- *Pentecostal churches*. These grew up in the twentieth century mainly in America from a tradition of preaching the Gospel through the fire of the Spirit. The largest is the Assemblies of God but many small evangelical church units have evolved from this tradition and are growing in popularity in England in the latter part of the century.

3.4 Ecumenism

Despite the large numbers of Christian denominations and the fact that new churches are emerging all the time, there is a strong movement in favour of church unity. This is the ecumenical movement. Church leaders meet regularly to concentrate on shared beliefs and ideals so that on common ground they can move forward together as much as possible. In practice this means that there are shared services and sometimes, in more remote areas, shared churches. Some schools are becoming joint church schools to emphasise the commonality of shared beliefs.

3.5 Christians working together

On a spiritual level Christians are able to share the **charismatic** movement which is embraced by some people of all denominations and emphasises spiritual gifts such as praying in tongues and healing in the Spirit. Christians come together at centres for spiritual enrichment through shared prayer and praise. This happens, for example, at Taize in France, which is known especially for sung prayers which are meditative chants.

On the wider scale Christians in many parts of the world (e.g. Africa and South America) have been united by the idea of **liberation theology**. (see page 99 for a definition of Liberation theology.) The Gospel is used in an effort to bring about justice and peace for the poor and oppressed. Liberation theology is promoted through teaching, through infiltrating the infrastructure of a country by working in schools and hospitals, and sometimes through active protest against the oppressors. Christians of all denominations have been martyred for their efforts to liberate the poor. A martyr is one who dies for what he or she believes in.

3.6 The nature of the Church

Despite differences in the nature of their leadership, Christians of all denominations share a common purpose. St Paul describes the church as the body of Christ on earth and *the work of the Christian church is to reveal Christ to the world*. This is mainly to be brought about through witness, which means the churches must try to unite in a way which enables them to work together to spread the good news in the world through teaching and practice. This is what Jesus would have taught.

It is for this latter reason that the churches are involved in social projects in Great Britain and the world. This involvement takes the form of work which helps all sectors of society in need, e.g. the aged, handicapped, unemployed and families in distress. Agencies such as Christian Aid and Cafod, the Church of England Children's Society and a plethora of local church groups play a leading part in providing this help.

In addition, local aid is given by church members and ministers. Enormous demands are made on ministers to counsel people in difficulty.

Summary

1. The Roman Catholic church has a clear hierarchical organisation headed by the Pope and followed by cardinals, archbishops, bishops and priests.
2. Authority vested in the bishops in the Roman Catholic Church is known as the Apostolic succession.
3. In the Orthodox church all have equal authority. The Bishop of Constantinople is the senior patriarch yet he has no extra authority except as a leader in any decision making.
4. In the Orthodox church married men can become priests but priests cannot marry or remarry. Only celibate priests become bishops.
5. The sovereign is head of the Church of England.
6. The governing body of the Church of England consists of bishops, clergy and laity and it is called the Synod.
7. Baptist chapels and churches are run by ministers and their congregations.
8. The United Reformed church is run by a general assembly, 12 synods and district councils.
9. Quakers do not have ministers but elect their own elders to take charge of meetings.
10. The Methodist church has superintendent ministers assisted by lay preachers. The country is divided into 900 circuits, each with a superintendent.
11. The Salvation Army uses military ranks for its ministers and there is a general in overall charge.
12. Ecumenism is a movement which aims to unite the Christian churches through what they hold in common.
13. The Christian churches are the body of Christ and all members work to bring Christ into the world through prayer and good works.
    This is known as Christian witness.

Quick questions

1. Draw a pyramid which shows the hierarchical organisation of the Roman Catholic Church.
2. What does the Apostolic succession mean?
3. What role does the senior patriarch have in the Orthodox church?
4. What is the difference between Roman Catholic priests and Orthodox priests?
5. How is the Church of England organised?
6. Which churches organise themselves in areas?
7. What is the main mission of the Salvation Army?
8. What is the nature of the Christian Church in the world?
9. What practical ways do churches have to help ecumenism?
10. How do certain agencies try to reveal the church to the world?

Chapter 4
Christian practices

4.1 Worship

Worship is understood by Christians to mean prayer and praise. People worship personally, in small faith groups or as a corporate body in a designated place of worship. The main form of Christian worship is the celebration of the Lord's Supper. This is given different names by different denominations.

Worship in the Orthodox Tradition

In the Orthodox Church the Lord's Supper is called The Liturgy; the bread is broken and the wine blessed using words similar to those in the Gospel. Those present believe that although the substance of the wine doesn't change, Christ becomes really present in a special way which cannot be understood because it is one of the mysteries of faith. Unusually, ordinary bread is used. Some of it is taken to the Holy Table and is called **prosphora**. The rest can be taken home by the congregation. This is called **antidoron** and is a reminder of early Christian Communion in which Christians shared meals together. Some worshippers only take the antidoron after the service because they feel the prosphora is so special it should only be taken on certain major feasts.

Orthodox believers also pray privately. They make the sign of the cross by moving the hand from head to chest,
then from right shoulder to left shoulder.
They use the thumb, index and middle fingers
to indicate the Trinity and have the ring and
little finger folded to remember the humanity
and divinity of Christ.

An important personal prayer for Orthodox Christians is a meditation using the words, 'Jesus, Son of God, have mercy on me, a sinner.' Believers will also use external stimuli to help them pray. Statues, pictures and icons are examples. These are a focus for the mind, as are candles and incense; these are used in church to create a prayerful atmosphere.

Worship in the Roman Catholic Tradition

Hail Mary, Full of Grace
The Lord is with you
Blessed are you among women
And blessed is the fruit of your womb, Jesus.
Holy Mary, Mother of God,
Pray for us sinners,
Now, and at the hour of our Death.
Amen

Roman Catholic Christians also use external stimuli as a help to personal prayer; they use statues and pictures of saints as well as images of nature to provoke thought. Believers are taught to pray through saints as intermediaries to the Father God. It is also common practice to pray through Mary, the mother of Jesus. She is held in the highest regard and there are many prayers which praise and honour her. The most widely used devotion to Mary is the rosary, a series of beads grouped into five sets of ten with a single bead between each ten. As the believer moves his hands onto each bead he intones a 'Hail Mary'. Each ten beads represent a 'mystery of the rosary'. In a whole rosary the prayer will consist of fifteen mysteries – five joyful, five sorrowful and five glorious. The idea is to enter into a meditative state through repetition of the prayer; this empties the mind and allows the believer to focus on the purpose of the prayer.

4.1 Worship

Vehicles to prayer are available to suit all types of people. There is a tradition of prayer through fasting, especially during lent and on the first Friday of every month. On such days some Catholic churches encourage the people to fast and pray and donate the proceeds to the hungry in the world. There are also many places of pilgrimage for Catholics in the world. A journey to Lourdes, Walsingham, Fatima, Medjugore or Knock, sustained by prayer, is another way in which a Catholic can come closer to God. In an informal way Catholics also worship individually and in groups. They may use the Bible, recite known prayers or join together in spontaneous prayer. Communities are at liberty to plan and carry out their own liturgies, including spiritual readings, hymns, prayers and even dance and drama.

Roman Catholics also have an active element in Worship, symbolised by bending the right knee (genuflection) before the Blessed Sacrament and making the sign of the cross. Roman Catholics genuflect each time they pass before the Blessed Sacrament. The sign of the cross is made with the right hand which touches:

- the forehead as the worshipper says, 'In the name of the father;
- the heart as he or she says, 'And of the Son';
- the left shoulder as is said, 'And of the Holy Spirit'; and
- the right shoulder as is said, 'Amen'.

This emphasises belief in the Trinity.

The Roman Catholic Mass

The most important aspect of Roman Catholic worship is the Mass; it is here that the bread and wine are consecrated. The Mass is divided into clear parts:

1. The penitential rite where participants ask God (and one another) for forgiveness for their sins.
2. The Liturgy of the word where they hear readings from the Old and New testaments, a psalm and a passage from the Gospel.
3. The liturgy of the Eucharist: the priest speaks the words of the last supper over the bread and wine and Catholics believe that the substance of the bread and wine are changed and become the body and blood of Jesus. This is the doctrine of 'transubstantiation'.
4. The Communion Rite. After the consecration all recite the Lord's Prayer. This is often called the 'Our Father' and is an essential part of the Mass as a further confirmation of belief. The consecrated bread is received as a sacrament called Holy Communion and is taken by all Catholics once they have been prepared and have received for the first time.

Take this all of you and eat it: this is My Body which will be given up for you.

Take this all of you and drink from it: this is the cup of My Blood, the blood of the New and Everlasting Covenant. It will be shed for you and for all men so that sins may be forgiven. Do this in memory of Me.

For centuries the Mass was spoken in Latin but today it is said (or celebrated) in the language of the worshippers, so that all can follow. The altar is close to the congregation to emphasise the idea of sharing a meal together. It is compulsory for all Roman Catholics to attend Mass on Sundays and many like to attend on other days also.

Worship in the Protestant Tradition

The Bible is the basis for worship in the Protestant churches. Services consist of readings, hymns and prayers and a recitation of the creed. Communion services are also held with varying regularity, depending on how *high* or *low church* the church community is. Protestants use the phrase *high church* to describe a community which is Anglo-Catholic and has retained regular communion and a service similar to that of the Mass in the Roman Catholic church – indeed it is sometimes called the Mass. A *low church* is likely to have communion services less frequently. The way services are conducted depends on the individual church tradition. They can be very quiet, sombre affairs or very lively, with much singing, dancing and loud praising such as occurs in the pentecostal churches.

The Lord's prayer of all Christians

Our Father, who art in heaven,
hallowed be your name;
your kingdom come;
your will be done;
on earth as it is in heaven.
Give us this day our daily bread.
And forgive us our trespasses,
as we forgive those who trespass against us.
And lead us not into temptation;
but deliver us from evil.

(In the Anglican tradition) For thine is the Kingdom, the power, and the glory, for ever and ever. Amen.

Protestant Eucharist

The Communion service is often called The Lord's Supper or Eucharist and there is the Liturgy of the Word when the Scriptures are read and then the blessing of the bread. The words of the last supper are used but in the Protestant tradition it is taught that this is in memory of Jesus, it is a re-enactment of the last supper and nothing mystical is thought to happen to the bread and wine. Communion services are held about once a week in the Anglican church and there is no compulsion to attend.

Worship in the Free Church Tradition

The Free churches place even greater emphasis on the Bible as a central part of worship. They have readings, hymns and periods for personal prayer either out loud or quietly. They do not recite the creed because a commitment to Christ is all that is necessary to be members of the community. Quakers have a simple silent ceremony where they 'quake' in the presence of God. Someone speaks only when moved by the Holy Spirit; believers might then read a passage, pray out loud or share a thought.

4.2 Rites of passage

Rites of passage are also sacraments. The Roman Catholic and Orthodox churches have seven of these while the Protestant churches recognise only two (baptism and marriage). A sacrament is an external ritual which signifies that an internal change of a spiritual dimension is believed to have occurred or be occurring for the participant.

Baptism

Baptism is common to the Roman Catholic, Orthodox and Protestant traditions. In the Orthodox baptism the baby is immersed in water, then dressed in white and anointed with oil. The priest uses the oil to make a cross on the forehead, eyelids, nostrils, ears, lips, chest, hands and feet, saying the words 'the seal of the gift of the Holy Spirit'. A lock of hair is taken to show the baby is committed to Christianity and he or she is given a cross to wear.

Once baptised, the child is a full member of the church and able to receive Communion. The chrismation (or anointing) takes the place of the Protestant confirmation. The actions are all symbolic. The water is a symbol of cleansing of sin and finding a new life in Jesus. The oil is chrism and it is a symbol of healing to confirm the child will grow strong in Christ.

In the Roman Catholic tradition membership of the church is by baptism. The parents choose godparents to help guide the child on the faith journey. They all present the child for baptism, affirm their faith (in renewing baptismal promises) and renounce evil on their own behalf and that of the child. The priest makes a sign of the cross on the baby's head; he uses a special oil called the oil of catechumens to signify the child is becoming a member of the Christian community. The child then has water which is blessed poured over the head as the priest says, 'I baptise you (name) in the name of the Father and of the Son and of the Holy Spirit, Amen.'

The child is often named after a saint of the church; this provides a positive role model for the infant. The baby is anointed with oil of chrism on the chest, and clothed with a white garment (baptismal shawl); the parents are given a candle which has been lit from the Paschal candle.

The water represents death to a life of sin and a new life in Jesus. The oil of catechumens is used to welcome new members and the chrism is holy oil used to anoint kings; chrism is a sign of special calling – that the child is to share in Christ's Kingdom. It is also a symbol of healing. The white garment is a symbol of purity: that the child is now without sin. The candle is a symbol of Christ the light of the world. It is lit from the Paschal candle.

Baptism is also a sacrament in the Church of England. The child is brought to the font and the minister reads from the Gospels about Jesus welcoming children. He prays for the child and the child's carers and addresses the parents about their responsibilities in the Christian upbringing of the child. The infant is then baptised with water as the priest says, 'I baptise you (name) in the name of the Father and of the Son and of the Holy Spirit. The child is then blessed and is officially a member of the church.

Some free churches and some ministers of the Protestant churches are opposed to infant baptism and practise believer's baptism. An adult or young believer is immersed in water and baptised in the name of the Father, Son and Spirit. The believer must be completely immersed as a sign of drowning to sin and being born again in Jesus. This practice has given rise to the term 'born again' Christian. Even some Christians who have been baptised as infants feel it is more important to be baptised as a believer.

Reconciliation/penance/confession

This Sacrament is part of the Faith Journey in the Roman Catholic and Orthodox churches.

The different names given to this Sacrament indicate its constantly changing nature. Originally *Confession* was for the sinner to confess (that is acknowledge) his or her sins before a priest and before God. Provided the sinner was prepared to make amends for the sin and was genuinely sorry and ready to promise to try not to sin again, it was recognised that the priest was able to grant absolution in the name of God. The emphasis was moved to *Penance* to show that the sinner was prepared to make amends for his or her wrongs. The term *Reconciliation* is now preferred. This is because it is understood that sin creates a barrier between people and between God and his children. To sin is to reject Jesus and turn away from God. Then, in recognising the sin and showing sorrow, a sinner is able to find forgiveness from God, to forgive self and thus be reconciled with the Father. It is still necessary to show sorrow and commitment to change but the emphasis is on forgiveness and a loving God, not a punishing God.

The practice of Confession is still continued in some branches of the Anglo-Catholic Protestant tradition.

Communion

Communion, the celebration of the Last Supper in the form of receiving bread and wine, is common to all Christians. It is the main focus of Christian worship. In the Roman Catholic Tradition believers are expected to receive the Body of Christ every Sunday. Children are taught that they should be 'free from sin' to receive. (This used to be known as 'a state of Grace'.) Before being permitted to receive Communion Roman Catholic children must be able to understand the meaning of Reconciliation. They are therefore normally at or beyond seven years of age, which is regarded as the age of reason.

In the Protestant tradition receiving Communion is seen as a mark of adult participation in the Faith and is allowed after confirmation. In both traditions the first occasion is marked by special ceremonies and followed by celebrations. People wear their best clothes and many young girls still wear white dresses.

There is no special initiation into this sacrament in the Orthodox church as all baptised members may receive.

First Holy Communion

Confirmation

Confirmation is practised in the Protestant and Roman Catholic traditions. In Confirmation a Christian is confirming the commitment to faith which was made on his or her behalf at baptism. The candidate is prepared by the faith community and should be capable of making a free and independent decision to be an adult follower of Christ. At the ceremony the candidate repeats the vows that were made at Baptism to renounce evil and accept Christ. The Bishop then lays his hands on the head of the candidate as a sign of the power of the Spirit coming upon him or her; the candidate is thus blessed and is regarded as a full member of the Christian church.

In the Church of England only confirmed Christians should receive communion. In Roman Catholicism children receive earlier. A candidate for confirmation has a sponsor who is a committed adult Christian. This person acts as companion and guide to the preparing and newly confirmed Christian.

In the Orthodox church Confirmation is part of Baptism. It is not an adult ceremony. If an adult becomes a Christian he or she can be baptised and confirmed at the same time.

Holy Orders

Being ordained as a priest is called receiving the Sacrament of Holy Orders in the Roman Catholic Church. Ordination is regarded as entering into a permanent state in the same way as someone making the marriage vows. Roman Catholic priests cannot be married and have a special role as spiritual leaders in the community. They are all male and only an ordained priest can celebrate the Mass and preside over the Eucharist.

Marriage

Marriage is a sacrament in all three Christian traditions and is regarded as a lifelong commitment. It ensures companionship and provides a secure and loving environment for children. (Marriage is described fully in Section 2, Chapter 6.)

Sacrament of the sick

This is a rite of passage available to Roman Catholics. In this rite a dying person is specially anointed with oil as prayers are said.

The Funeral rite

The final stage of life on earth in the Christian journey is death, and the passing of a believer from this life to eternal life is marked by a Christian funeral service. After death the body is washed and placed in a coffin which sometimes bears a Christian symbol. The coffin is taken to a church or chapel where the mourners meet. Prayers, readings, hymns and a sermon about death and resurrection and the life of the deceased form part of the service. There then follows either the cremation of the body or its interment in a consecrated graveyard.

The Roman Catholic funeral service is sometimes a special Mass called a Requiem Mass which has prayers and readings for the dead. During the service and at the point of committal to the ground the coffin is blessed with holy water as a sign of the cleansing of sins.

Christians all believe that every one of them can be reunited with Christ after death. The words of the ceremony reflect this as they remind all present that life is short and the body must be returned to the earth; but the person will rise again and enjoy eternal life which has been assured by the sacrifice of Jesus.

4.3 Festivals and feasts

The most important Christian festival is Easter and this is preceded by a period of preparation called Lent. Lent lasts for six weeks and is reminiscent of the time Jesus spent in the desert wilderness undergoing temptation.

4.3 Festivals and feasts

Shrove Tuesday

Lent begins one day after Shrove Tuesday or 'Fat' Tuesday. It is traditional to use up all fat and sugar in the house in preparation for fasting: hence the Christian orgy of eating pancakes with tasty fillings.

Ash Wednesday

Ash Wednesday marks the beginning of Lent. Some Christians – i.e. Roman Catholics and high Anglicans – may receive a cross of ashes on the forehead and are reminded that it is their duty to repent of their sins and believe the Gospels.

During Lent adult Christians focus on how they can change their lives and become closer to Christ. This is attempted through prayer, sacrifice and good works such as almsgiving and charity. Lent is immediately followed by Palm Sunday when the triumphant entry of Jesus into Jerusalem is re-enacted in churches. The following week is Holy Week during which devout Christians enter into remembrance of Christ's passion and death.

Holy Week (students should also refer to the Gospels account of Jesus' passion and death.)

Spy Wednesday
This day recalls the betrayal of Jesus by Judas.

Maundy Thursday
Maundy Thursday is in memory of the Last Supper. Some believers attend special communion services and often the priests wash the feet of some of the congregation as a sign of humility. In the Church of England the Queen distributes specially minted Maundy pennies to the poor.

Good Friday
This is the day on which the death of Christ is remembered. Many churches have services at 3 o'clock when *the passion* is read from the Gospel and the faithful depart in silence after reading of Christ's death on the cross.

In Roman Catholic churches these services are always Masses and include a ritual of venerating the cross in which believers kiss the feet of Christ on a crucifix. Christians follow the tradition on this day of eating Hot Cross Buns: spiced buns with crosses on them.

Holy Saturday
On Holy Saturday the resurrection of Jesus is celebrated after sundown and Easter has begun. The vigil service takes place and the Easter (paschal) candle is lit from a special fire as a sign of the light of Christ. At the Easter vigil the faithful repeat their baptismal vows and rejoice with hymns, reading and prayers in the risen Christ who they believe is truly alive today.

Easter Sunday
Easter Sunday is a day on which many Christians attend church even if they have not done so throughout the year. At Easter Sunday services the Gospels of the resurrection are read and prayers and hymns of rejoicing in the risen Lord form the most important services of the year. The church is decorated with many flowers symbolising spring and new life.

On Easter Sunday throughout the Christian world millions of people exchange chocolate eggs. The eggs are a symbol of new life. In some parts of the world eggs are rolled down hills as a sign of the stone rolling away from the tomb.

All Roman Catholics are obliged to receive the sacraments of reconciliation and Eucharist at some point during the Easter period. This is known as the Easter Duty.

The Ascension

The Ascension of Our Lord into heaven is celebrated six weeks after Easter and Christians read the Gospel accounts at services or Mass.

'And so the Lord Jesus, after He had spoken to them, was taken up into heaven ...' (Mark 16:19).

Pentecost

Pentecost, usually called Whitsun, is celebrated several weeks after Easter. Christians recall when the Holy Spirit visited the terrified disciples. The Gospel accounts speak of a roaring wind and the appearance of tongues of fire. The disciples received the gift of tongues and were able to spread the good news about Jesus to people of all nationalities.

It is important for Christians today that the power of Jesus was seen to return in the form of the Holy Spirit and it is this almost invisible force that many Christians are able to relate to as the real presence of God in the world. Many believers call on the Spirit in prayer to help them find courage and strength and wisdom.

Advent

The second most important celebration for Christians is advent, leading up to Christmas. Advent begins five Sundays before Christmas and literally means 'coming towards'. During advent Christians can reflect upon their beliefs in the light of the impending celebration of the birth of Jesus. It is traditional to have advent wreaths of five candles. By lighting one each Sunday Christians offer a reminder of the light that is about to enter the world.

Christmas is celebrated with religious services. Old Testament prophecies of the coming of the Messiah are read; New Testament stories of the nativity are told; and traditional Christmas carols are sung. Presents are exchanged on Christmas Day.

The Epiphany

Christmas is followed by the celebration of the Epiphany when the wise men visited Jesus. This is to show that Christ came to save all the world.

Harvest Festival

In September it is becoming more widespread to celebrate the Harvest. This is done particularly now in the affluent world to thank God for the bounty that is enjoyed, raise awareness of the hunger in the world and use harvest time to contribute to helping those in need of food.

4.4 Pilgrimage

Christianity is a journey into Christ – a journey which mirrors every Christian's mystery journey through life. As a Christian grows and changes so he or she tries to move nearer to Christ. A believer's ultimate hope is to be completely at one with Him in eternity. While on the journey Christians may use the physical act of pilgrimage to help them focus on the need for spiritual nourishment. Any place of holy significance is an appropriate destination for pilgrimage. Thus Christians journey to the Holy Land, to Bethlehem and Jerusalem. Other important destinations are:

- Lourdes, where St Bernadette saw a vision of the Virgin Mary and a healing spring was revealed.
- Walsingham in England, site of Anglican and Roman Catholic shrines to the Virgin Mary.
- Medjugore in Bosnia and Fatima in Portugal, where visions of the Virgin Mary were seen and secret prophecies given.
- Lindisfarne and Iona, sites of the early Christian presence of the communities of Saints Aidan and Columba.
- The Holy Land and places of significance described in the Gospels, for example, Bethlehem, Jerusalem and Nazareth.
- Rome and St Peter's, a centre of pilgrimage for all Christians, especially Roman Catholics.

Throughout the world there are many Holy places to which Christians become especially devoted, and these vary with the times.

4.5 Places of worship

The Christian place of worship is called a church or chapel. Every diocese in the Church of England and the Roman Catholic church has its own cathedral church. This is always large and imposing and is the focal point for all diocesan services; it contains the seat of the bishop of the diocese. There is a standard layout for most parish churches, many of which were built before the reformation.

Few new churches are built today because of dwindling congregations in most areas, but those that are built often have different shapes while still retaining the usual features. A chapel is normally smaller and less ornate. Chapels are favoured by nonconformist Christians.

The Orthodox Church

Orthodox churches are square with a dome on top. The square represents order and equality. The floor of the nave represents the earth and the four corners represent the four evangelists. Seats are provided only for the old and weak and people can move about during services; usually they stand still to worship.

The churches are richly decorated. The circular dome, located above the apex of the cross formed by the transepts, represents eternity. Around the walls are pictures of saints. On the altar table is a seven-branched candlestick which represents the seven sacraments and the seven gifts of the spirit.

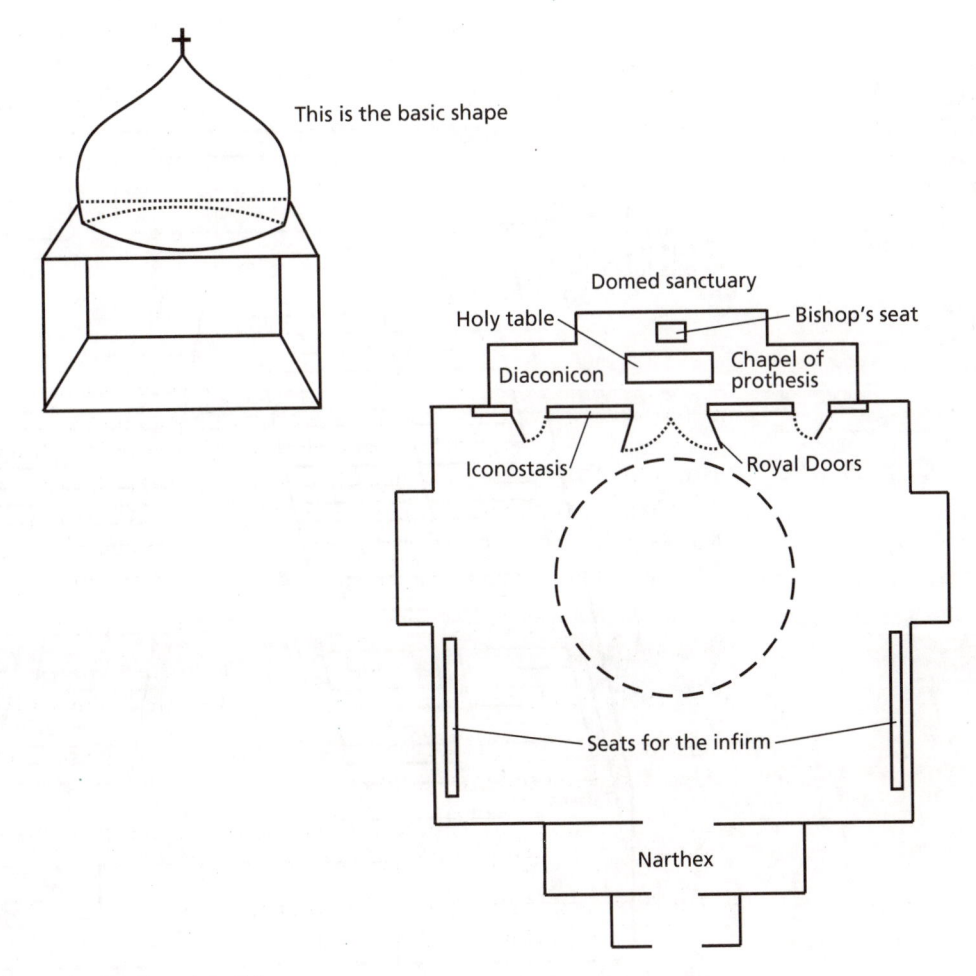

This is the basic shape

Domed sanctuary
Holy table
Bishop's seat
Diaconicon
Chapel of prothesis
Iconostasis
Royal Doors
Seats for the infirm
Narthex

An Orthodox church building

Chapter 4 Christian practices

At the entrance to the church is the narthex; this is the stage traversed by novitiate Christians and people wishing to enter Christianity. Across the front of the church is a huge screen decorated with pictures of the evangelists. This is called the iconostasis. Behind this are three areas:

1. *The diaconicon*, where robes and equipment are kept and where the priests dress;
2. *The chapel of prothesis*, where the bread and wine are prepared; and
3. *A domed sanctuary*, where the Eucharist takes place. This is entered by the curtained royal doors. The priests carry the Gospels and the bread and wine through these doors.

The Roman Catholic Church

Roman Catholic churches vary in shape. The table on which the bread and wine are consecrated is the focal point of the building. This is the Eucharistic table, the Mass being a celebration of a Christian community breaking bread together. In the modern church this feature is combined with some of the more traditional aspects which are important to people. Typical features include:

- a *Blessed Sacrament chapel/area*; the tabernacle housed here contains any consecrated bread and wine;
- a *Lady chapel* with a statue of the Virgin Mary and a *prie-dieu* for private prayer;
- the *baptismal font*. This is near to the altar. Often, however, there is no font, and the priest brings a bowl of water to the altar for baptism;
- pictures or carvings of the stations of the cross. These are found at intervals around the church;
- a *confessional* (in some churches), with two adjoining rooms for private confession;
- a *sacristy* where artefacts are kept and where the priest robes.

Readings and sermons are delivered from small, plain lecterns to emphasise that the words are important – not the grandness of the reader. Few churches have large organs and choir lofts. Music is communal and the leader of liturgical music sits with the congregation or as close as possible.

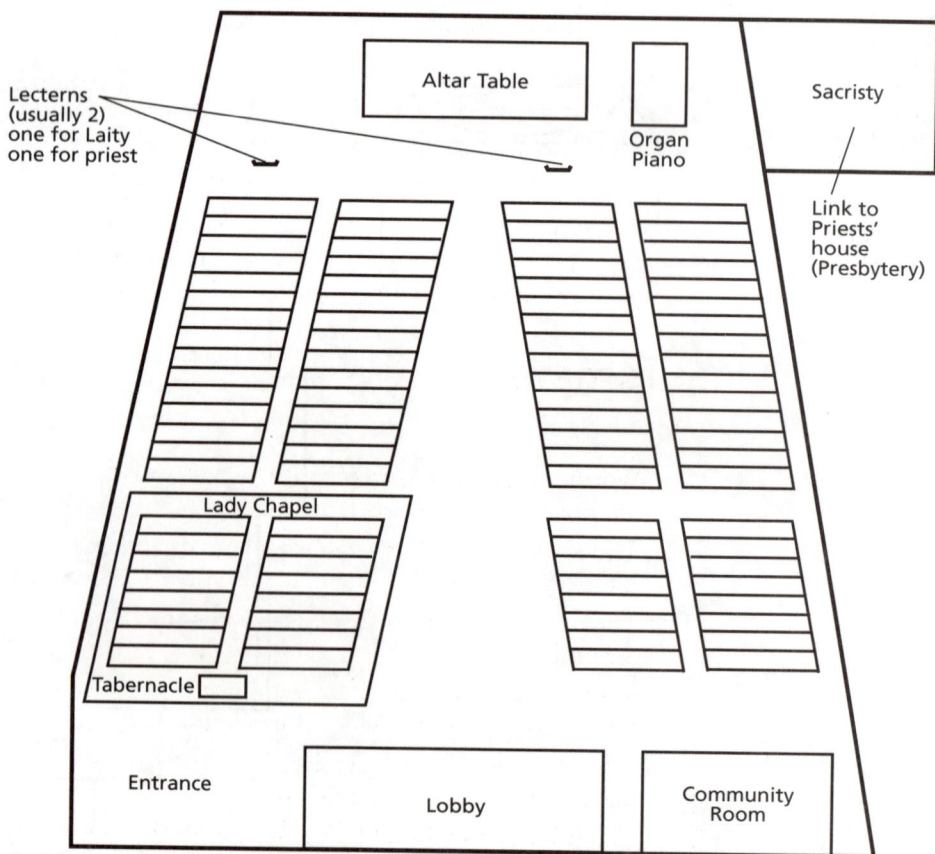

A typical Roman Catholic church

4.5 Places of worship

The Anglican Church

Many Anglican churches were built before the reformation and tend to remain traditional in layout. They are usually rectangular or in the shape of a cross. Cathedrals are particularly likely to be cross-shaped. A traditional church has a door at one side with a belfry to the rear of the nave. The baptismal font is close to the rear of the church in the nave. At the front of the church is the raised pulpit from which the sermon is given, and there is a lectern for scripture readings. At the very front is the high altar where communion services are conducted. Directly in front of this is the chancel and the choir stalls.

A cathedral traditionally has transepts and contains the bishop's throne. Sometimes there are side chapels, many of which date from before the reformation and were used for private Masses. A number of cathedrals still preserve their Lady chapels. Anglican churches do not often have statues or pictures although some high churches retain images from pre-reformation tradition.

Nonconformist churches

Nonconformist tradition is such that the churches have a much less formal design; this emphasises the equality of the worshippers. The churches are more modern and so have been designed with practicalities in mind. Many nonconformist churches are basically rectangular in shape but they may be organised to allow for conversion for social functions. Often the pulpit is at the centre of the front behind the communion table to show the centrality of the teaching of the Word of God. They are plain with no artefacts or statues.

Left: The Anglican church is cross-shaped. The altar is the focus of the building. It is set apart to create a feeling of mystery and awe. The central part of the church is the nave where the congregation sits.

Right: The furnishings of a nonconformist church are usually less ornate. The focal point is the elevated pulpit, in front of which is a far less noticeable Communion table.

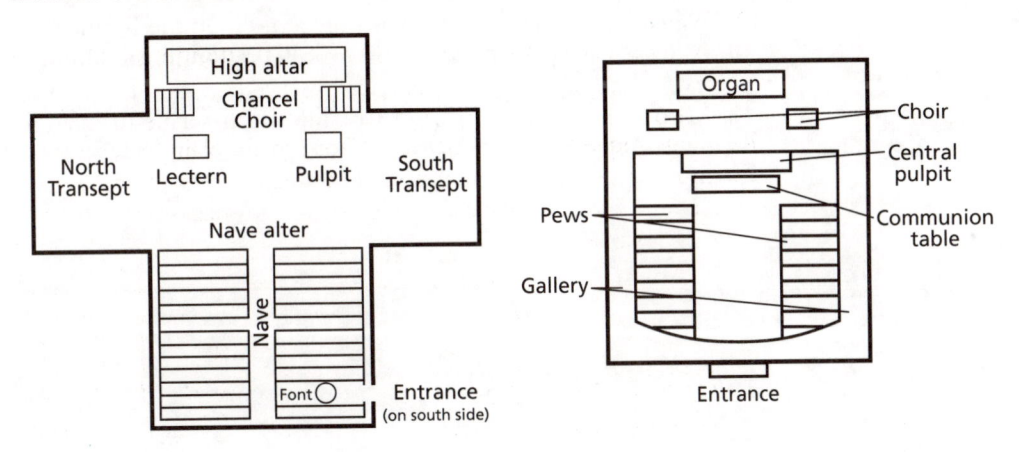

An Anglican church

A nonconformist church or chapel

Summary

1. Worship is giving regard to that which is worthy. In Christianity this means offering prayer or praise, thanksgiving and supplication to the Lord God.

2. The main form of Christian worship is the celebration of the Lord's supper: bread is broken, wine is blessed and the minister speaks the words of the last supper.

3. The meaning given to the celebration of the last supper is subtly different in the denominations.

4. Roman Catholics use external stimulants to prayer and sometimes pray through the intercession of the virgin Mary and saints.

5. Fasting and making pilgrimages are methods of showing devotion and praying that are customary for Christians but not obligatory.

6. The Bible is used by all Christians for private prayer, group study/prayer and in corporate worship.

Chapter 4 Christian practices

7   Protestants recognise two sacraments, Baptism and Marriage.

8   Roman Catholic and Orthodox Christians have seven sacraments – Baptism; Reconciliation; Communion; Confirmation; Holy Orders; Marriage; Sacrament of the sick.

9   All Christians follow the same calendar and observe the same festivals – Christmas; Lent: Easter; Pentecost.

10 The Christian Holy Day is Sunday and Christians mainly hold their services in cathedrals, churches or chapels. The Salvation Army has a citadel while Quakers have a meeting house.

Quick questions

1   What is the purpose of Christian Worship?
2   What do Orthodox Christians believe happens at the Lord's Supper?
3   What do Roman Catholics believe happens at the Consecration?
4   What do Protestants believe the breaking of bread represents?
5   Why are Protestant churches less ornate than Roman Catholic ones?
6   What is the purpose of statues and holy pictures for Roman Catholics?
7   How is making a pilgrimage helpful to Christians?
8   In what ways do Christians use the Bible to pray?
9   What are the seven Sacraments recognised by the Roman Catholic church?
10 Why is Easter the most important celebration in the Church's year?
11 For what purpose do Christians observe lent, and how do they do this?
12 Choose a Christian place of worship and describe its main features.

Chapter 5
Jesus and the Gospels

5.1 Using this chapter

In order to make the best use of this chapter, make sure you know which Gospel passages you need to be familiar with for your course before following the structure indicated below.

The first source is Mark's Gospel. Many courses ask you to become familiar with the basic ideas in this Gospel. If you need Luke's Gospel, read the section on Luke and refer to the passages in Luke as necessary – but where a title is given, and a reference, this means that the episode has been explained at length as it appears in Mark; any important differences will be highlighted. If you need passages from Matthew for your course, read the section on Matthew in the same way. Any passage which is titled is described fully in the sections on Mark and Luke and any differences explained.

It is not possible to go into every episode in complete detail but the major passages and the salient points are all covered here.

5.2 The person of Jesus

The Gospels are about Jesus, the great founder of Christianity, with one billion followers worldwide.

Jesus is the Christ from the Greek word *Christos* meaning Messiah or anointed one. Jesus is anointed by the woman at Bethany who pours nard on his head (Mark 14:3–9; Matt. 26:6–13). Jews had long been awaiting a Messiah, someone set aside for a special task. One had been prophesied in the Old Testament but they had fixed ideas about what the Messiah would be like. Some expected a prophet like Moses.

Suffering Servant

There are indications in the Gospel that Jesus saw himself more as the 'suffering servant', prophesied in Isaiah (Isa. 35:4; 53:2–12). He often told his disciples that the Son of man would suffer and die; and He put great emphasis on the need to put self last and be servant of all.

King

The promised Messiah was expected by many to be a King descended from David who would lead the Jews as a warrior against their enemies.

Chapter 5 Jesus and the Gospels

Human or Divine

Some Jews expected God to come and make his Kingdom on earth; so they waited and looked for a Son of God or a Son of Man. Jesus uses the term Son of man frequently when speaking of his ministry on earth, his suffering and death and of his future glory. The title has the meaning of ordinary man and also divine authority. Christians hold the doctrine that Jesus is both human and divine at once.

5.3 The importance of the Gospels

The Gospels are your most important resource in a study of Christianity. From the Gospels Christians obtain most of their knowledge and understanding of Jesus. You can base your answers on words Jesus has said and deeds that he has done as well as on the specific teachings of the church or churches you have learnt about. The churches' teachings are all interpretations which they have put on the teachings of Jesus in the Gospels. Christians regard the Gospels as the Word of God and often treat them with more awe and reverence than other parts of the Bible.

Some examining boards (see tables on pages 4–13) offer papers which are centred around a particular Gospel or Gospels. So for these papers you need to be able to demonstrate a very detailed knowledge of the texts which are prescribed. Many Gospel passages also help us understand Christian views on today's issues and it is important to understand the teachings of Jesus which are the inspiration behind Christian action.

Gospel

Gospel means 'good news'. It comes from the Greek word *evanglion*; hence the Gospel writers are called evangelists because they are proclaiming the 'good news': the good news that Jesus is the Messiah and came to show people a new way of living.

The bulk of the Gospel texts are concerned with the last three years of Jesus' life, when he was teaching, and they also give much space to a description of his arrest, trial, death and resurrection.

The Synoptic Gospels

The Gospels of Mark, Luke and Matthew are called the synoptic Gospels because they are all similar to one another, containing much information which is common to all three. Mark was written first but Matthew and Luke share information not contained in Mark; this information is believed to have come from a source now lost but known as Q. Similarly, information which is unique to Matthew and Luke is respectively referred to as arising from sources known as *L* and *M*.

The context in which Jesus lived

The geography of Palestine has not changed. It contains both desert and fertile areas. The people were mainly illiterate and subsisted by farming, keeping sheep or providing simple services like carpentry and pottery.

Palestine was occupied by the Romans and was multiracial with many languages and cultures. Jesus was born a Jew and therefore is identified with that culture.

When Jesus began his ministry he came into contact with the influential people of Palestine and of His own community, and the Gospels show how conflict arose between them because he was declaring a completely new and radical way of looking at life.

You should be familiar with the groups of people listed below:

- Pharisees: in the Gospels they are shown by Jesus to be Jews who put the letter of the law above the needs of men. They were completely committed to observance of the oral law and the Torah but also accepted the Prophets and Writings as Scripture. Jesus often challenges them and calls them hypocrites.

- Sadducees: a politically influential group who recognised only the Torah as law and compromised with the Roman authorities to keep their influence.
- The Sanhedrin: the Jewish Council which decided religious matters. It had 70 members and was presided over by the high priests.
- Herodians: supporters of Herod the Great; mainly wealthy Jews who wanted a nationalist party,
- Zealots: Jews who wanted to overthrow Roman rule by terrorism,
- Tax collectors: Jewish employees of Rome regarded as outcasts by the rabbis,
- Samaritans: A race of people living between Judea and Galilee who accepted the Torah but were not regarded as Jews and were much despised.

The Synagogue was the place of worship for the Jewish community to which Jesus belonged and the Sabbath was the Holy Day.

5.4 Mark's Gospel

Mark's Gospel is ascribed to a certain Mark, or John Mark, although it is by no means certain who wrote it. It is accepted that this Gospel was written in about AD 60–70 in Rome and seemingly the writer had the persecuted Christians in mind. There are two good reasons to believe that Mark's Gospel is written for a non-Jewish readership:

1. words are translated from Aramaic; and
2. there is strong emphasis on the suffering of Jesus and on the necessary acceptance of possible suffering on the part of the disciples.
   You need to concentrate on Mark if you are studying for:
   - NEAB Syllabus B, Section 1C, and
   - ULEAC 1477, Unit 5.
   In both of the above, contemporary issues are related to teachings in Mark.

Most of what Mark has to say about Jesus can be understood by looking at five major themes: miracles; parables; episodes of conflict; discipleship; and Jesus' arrest, trial and death.

Miracles in Mark

In Mark's Gospel Jesus performs many different types of miracle to demonstrate the nature of Jesus. Jesus performs miracles to show that he has God's power over nature and physical and mental illness. He also shows that it is necessary to have faith in order for a miracle to happen. The occurrence of miracles does not lead to faith.

It does not matter whether Christians believe the miracles really happened in a supernatural sense. A miracle is simply an event which is not explicable in any normal way. Today some scientists say there is a logical explanation for every miracle but most believers do not mind. The miracle accounts and what Jesus teaches about faith are part of the Gospel writers' good news. They tell the reader about the person, Jesus.

You may find it helpful to look at miracles in the light of three key words.

- *Terras* is the awe and wonder, the amazement, in which onlookers regarded miracles.
- *Dynamis* is the power that was displayed.
- *Semeion* is the meaning which may be apparent to the healed and those witnessing the event.

Nature Miracles
Jesus calms the storm (Mark 4:35–41). When Jesus calms the storm He says to his frightened disciples, 'Have you no faith?' Then they ask one another who He can be; they are filled with awe (*terras*) at the power (*dynamis*) of Jesus and they wonder what it can mean (*semeion*).

Jesus feeds five thousand (Mark 6:30–44). When Jesus has a large crowd to feed He gathers five loaves and two fish. He looks up to heaven and gives thanks to God; then He breaks the bread. When the disciples distribute it to the crowd there is enough for all of them with twelve baskets of leftovers.
Jesus is always recognised by Christians in the breaking of bread.
He is the source of all life.
Jesus walks on water (Mark 6:45–52). Jesus comes to the disciples in their boat by walking on the water and they are terrified, thinking He is a ghost. He calms them but they are amazed because, despite the feeding of the 5000, they still do not understand His power.

The water is symbolic of chaos, evil and darkness. Jesus shows his power over these things. Water is also a symbol of new life and is constantly referred to in the Bible. Walking on water is showing power like the power God demonstrates in the parting of the Red Sea at the Exodus (Exod. 14).

In Mark 8:1–9 Jesus again feeds a large crowd; this time there are 4000 people. Jesus uses the same method but only seven loaves. Again there are seven baskets of leftovers.

Healing (mental illness)

Jesus is seen to heal many people who are possessed by evil spirits. They seem to have symptoms which might today be regarded as those of mental illness.
A man with an evil spirit (1:21–28). Jesus is preaching in the synagogue on the Sabbath when a man with an evil spirit says to him, 'What do you want with us Jesus of Nazareth? Are you here to destroy us? I know who you are, you are God's holy messenger!'

Jesus replies, 'Be quiet and come out of that man.'

The evil spirit shook the man hard, gave a loud scream and came out of him. The people in the synagogue were amazed and questioned Jesus' authority.
A man with evil spirits (The Gerasene Demoniac) (5:1–20). This man lived in the territory of Gerasa and was possessed by so many evil spirits that his feet and hands had been chained. He smashed the chains and roamed the hills, screaming and cutting himself with stones.

When he sees Jesus he calls him the Son of the most high God and begs him not to punish him. Jesus is quietly ordering the evil out of the Man. Jesus asks, 'What is your name?' and the man replies, 'Mob, there are so many of us.'

Jesus sends the spirits from Mob into the pigs feeding nearby and they all rush over the cliff into the lake and drown. After this Mob is sensible and quiet. He wants to go with Jesus but Jesus orders him to go through the ten towns telling people what Jesus has done for him.
The Syro-Phoenician woman's daughter (7:24–30). This woman came to Jesus and told him her daughter had an evil spirit. She begged Jesus to drive out the demon and Jesus said, 'Let us first feed the children.' The woman, who was a gentile, agreed, saying that the dogs could even eat the scraps first. Jesus told her that because of her answer she would find her daughter cured when she returned home, as indeed she did.

It is important in Mark that Jesus heals all people, including Gentiles, and the Jewish term for dog was used for Gentiles. The woman had absolute faith that Jesus would heal her daughter and did not rush him.

The boy with the evil spirit (9:14–29). This is an important story, illustrating the importance of faith in the working of miracles. A boy has fits and the disciples cannot cure him. (These fits are described as similar to epilepsy.) Jesus chastises the disciples for their lack of faith and asks for the boy to be brought to him.

The 'spirit' throws the boy on the floor and Jesus tells the boy's father that his son can be healed if only the father has faith. The father says he has faith but begs for more. Jesus then heals the boy, and, in reply to the disciples' questions, says that only prayer can drive out demons of this sort.

It is important to search for faith, to pray for faith rather than to pray for miracles.

Miracles of Healing (Physical)

Jesus heals many people (Simon's mother-in-law) (Mark 1:29–34). Jesus very quietly heals Simon's mother-in-law of a fever and then goes on to heal many who are brought to him when the Sabbath is ended.
Jesus heals a man with a dreaded skin disease (Mark 1:40–45). A man approaches Jesus and says, 'If you want to, you can make me clean.' Jesus says he wants to, and cures the man,

saying, 'Be clean'. He tells the man to keep the healing a secret but the man tells many people, thus increasing Jesus' fame and notoriety.

This miracle shows the faith of the man and Jesus as an emerging public figure.

Jesus heals a paralysed man (Mark 2:1–12). Jesus is surrounded in a house and some men bring their friend to be cured. When they cannot reach Jesus they lower the man through the roof on his mat. Jesus tells the man his sins are forgiven and some in the crowd are astonished, saying, 'It is blasphemy, as only God can forgive sins'.

Jesus asks which is easier, to forgive sins or cure the Man. Then he tells the man to pick up his mat and walk. The man does so. Jesus says, 'I will prove to you that the Son of Man has authority on earth to forgive sins.'

Jesus calls himself the Son of Man and shows He has God's power not only to heal but to forgive as well.

The man with the paralysed hand (Mark 3:1–6). A man with a paralysed hand is in the synagogue on the Sabbath and Jesus calls him up and asks, 'What does our law allow us to do on the Sabbath? To help or to harm? To save a man's life or to destroy it?' Jesus heals the man and we are told that some Herodians met with some Pharisees to plot to kill Jesus.

It is an important part of Jesus' developing ministry that He challenges the Pharisaical application of the Sabbath laws. When He makes this challenge by performing spectacular miracles it is very threatening to the authorities.

Jesus heals the haemorrhagic (Mark 5:25–34). A woman touches Jesus' cloak because she believes she can be cured of the bleeding which has afflicted her for years. She is healed and Jesus feels the power leave him. He asks who touched him and when the woman comes forward he tells her that her faith has cured her.

Mark shows that people do not need to ask for healing – they only need faith.

Jairus' Daughter (Mark 5:21–42). Jairus begs Jesus to heal his daughter but they hear the girl is dead. Jesus goes with Jairus to his house, telling Jairus to 'believe'. When he arrives he says the child is sleeping and goes to her, telling her to get up. He then says she should be given something to eat.

Mark quotes the original Aramaic 'Talitha Kum', which Jesus might have used, and translates for the reader, 'Little girl get up'.

Jesus heals a deaf mute (Mark 7:31–37). This man is brought to Jesus by his friends and Jesus heals him in a very physical way. Jesus puts his fingers in the man's ears, spits and touches the man's tongue, saying, 'Ephphatha' (open up). Jesus does this away from the crowd and the man is cured. When the crowd see what Jesus has done they are filled with wonder.

The Blind man at Bethsaida (Mark 8:22–25). This man is also presented to Jesus by his friends. Jesus leads the man from the village, spits on his eyes and also touches his eyes until he can see clearly. The man is asked not to return to the village.

It is not clear why Jesus orders secrecy. It is possible He does not want to draw too much attention to Himself or appear too threatening. Performing miracles is not His major task; it is part of His ministry to the sick.

Parables in Mark

The second area to consider in the Gospels is that of the parables Jesus told. Many of them are called *The parables of the Kingdom* because these parables begin, 'The Kingdom of God is like this...'.

What is a parable?
A parable is usually a simple story with a clear and simple meaning. Jesus used the medium of parables because storytelling was part of the Palestinian culture. He utilises the imagery of farming and shepherding because those are the contexts which were familiar to his listeners. Sometimes the parables are quick and simple messages and at other times they are turned into allegories, each part particularly representing something different.

Parables of the Kingdom

The Kingdom of God is not seen as a place somewhere in the future. At the beginning of the Gospel Jesus preaches the good news, which is: '*The Kingdom of God is near. Repent and believe the Good News.*' The Kingdom of God is realised when all people turn to follow the way of God which is shown to them by Jesus. This news about the Kingdom is illustrated in the parables.

In Mark's Gospel, Christians learn that the Kingdom is like:

A growing seed (Mark 4:26–29). A seed is planted and grows in good, fertile soil when the farmer sleeps. When it is fully developed the farmer harvests it.

So too the Kingdom of God – and it grows silently, waiting for the harvest.

A mustard seed (Mark 4:30–34). The mustard seed is the smallest of seeds, which grows into a huge plant with large branches to shelter birds.

So the Kingdom of God grows and is a haven, a resting place for all who wish to shelter in it.

The New Way

Through the teachings in the parables Jesus emphasises the fact that his way is a new way.

The patches and the wineskins (Mark 2:18–22). This is one of the parables Jesus told which challenged the Pharisees. He tells them no one would use new cloth to patch an old coat as the new cloth would tear the old; and no one would put new wine into old skins as the skins would swell and burst. New wine must be poured into fresh skins.

Jesus is clearly telling the Pharisees that His way is completely new. It is not an adaptation of old ways but a fresh and radical way of living.

Allegories in Mark

The Parable of the Sower (Mark 4:3–9;13–20). In this parable Jesus likens the farmer sowing his seeds to someone sowing God's message. The seeds represent the word of God.

Seeds which fall on the path represent words which fall on willing ears but are quickly forgotten because of temptation (snatched away by Satan) just as seeds on the path are snatched away by birds.

Seeds which fall on rocky ground take root and grow but die quickly. As the soil dries the roots die, and so sometimes the word is rooted weakly and is lost in times of trouble and persecution.

Seeds which fall among the weeds and thorns grow well until they are choked by other growth, just as the word is choked by those who become worried about riches and things of the world.

Seeds which fall on fertile soil grow and multiply to produce a rich harvest, just as words are heard by accepting people and the message is accepted and it multiplies.

Jesus is explaining the message in order to make clear that everyone should listen to the Word of God and allow nothing to detract from it in order that the Kingdom can grow and flourish in each person.

The parable of the Tenants in the Vineyard (Mark 12:1–12). This parable is to be found in Chapter 12, whereas the others are in the early part of the Gospel. It is quite different in meaning and speaks of Jesus' purpose on earth. It has been turned into an allegory, with each part representing something about the life of Jesus.

A man plants a vineyard and leaves it in the hands of tenants. When he sends servants to collect the profits they are beaten, so he finally sends his son. The tenants decide to kill the son, believing that the vineyard will then be theirs. The owner returns, throws out the tenants and hands the vineyard to others.

Jesus concludes that the stone the builders rejected was the most important stone. Once again the reader is told that the Pharisees plotted to kill Jesus because he told this parable against them.

In this parable:

- the vineyard represents Israel
- the tenants represent the Jews
- the servants represent the prophets
- the Son represents Jesus
- the owner represents God

The teaching of Jesus through the parables was controversial and challenging. It was uncompromising in its rejection of the way of the Pharisees. Jesus knew that He was making enemies but He did not flinch from his dangerous path and radical message.

The messages of the parables can be used to demonstrate Christian inspiration for working for the true meaning in the Gospels. Jesus was more concerned about people and their understanding of the Kingdom and he came with a simple, clear message.

Episodes of conflict

Jesus directly challenged the established authority, not just through his parables but with direct action and teachings.

The Sabbath Laws

The Pharisees applied the Sabbath Laws very rigidly. They had hundreds of these and numerous subclauses about what constituted work on the Sabbath. No one was allowed to carry more ink than was necessary to write two letters or more oil than was needed to anoint the nail of the smallest toe. Jesus cast these petty rules aside.

When the disciples pick ears of corn on the Sabbath they are accused of 'working'. Jesus responds by reminding the Pharisees that David and his men ate bread designated for priests on the Sabbath because they were hungry. He tells them the Sabbath is made for man, not man for the Sabbath. (Mark 2:23–27).

He says the same thing when he heals the man with the withered hand, making it clear that it is more important to do good on the Sabbath, to help not to destroy (Mark 3:1–6).

Ritual washing

Jesus challenges the Pharisees about their elaborate teaching on cleanliness. It was considered necessary to wash hands in a ritual way after they had touched anything which might make them unclean. Food from the market and other items had to be ritually washed.

Jesus chastises the Pharisees, saying they only apply the law when it suits them and yet treat their parents badly by declaring that all their goods are 'Corban' (belonging to God) and cannot be used to help the elderly. Jesus says it is the things which come out of a person which make him unclean – immoral things like murder, slander, adultery, jealousy, indecency, pride and deceit. What a person takes in physically does not make him unclean in a real sense as a person.

Paying Taxes

Some Pharisees and Herod's men try to trap Jesus by asking Him who they should pay taxes to. Jesus shows them the Emperor's head on a coin and tells them to pay to the emperor what belongs to him and to God what belongs to God.

Jesus has the measure of the Pharisees and is not afraid to confront them and outwit them if necessary to underline his message. He is not a revolutionary about to overthrow the government. He is there to challenge the distortions in following the way of God.

Discipleship

The most important aspect of Mark's Gospel is the message he conveys about what is necessary to be a follower of Jesus – to be a disciple. *It is from these passages that you can find much evidence to support Christian teachings on attitudes to contemporary moral issues.*

The section on discipleship is mainly contained in Mark 8:22–10:52. The section begins with the curing of the blind man at Bethsaida and ends with the curing of blind Bartimaeus. These episodes can be seen as symbolic. Until people recognise the way of discipleship they are blind. Only when they understand the cost of being a follower of Jesus can they be considered to have seen the new way and become enlightened.

Peter's declaration

Jesus asks the disciples who people say He is and they tell him that some say John the Baptist and some say Elijah. He asks, 'Who do *you* say I am?' and Peter replies, 'You are the Messiah.'

When Jesus goes on to explain that the Son of Man must suffer and be rejected and put to death and that he will rise again, Peter rebukes him. Jesus tells Peter, 'Get away from me, Satan. Your thoughts are not from God but from man.'

Peter loves Jesus and although he recognises Jesus as the Messiah he is not able to see what kind of Messiah Jesus is.

Taking up the cross

Jesus tells the crowd and his followers: 'If anyone wants to come with me, he must forget self, carry his cross and follow me. For whoever wants to save his own life will lose it; but whoever wants to lose his life for me and for the Gospel will save it. Does a person gain anything if he wins the whole world but loses his life? Of course not.' (Mark 8:34–36).

Taking up the cross had a literal connotation for Mark's readers who were faced with death for their Christian beliefs. Even today Christians in many areas are killed for their beliefs. Roman Catholic priests and nuns, for example, have been murdered in El Salvador because their work with the poor was seen as a threat to the government.

This idea is reinforced when Peter, James and John witness the transfiguration of Jesus on the mountain (Mark 9:2–9), and see Him with Moses and Elijah. Jesus tells them the Son of man will suffer and die. The Scriptures will be fulfilled, just as they were when people treated Elijah as they pleased.

Qualities of a follower (disciple)

There are, then, certain passages which allow the reader to see the qualities that are necessary to be a follower of Jesus carrying the cross.

- A follower must have *faith* as the father of the boy with an evil spirit has faith and prays for more faith, believing anything is possible for those who have faith.

- A follower must have *humility*. Jesus says, 'Whoever wants to be first must place himself last of all and be the servant of all' (Mark 9:35).

- A follower should *love children*. Jesus says, 'Whoever welcomes in my name one of these children, welcomes me; whoever welcomes me, welcomes not only me but the one who has sent me' (Mark 9:37).

- A follower is anyone who is *for* Jesus. 'For whoever is not against us is for us' (Mark 9:40).

- A follower must have *fidelity in marriage*. Jesus says, 'Man must not separate what God has joined together' (Mark 10:9), and, 'A man who divorces his wife and marries another woman commits adultery against his wife. In the same way, a woman who divorces her husband and marries another man commits adultery' (Mark 10:11–12).

- A follower must *receive the Kingdom of God like a child*. 'Let the children come to me and do not stop them for the Kingdom of God belongs to such as these. I assure you that whoever does not receive the Kingdom of God like a little child, will not enter it' (Mark 10:14–15).

Children receive and believe in innocence which is often lost through the trials of life. Adults have to struggle to hold on to a childlike faith.

- A follower must *sell all he has and give it to the poor*. When the rich young man asks Jesus what he must do to enter the Kingdom of heaven, Jesus tells him to obey the commandments. He says he has done this since childhood so Jesus tells him he must sell everything, give it to the poor and follow Jesus. The rich man goes away sad because he is very rich and Jesus tells the disciples, 'It is much harder for a rich person to enter the kingdom of God than for a camel to go through the eye of a needle' (Mark 10:17–31).

This is a radical aspect of Jesus' teaching which many Christians cite as inspiration for working with 'the poorest of the poor' and for lives of poverty.

- A follower must be *servant of all*. When James and John ask if they can sit either side of Jesus on his glorious throne He tells them they have no idea of the suffering He must endure. He tells them, 'If one of you wants to be great, he must be the servant of the rest' (Mark 10:43).

Great people in Christian tradition are those who live and give unstintingly of themselves to others, e.g. Mother Theresa.

These passages spell out clearly that Mark's message is that the Gospel values are difficult to hold on to; they are difficult ways to follow and Jesus sets a hard path for his would-be followers.

The Passover meal

Jesus is asked by his disciples where He wishes them to prepare the Passover meal. He instructs them to follow a man carrying a jar into a house and tells them that the owner of the house will lead them to an upper room.

When they are all assembled in the upper room Jesus says one of them will betray Him and they all deny it. Jesus tells them that the one who dips his bread with Him will be the traitor and 'It would be better for that man if he had never been born' – because he will betray the Son of Man.

The Lord's Supper

During the meal Jesus breaks bread, says a prayer of thanks, and says, 'Take it, this is my body.' He gives the cup of wine, and says, 'This is my blood which is poured out for many, my blood which seals God's covenant.' He also predicts that Peter will deny Him.

The Lord's Supper is the Institution of the Eucharist and is the central part of much Christian worship. The remembrance of Christ and His sacrifice is commemorated at the breaking of bread by Christians together.

The Last Supper

The arrest, trial and death of Jesus

In Mark's Gospel a great deal of emphasis is placed on Jesus' suffering and death. Mark wishes to convey the extent of the suffering of Jesus, His humiliation, the injustice of His situation, His own fear and the horrible pain of His crucifixion.

The Garden of Gethsemane

When Jesus prayed in the Garden of Gethsemane, He asked His Father to take away His cup of suffering because He was deeply distressed by the fear of His coming death. Jesus nevertheless told His Father that He would do what His Father wanted Him to do, not what He Himself wanted (Mark 14:32–41).

This passage shows what is expected of Christian disciples; they are expected to follow God's will even if this means death.

Jesus is betrayed

Jesus was arrested when Judas betrayed Him by a kiss; this was a signal to the chief priests, teachers of the law and the elders (Mark 14:43–52) to seize Him in the garden. Jesus did not resist the arrest. He knew that His teaching and actions had threatened the religious authorities.

Trial before the Sanhedrin

At His trial before the council of religious leaders (Mark 14:53–65) many witnesses told lies about what Jesus had said and contradicted one another. The High Priest finally asked Jesus whether he was the Messiah, and Jesus replied, 'I am, and you will all see the Son of Man seated on the right of the Almighty coming with the clouds of heaven.'

The Jewish leaders were very angry to hear these words because the words 'I am' were sacred – suggesting that Jesus was divine. He was declared guilty of blasphemy.

During the trial Peter, the leader of the disciples, denied to a waiting crowd that he knew Jesus (Mark 14:66–72). He was afraid that he would also be arrested for being a follower of Jesus. After the cock had crowed twice Peter remembered that Jesus had told him that Peter would deny that he knew Jesus. Peter broke down and cried.

Peter's story was an example to the followers of Jesus of a man, their leader, who had turned away from following Jesus, but then returned to following Jesus after Jesus had forgiven him.

Trial before Pilate

The high priests had Jesus taken before Pilate. They had declared Him guilty of blasphemy but had no power to condemn Him to death. Only the governor had that power. The high priests had already spread rumours that Jesus had called himself the King of the Jews, and that was treason. Pilate asked him, 'Are you the king of the Jews?' and Jesus replied, 'The words are yours.'

Jesus did not reply to any of the accusations made against him. Pilate decided to offer Jesus as one of the prisoners for release for the Passover alongside a murderer called Barabbas. The crowd called for Barabbas and when Pilate asked what he should do with the one they called the King of the Jews they called out, 'Crucify him!'. So Pilate (to satisfy the mob) had Jesus flogged and handed Him over to be crucified (Mark 15:1–15).

The Death of Jesus

Jesus was mocked. The soldiers took him into the governor's headquarters. They put a purple robe on Him and twisted some thorns into a crown for His head. They called him 'King of the Jews' and bowed down and spat on Him. Jesus was helped by Simon from Cyrene as He carried his own cross to the place called Golgotha (the Place of a Skull) where he was to die. Jesus refused the drugged wine He was offered. He was fixed to the cross and His executioners cast lots for His clothes. He was crucified at 9 o'clock in the morning and a sign was put over him, which said, 'The King of the Jews'.

Passersby mocked Him, telling Him to save Himself as He had saved others or to come down from the cross and save Himself if He really had the power to rebuild the temple in days.

At 3 o'clock the land was covered in darkness and Jesus cried out, 'Eli, Eli, lema sabachthani?' (My God, My God, Why have you abandoned me?) Then Jesus gave a loud cry and died and the curtain in the Temple was torn in two. The centurion looked on Jesus and said, 'Truly this man was the Son of God.'

Note: *It is thought that Jesus may have been crying out in the agony of his humanity that God had abandoned Him. Some scholars say that Jesus was uttering the beginning of Psalm 22, which ends joyously. The Temple curtain tearing can be seen to symbolise that through his death Jesus had allowed all men to enter the 'Holy of Holies' which was a special curtained-off area of the Temple where only high priests could go. This would be constant with Mark's theme that Jesus was clearing a path for a new way of living. The centurion's comments confirm that for Mark, Jesus was very much the Son of God, as even one of his murderers realised.*

The Resurrection

On the day after the Sabbath Mary Magdalene, Mary the mother of James and Salome go to anoint the body, as is the custom, and they find the stone rolled away and the body gone. A young man tells them to go and tell Peter and the disciples that Jesus has gone to Galilee ahead of them. The women run from the tomb in distress. Readers are told that Jesus appears to Mary Magdalene, to two disciples in the country and to eleven disciples when they are eating. He scolds them for their fear and orders them to go out and preach the Gospel, driving out demons and performing miracles in His name.

Jesus is then taken up to heaven.

5.5 Luke's Gospel

Several examination syllabuses call for a detailed study of Luke's Gospel, including:

- MEG Paper 1;
- SEG Syllabus C, Unit 3 (Roman Catholic Tradition)
- SEG Syllabus A, Section 7 (selected passages);
- WJEC, Group 2.

Use the tables on pages 4–13 to remind yourself what you are studying and use these summaries in conjunction with your own reading of the Gospel passages.

Luke was a Gentile and wrote his Gospel in a way that emphasised that Jesus was the saviour of all, Jews and Gentiles alike. It seems that Luke travelled with Paul and spoke to many people who had known Jesus although he had not known Him. It is believed the Gospel was written in Rome in about AD 80–90.

Much of the detail in Luke is also to be found in Mark. In the following paragraphs, however, you will find indicated areas which are unique to Luke.

The Infancy Narrative

Luke includes a section on the birth of Jesus which is absent from Mark; these passages are widely read in Christian churches at Christmas time.

An old man called Zechariah is promised by the Angel Gabriel that his wife Elizabeth will have a child whom she will name John. Zechariah is struck dumb until the birth because he has difficulty believing what the angel has to say (Luke 1:11–20). Elizabeth had been thought to be barren (unable to bear children).

The Annunciation

The Angel Gabriel visits the Virgin Mary and tells her she will conceive a son and give Him the name Jesus. Mary is deeply troubled but the angel tells her not to be afraid and says he will be called, 'Son of the Most High.' Mary asks, 'How can this be, I am still a virgin?' She is told the Holy Spirit will come upon her and the child will be called, 'Son of God'. Mary says, 'Here am I. I am the Lord's servant; as you have spoken so be it' (Luke 1:26–38).

It is very important in Christian understanding that a young, vulnerable virginal girl accepted what she believed to be the will of the Lord in such a trusting way despite the fear and uncertainty that the pregnancy would bring to her.

The Visitation

Mary visits Elizabeth and Elizabeth's child moves in her womb. Elizabeth says, 'Who am I that the mother of my Lord should visit me?' and 'How happy is she who has had faith that the Lord's promise would be fulfilled.'

Luke then writes the 'Magnificat' (Luke 1:46–56), which is Mary's song of praise for the work of the Lord and is an important prayer and a hymn of praise for Christians; it is used more often in Roman Catholic worship, taking a prominent part in the Office (a series of special prayers read by religious three times a day).

The Birth of John the Baptist

When Elizabeth's baby is born she insists on calling him John, at which point Zechariah recovers his speech and praises the Lord in prophecy (Luke 1:68–79).

The Nativity

Luke tells how Mary and Joseph have to travel to Bethlehem for the census which has been ordered by Caesar Augustus. (Luke is noted for his historical accuracy as a census did take place at about this time.) Mary gave birth to Jesus there and, 'wrapped Him in swaddling clothes, and laid Him in a manger because there was no room for them to lodge in the house.' (Luke 2:6–7).

The Shepherds

Some Shepherds are visited by angels who tell them a Messiah has been born and He is in a manger. The shepherds hurry to Bethlehem to see the baby and tell Mary and Joseph what they have been told. Mary stores up this news in her heart while other listeners are astonished (Luke 2:8–19).

The Presentation

Jesus is taken to be circumcised on the eighth day according to Jewish custom. Simeon visits Him at the Temple. Simeon has been told by the Holy Spirit that he will not die until he has seen the Messiah. Simeon tells Mary that the child is destined to be a sign rejected by men and that Mary herself will be pierced to the heart.

A woman, Anna, who prays every day in the Temple, tells Mary and Joseph that the child is the one to whom all are looking for the liberation of Jerusalem.

Jesus in the Temple

When Jesus is twelve years old Mary and Joseph make a pilgrimage to Jerusalem; after they've left the city they cannot find Jesus and have to return. Eventually they find Him in the temple talking and answering questions. When Mary chastises Him Jesus answers that she should expect to find him in his Father's house (Luke 2:41–50).

Luke is very clear from the start that Jesus is the Messiah, the Son of God, the Son of the Most High, and that Mary treasures her knowledge about Jesus.

John the Baptist

Luke gives more emphasis to John the Baptist than Mark. Both Gospel writers tell how John says he baptises with water but that the one who will come after him will baptise with the Holy Spirit. But John also warns people to share their shirts and food, and live good lives.

John baptises Jesus and the Spirit descends on Him in the form of a dove. A voice from heaven is heard, saying, 'Thou art my Son, my Beloved, on thee my favour rests.' (Luke 3:21,22) (also Mark 1:10,11)

The Temptations of Jesus (Luke 4:1–13)

Mark merely mentions that Jesus was tempted by the devil in the wilderness. Luke tells his readers about the temptations. The devil tempts Jesus:

- to turn stone to bread, but Jesus replies, 'Scripture says, "Man cannot live on bread alone".'
- to become master of all the Kingdoms of the world by doing homage to him (the devil), but Jesus tells him, 'Scripture says, "You shall do homage to the Lord your God and worship him alone".'
- to throw Himself off the parapet of the temple and the angels of God will save Him but Jesus replies, 'It has been said, "You shall not put the Lord your God to the test".'

> **Application for today:** Christians recall the temptations and the wilderness during a time of fasting and abstinence in Lent. At this time they pray and reflect, trying to make spiritual ideas the focus of life and grow closer to Christ.

Miracles in Luke

Luke includes the following miracles:

Mental illness
The man with an evil spirit in the Temple (Luke 4:31–37)
The man at Gerasa (Gerascene Demoniac) (Luke 8:26–39)
The epileptic boy (Luke 9:37–43)
Jesus heals a crippled woman (Luke 13:10–17). A woman had been possessed by a spirit which caused her to be crippled for 18 years. When Jesus saw her He simply said, 'You are rid of your trouble.' and the woman was cured. He was criticised for doing this on the Sabbath but argued that the woman had been bound by Satan and it was appropriate that she should be released on the Sabbath.

Physical Illness
Simon's mother-in-law (Luke 4:38–39)
Many people (Luke 4:40–41)
A leper (Luke 4:12–16)
The paralysed man (Luke 5:17–26)
The man with the withered arm (Luke 6:6–11)
The Centurion's servant (Luke 7:1–10). A centurion's servant is ill so he sends some Jewish elders to ask Jesus to cure the servant. Jesus goes to the house but the centurion sends a message that he is not worthy to have Jesus in his house and asks Jesus only to speak to cure the servant. Jesus admires the man's faith and the servant is cured.
The Haemorrhagic woman (Luke 8:43–48)
Jairus' Daughter (Luke 8:49–56)
A man with dropsy (Luke 14:1–6) Jesus uses this episode to cure a man of dropsy on the Sabbath and at the same time challenge the Jewish Sabbath laws about work. He says to the Pharisees, 'Who among you would hesitate to haul his ox or ass to its feet if it fell on the sabbath?'
The Blind man of Jericho (Luke 18:35–43). As Jesus passes by, the blind man calls out, 'Jesus, Son of David, have pity on me!' and Jesus asks the man what he wants. The man replies that he wants his sight and Jesus cures him because of the faith he has shown. (This is the story of Bartimaeus given in Mark)
The thankful leper (Luke 17:11–19). Jesus cures ten lepers, telling them to go and show themselves to the priests. One, realising he is cured on the way to the priests, turns round and goes back to thank Jesus. Jesus tells him, 'Go, your faith has cured you.'

Nature Miracles
Jesus calms the storm (Luke 8:22–25)
Jesus feeds the 5000 (Luke 9:10–17)

Parables in Luke

Luke includes more parables than Mark. His Gospel is perhaps more of a teaching Gospel whereas Mark's is very emphatic about discipleship.

Parables that are equivalent to those in Mark
The Patches and the wineskins (Luke 5:36–39)
The Sower (Luke 8:4–8)
The lamp under the bed – No one hides a lamp under a bed; it is put out for all to see. (Luke 8:16–18)
The Mustard Seed (Luke 13:18–19)
The tenants in the vineyard (Luke 20:9–18)

Parables which do not appear in Mark and may be from Luke's source *L* or from Q.
The Good Samaritan (told in response to the question, 'Who is my neighbour?') (Luke 10:25–37). A man is attacked, beaten, robbed and left for dead. A priest and a levite pass him by but a Samaritan (regarded by the Jews as an enemy) stops, tends his wounds and takes the man to an Inn, leaving money for him to be looked after till he has recovered.
   The neighbour is thus shown to be the one who showed the man kindness.
The Rich Fool (Luke 12:13–21). A rich man grew many crops and decided to store them all in a barn and then take life easy; but that night God said to him, 'You fool, this very

night you must surrender your life; you have made your money – who will get it now?' (This is how it is for a man who amasses wealth for himself but remains a pauper in the sight of God.) Jesus teaches that God clothes even the lilies in the fields and how much more will he look after his little ones. 'Set your mind upon His Kingdom and all the rest will come to you as well.

The Watchful Servants (Luke 12:35–40). Jesus teaches that servants should be alert for the master can return at any time. He says if the Master comes and finds his servants ready he will seat them and wait on them. He reinforces His point by saying that if the householder had known about the burglar, he would not have left his house. (From this story Christians understand that death comes like a thief in the night, stealing up on the unprepared.) This is a message to the Jews who use the comparison of the Messiah coming like a banquet.

Jesus says all must be careful of their power. A servant without a master must not be too severe on others. From he who has much, much will be expected. Thus rights bring responsibility. (Luke 12:41–48).

The Great Feast (Luke 14:7–24). A man prepares a feast (verse 16) and invites his friends; they do not come, pleading business, possessions and relationships as excuses. The man sends his servants to find the poor and the beggars to sit at his table. He says 'Not one of those who were invited shall taste my banquet.'

This is a parable about the Messianic banquet to which many are called and should respond.

The Lost Sheep (Luke 15:1–7). A farmer who loses one sheep leaves the other 99 to search for it and on finding it rejoices. There is more rejoicing in heaven over one repentant sinner than over 99 righteous people who do not need to repent.

Jesus emphasises his call to sinners, the weak in every way, the outcasts of society.

The Lost Coin (Luke 15:8–10). This parable has a message similar to that of The Lost Sheep (above)

The Prodigal (lost) Son (Luke 15:11–32). A younger son asks for his inheritance, takes it and spends it having a good time and winning many friends. When he has no money he has no friends and has a job tending pigs and eating their swill. He decides his Father's servants are better off so he returns home.

When his father sees him he kills the best calf and has a big party. The elder son, who has stayed at home, says, 'Why do you never have a party for me?' His father tells him, 'Everything I have is yours but how can I help welcoming my son who was lost and is found?'

This parable teaches about the constant forgiveness of the Father, God's unconditional love.

The Shrewd Manager (unjust steward) (Luke 16:1–17). The shrewd manager uses his master's debts to win friends for himself. Jesus teaches that money can be put to good purpose but that someone untrustworthy in small things is untrustworthy in great things. He also says you cannot serve God *and* money.

The Rich Man and Lazarus (Luke 16:19–31). This is the story of a rich man who is separated from Abraham after his death; he sees Lazarus, once a beggar, sitting with Abraham at a feast in heaven. The rich man begs that Lazarus might bring him water but Abraham tells him that no one can cross the chasm between heaven and hades. On earth the rich man had everything and Lazarus nothing – now it is for Lazarus to have consolation.

The rich man asks that someone be sent to warn his brothers of what will befall them, but Abraham says, 'If they pay no heed to Moses and the prophets, they will pay no heed to someone who rises from the dead.'

The Gold Coins (Luke 19:11–27). A master goes away, giving each of his ten servants one pound to trade with. One of them makes ten pounds from one, another makes five pounds, while a third makes none and only has the one pound to return to his master. His pound is taken from him to be given to the one with ten, and the master says, 'The man who has will be given more and the man who has nothing, even what he has will be taken from him.'

The purpose of the parables in Luke is to demonstrate Jesus' commitment to the poorest of the poor, to the outcasts, to sinners and the marginalised in society. They emphasise that Jesus was the Saviour of all.

Discipleship in Luke

Much of Luke's Gospel indicates what is necessary for true disciples of Jesus. It is important to be humble, giving of self, forgiving of others – and to spend time with the poor and outcasts of society.

Jesus sends out twelve disciples (Luke 9:1–6). The disciples were told to go out and spread the good news, heal people and drive out demons. This was their work and they were to travel light with only a staff and a shirt.

In Luke's Gospel the following qualities are seen to be necessary in a disciple:

- to be prepared to take up the cross day after day (Luke 9:23–27).
- to be prepared for homelessness (Luke 9:58).
- to be prepared even to put aside family responsibilities (unlike the man who wants to bury his dead father, Luke 9:59,60).
- not always to look back to the family (Jesus fears that the man who wants to say goodbye to his family will be persuaded to change his mind, Luke 9:61,62).
- not to stop or be deterred from a task (Jesus sends out the 72, Luke 10:1–24).
- to put listening to the Word of God before all things (Mary listens to Jesus while Martha fusses and works, Luke 10:38–42).
- to consider the implications of being a disciple carefully. As an owner counts the cost of constructing a tower over his vineyard and a soldier weighs up the implications of mustering his armies so must a would-be disciple make sure he is prepared to give all with total commitment (Luke 14:25–33).
- to sell all and give it to the poor (Luke 18:18–30) (as Mark 10:17–31)
- being prepared to give willingly, as in the case of Zacchaeus (Luke 19:1–10).
- being a servant of all, including children (Luke 9:46–48)
- always being prepared to forgive – even up to seventy times seven (Luke 17:1–4)

Episodes of conflict

Luke does not put too much emphasis on conflict between Jesus and the Jewish leaders or that between Jesus and the Roman authorities since he is anxious to show that Jesus had a message for all people. He does, however, include conflict over the Sabbath laws:

Disciples picking corn on the Sabbath (Luke 6:1–5)
Healing the man with the withered arm (Luke 6:6–11)

Stewardship in Luke

Stewardship of possessions is emphasised in Luke. Jesus' parables in Luke have particular relevance to life in the late twentieth century. People are aware today of a world being stripped of its natural resources; and many are also aware of the futility and worthlessness of material possessions.

A man who is ready to sit back and enjoy the fortune he has amassed but could die that very night (Luke 12:13–21).

A steward who misuses the assets of his master (Luke 16:19–31) (people are misusing the assets God gave them when he created man to have dominion over the earth.

The parable of the rich young man (Luke 18:18–30) is another warning of the folly of treasuring the things of the world.

The parable of the servants with the master's coins (Luke 19:11–27) teaches the need to care for gifts that have been given and use them wisely. In the same way modern Christians believe man is cautioned to use the earth and its resources wisely.

The Passover meal

Luke's account is similar to Mark's (Luke 22:7–20). However, Luke mentions *Peter and John* as the disciples who arranged the room for the Passover.

The Lord's Supper

Luke writes of Jesus instituting the Eucharist *after* giving out the cup of Passover. Luke also adds a teaching from Jesus to his disciples about humble service, leading to reward (Luke 22:24–30), which is a favourite theme for Luke. Luke also adds to Mark's account of Peter's denial of Jesus by saying that Peter would have a leadership role (Luke 22:31–34).

Luke also adds a message from Jesus to the disciples that each must carry a sword on his missionary work as they will be considered outlaws. This is a hint that their lives will be difficult and they might face death because of their work (Luke 22:35–38).

Christians see in this passage a call from God to follow Jesus' way and accept the difficulties that come their way as a result.

The Arrest, Trial and Death of Jesus

As in Mark's Gospel, Luke shows that the religious leaders were plotting against Jesus who prophesied He would suffer and be crucified by them.

The Garden of Gethsemane
Luke's version is shorter than Mark's account but includes an angel (Luke 22:43). Luke includes angels in the infancy narratives.

Jesus is betrayed
Luke adds to Mark's account the detail that the temple guard were among those who arrested Jesus and that Jesus healed the slave's ear after it was cut off by a disciple (Luke 22:49–53).

Luke also adds the idea that this was a time of darkness. Luke has already mentioned that Judas was under Satan's influence (Luke 22:3)

Trial before the Sanhedrin
Luke's account is similar to that in Mark but the trial is held in the morning. The witnesses who contradict one another, mentioned in Mark, are missed out in Luke. Luke's story of Peter's denial is also similar to Mark's but Luke adds a personal touch by writing of Jesus looking at Peter who then broke down.

Trial before Pilate
Luke's account is similar to Mark's but Luke notes the charges made by the Jews against Jesus. Luke emphasises that Pilate found Jesus to be innocent and harmless. Luke then writes of Pilate sending Jesus to Herod (Luke 23:6–12). Luke had written of Herod the fox wanting to kill Jesus (see Luke 13:31–45).

The Death of Jesus
Luke seems to have additional information to that used by Mark. According to Luke Jesus prophesies the violent destruction of Jerusalem (Luke 23:30–32). Luke also includes Jesus' words, 'Father Forgive them; they do not know what they are doing' (Luke 23:34), and his final words are '… into your hands I commit my spirit'.

These differences show that Luke's Gospel was written after the Romans destroyed Jerusalem and that Luke was concerned with the ideas of forgiveness. Jesus' first words according to Luke were about doing His Father's work (Luke 2:50) and Jesus' last words are about His Father.

The Resurrection

Both Luke and Mark record the fact that women found that Jesus was alive, that the stone was rolled away, and that the tomb was empty. Luke records that two men reminded the women of what Jesus had said about his death and resurrection. There is an inference that He has appeared to Simon, but it is vague.

This is significant for Christians since women were not highly regarded by men at this time and Peter was being singled out for leadership of the disciples despite his denial of Jesus.

Luke records more post-resurrection appearances by Jesus than Mark. Mark notes that Jesus appeared to two disciples who were on the way to Emmaus but Luke tells the story in detail — of how Jesus appeared to Cleopas and another disciple who did not recognise him. The desciples explained how they were depressed by Jesus' death since they had hoped He was the Messiah who would set Israel free.

Jesus told them that they were foolish not to believe the message of the Scriptures that the Messiah had to suffer and die before entering the glory of resurrection. Cleopas and the other disciple recognised Jesus when he broke and blessed bread with them and remembered that their 'hearts burned within them' when he spoke. They returned to Jerusalem to tell the others they had seen Jesus.

The story showed that even after being with him for three years the disciples did not understand what sort of Messiah Jesus was.

Jesus then appeared to His disciples, telling them not to be afraid and showing them His stricken hands and side. He ate fish with them to show he was not a ghost.

Luke was reminding the early Christians of their belief that Jesus was really alive.

Luke also records Jesus' teaching that the events of His death and Resurrection were a fulfilment of the Scriptures, and that the disciples had a mission to preach repentance and forgiveness to the whole world, starting in Jerusalem.

Jesus' ascension into heaven took place outside Jerusalem and the disciples were filled with joy and went to the temple praising God.

Luke's Gospel therefore finishes where it began, in the temple.

5.6 Matthew's Gospel

Only NICCEA requires you to have a detailed knowledge of Matthew. All the Boards expect some knowledge of the Sermon on the Mount (Matt. 5), which is an important teaching and a basis for Christian life alongside the ten commandments and the two great commandments.

If you are studying for SEG Syllabus A, Option 3, Christianity through the life and teaching of Jesus as demonstrated in the synoptic Gospels, you need to be familiar with the appropriate passages in Matthew, Mark and Luke.

The Infancy Narratives

Matthew's infancy narrative is less detailed. He tells the reader that Mary found she had conceived by the Spirit and that Joseph wanted to have the marriage contract set aside immediately. An Angel told Joseph the true situation and Joseph took Mary home and cared for her until the child was born (Matt. 1:18–25).

Matthew has the story of the magi (three wise men) who see the star which they believe signifies the birth of the King of the Jews and visit the baby, bringing gifts of gold (riches), frankinsense (Kingship) and myrrh (special calling). They warn the family that Herod is a danger to the baby and Mary and Joseph flee to Egypt until Herod has died. (Matt. 2:1–18).

The Temptations of Jesus (4:1–11)

Miracles in Matthew

Calming the storm (8:23–27)

Parables in Matthew

Parables of the Kingdom of Heaven (Matt. 13:1–50)
The Sower (13:1–9) and the mustard seed (13:31–32).

The foolish bridesmaids (Matt. 25:1–13) failed to preserve enough oil for their lamps and had run out when the bridegroom came. Jesus teaches 'Be prepared, you know not the day nor the hour when you will be called'.

Resurrection (Matt. 28)

When Mary of Magdala and the other Mary approach the tomb, there is an earthquake and an angel appears. He tells them not to be afraid, shows them the place where Jesus was and says he has gone to Galilee and they must tell the disciples. They see Jesus on the way.

Matthew emphasises that the chief priests sought to suppress stories of the Resurrection by bribing the soldiers. The disciples see Jesus and He sends them out to spread the good news, to baptise in His name and observe all that He has taught.

Worship in Matthew

Praying in secret (Matt. 6:5–8). Jesus teaches that hypocrites say their prayers standing up for all to see. You should pray in a secret place with the door closed to the Father who sees what is secret and will reward you. He knows your needs and you should pray thus:

Our Father in heaven,
thy name be hallowed; thy kingdom come,
on earth as in heaven.
Give us today our daily bread,
Forgive us the wrong we have done,
as we have forgiven those who have wronged us.
And do not bring us to the test,
but save us from the evil one (Matt. 6:9–13).

Answer to Prayer (Matt. 7:7–11)
Jesus teaches that a person only has to *ask* to receive, *seek* to find, *knock* and the door will be opened.

Fasting (Matt. 6:6–18)
Jesus teaches his followers to fast but not to be gloomy – and to show no sign to others, keeping it as a secret for the Father.

Authority

Peter's declaration (Matt. 16:13–17).
The Transfiguration (Matt. 17:1–8).
Jesus' Authority (Matt. 22:23–27). Jesus is asked by the Sadducees what the relationship of those who have been married to each other on earth will be after death. The Sadducees were trying to trick Jesus. They believed that at death the soul dies with the body. Jesus replies that after death people are like angels. Then Jesus says: God said, 'I am the God of Abraham, Isaac and Jacob, of the living not the dead.' People were astounded at his teaching. Jesus showed that God was constant to all generations in saying God was the God of all the Fathers of Faith.

Beliefs

Jesus proclaims the Kingdom (Matt 6:25–34) Consider the lilies of the field. Jesus teaches of the great love the Father has for all His creation and He will look after all His children.
The Grace of God, the tenants in the vineyard (Matt. 20:1–16)
The Kingdom of God is like a mustard seed (Matt. 13:31–33), a treasure, pearl, a net (Matt. 13:47–50)
How people will be judged (Matt. 25:31–46). Jesus cautions followers that God will judge people, bringing to Himself all those who gave food to the hungry, drink to the thirsty and clothes to the naked and who visited the sick and imprisoned, for '… whatever you do for the least of my brothers you do for me.'

It is important for modern Christians that Jesus teaches that care for others (neighbour) is the first duty of the Christian.

Community

Call to discipleship. As in Luke and Mark, the fishermen leave their nets and follow Jesus (Matt. 4:18–22).
The Apostles are commissioned and charged with their tasks (as Luke and Mark) (Matt. 28:16–20).
Christians are to be salt, light and leaven in a community (Matt. 5:13–16; 13:33).

Morality

The Golden rule: Always treat others as you would like them to treat you (Matt. 7:12).
On murder, reconciliation, retaliation, loving your enemies, reproving your brother – refer to beatitudes (Matt. 5:3–12).
Concern for the poor and oppressed (Matt. 6:19–21). Don't store up treasure on earth, store up treasure in heaven.
You cannot be the servant of two masters, you cannot serve God and mammon (Matt. 6:24).

Justice

The law and the prophets. Jesus says He did not come to abolish the law and the prophets but to complete it (Matt. 5:17–20).
Do not judge others; remove the log from your own eye before worrying about the speck in another's (Matt. 7:1–5).
Pay the right taxes to the right person – to Caesar what is Caeser's and to God what is God's. (Matt. 22:15–22).

Lifestyle and social practices

Christian values

- Do good secretly (Matt. 6:1–4)
- Honesty (Matt. 5:33–37)
- Beatitudes (Matt. 5:3–12)
- Taking up the cross – suffering (Matt. 16:21–26)
- Entering by the narrow gate (Matt. 7:13–14)
- Acting on the message. The man who acts on the words of Jesus is like a man who builds his house on a rock – his house has firm foundations (Matt. 7:24–29)

The Beatitudes (Matt. 5:3–12)

The Beatitudes stand with the Two great commandments as essential teachings about what is important for followers of Jesus. They are teachings about the way Christians should live and can be applied to all areas of individual and corporate lifestyles.

How Blest are those who know their need of God; the Kingdom of God is theirs.
How blest are the sorrowful; they shall find consolation.
How blest are those of gentle spirit; they shall have the earth for their possession.
How blest are those who hunger and thirst to see right prevail; they shall be satisfied.
How blest are those who show mercy; mercy shall be shown them.
How blest are those whose hearts are pure; they shall see God.
How blest are the peacemakers; God shall call them His sons.
How blest are those who have suffered persecution for the cause of right; the Kingdom of God is theirs.
'How blest you are when you suffer insults and persecution and every kind of calumny for my sake. Accept it with gladness and exultation, for you have a rich reward in heaven; in the same way they persecuted the prophets before you.' Matt. 5:3–12

Chapter 5 Jesus and the Gospels

5.7 The miracles of Jesus

The miracles Jesus is reported to have performed have been the subject of great debate. Jesus performed miracles to show God's great power over mental and physical illness and death and over nature. Jesus showed that for miracles to take place it is necessary to have faith. Miracles do not cause faith.

Syllabuses / Miracles	SEG Syllabus A Option 3	SEG Syllabus C Unit 3 (a)	NEAB Syllabus B Section 1C	MEG Paper 1	ULEAC Unit 5	(WJEC) GP 2 Christianity through the Gospels	NEAB Syllabus C Section 2	NICCEA Syllabus A & B
Exorcism 1. Legion (Gerascene demoniac)	Mark 5 1–20				Mark 5 1–20	Mark 5 1–20		
Possessed man in synagogue		Luke 4 31–37	Mark 1 21–28		Mark 1 21–28		Mark 1 21–24	
Epileptic boy		Luke 9 37–42	Mark 9 14–29		Mark 9 14–29			
Physical healing Syro-Phoenician woman's daughter	Mark 7 24–30		Mark 7 24–30		Mark 7 24–30			
Blind Bartimaeus	Mark 10 46–52						Mark 10 46–52	
Centurion's servant	Luke 7 1–10			Luke 7 1–10				
Widow's son at Nain	Luke 7 11–17							
Ten lepers	Luke 17 11–19	Luke 17 11–19						
One leper						Mark 1:40–45		Matt. 8 1–4
Man with withered hand	Mark 3 1–6	Luke 6 6–11	Mark 3 1–6		Mark 3 1–6	Mark 3 1–6		
Simon's mother-in-law		Luke 4 38–40		Luke 4 38–40				
Jesus heals many people		Luke 4 40–42						
The soldier's servant		Luke 7 1–17						Matt. 8 5–13
Crippled woman		Luke 13 10–17						
Paralysed man			Mark 2 1–12	Luke 5 17–26	Mark 2 1–12	Mark 2 1–12	Mark 2 1–12	Matt. 9 1–7
Woman with haemorrhage			Mark 5 25–34		Mark 5 25–34			
Feeding the 5,000	Mark 6 30–44	Luke 9 10–17	Mark 6 30–44		Mark 6 30–44	Mark 6 30–44	Mark 6 30–56	Matt. 14 13–21
Walking on the lake	Mark 6 45–52 Matt. 14 22–33				Mark 6 45–52			Matt. 14 22–33
Calming the storm		Luke 8 40–56			Mark 4 35–41		Mark 4 35–41	Matt. 8 23–27
Raising from dead of Jairus' daughter	Mark 5 21–24 35–43		Mark 5 21–24 35–43		Mark 5 21–24 35–43			Matt. 9 18–19 23–26

5.7 The miracles of Jesus

Miracles should be looked at on three levels:
- *Terras* (wonder): people were filled with amazement.
- *Dynamis* (power): people were aware of the great power Jesus demonstrated – the power of God.
- *Semeion* (meaning) – for witnesses or the healed miracles had a particular meaning or significance.

When you study a miracle, make sure you know exactly what happened and be sure which aspects of the miracles are significant, e.g.:

1. Was the miracle one of healing; exorcism; mastery over nature or raising the dead?
2. Was it on the Sabbath?
3. If someone was healed was that person a Jew or a Gentile?
4. Did the miracle take place in a synagogue?
5. Did Jesus speak or touch or heal from a distance?
6. Did Jesus speak of forgiveness?
7. What motive did Jesus show for the miracle?
8. Was faith specifically mentioned?
9. Did the miracle take place in secret?
10. Did Jesus ask for secrecy or order publicity?

Look at the table opposite and see which miracles you need to learn about; make sure you know the key facts about them.

For Christians today the happenings which gave rise to the miracle stories are not the most important thing. The miracles show how the Gospel writers perceived Jesus and what they believed Him to be. For early Christians the miracle helped them to understand and believe in the idea of Jesus as the good news and a new way. They can be regarded as literally true, explicable in modern science or simply symbolic but whatever a Christian believes about them does not diminish the person of Jesus.

Summary

1. The Gospels are the good news about Jesus.
2. Each Gospel is for a different readership and is slightly different in emphasis.
3. The synoptic Gospels are Mark, Luke and Matthew; they are called synoptic because they are similar to one another.
4. Mark's Gospel concentrates on the difficulties of discipleship: inspiring the readers with courage; Jesus as offering a new way; the conflict of Jesus with the authorities.
5. Luke's Gospel is one of more universal appeal. He writes for Jews and gentiles alike. He sees Jesus as the suffering servant and a teacher of the way of humility and service to the poor.
6. Matthew writes for Jewish Christians and portrays Jesus as the one who has come to fulfil the prophecies and complete what Moses began.
7. Jesus performs miracles to show the importance of faith and to demonstrate that He has God's power over nature and illness and death.
8. Jesus teaches parables because they are the medium of the day and He wants people to understand the nature of the Kingdom.
9. Jesus teaches that to be a follower demands very special personal qualities but in particular self-denial and helping the poor and sick.
10. The death of Jesus is described so that all readers can understand the suffering Jesus bore for the salvation of people.
11. The Resurrection is the hope that all Christians have needed since the early followers were martyred.

Chapter 5 Jesus and the Gospels

Quick questions

Luke
1. How does Mary respond when told of her expected child?
2. What is the purpose of the *magnificat*?
3. What is the importance of John the Baptist?
4. How do the shepherds know about Jesus?
5. How do the shepherds react when they visit Jesus?

Matthew
6. What is the significance of the visit of the three magi?

Matthew and Luke
7. How does the devil tempt Jesus in the desert?

Mark and Luke
8. What is heard at the baptism of Jesus?
9. How do Christians mark the temptation by the devil?
10. List the miracles in Mark or Luke that show Jesus' power over:
    - mental illness
    - physical illness
    - nature.
11. Explain the four types of seed in the parable of the sower and what they represent (Mark/Luke)
12. How does Jesus demonstrate that the Sabbath was made for man and not man for the Sabbath? (Choose one example from Mark or Luke.)
13. Why is it important for followers to 'consider the lilies of the field'?
14. List the miracles which demonstrate the importance of faith.
15. Describe an episode where Jesus explains the importance of repentance and forgiveness (Luke).
16. Describe an episode where Jesus points out the folly of worrying about worldly wealth.
17. From either Mark or Luke identify which qualities are important for a disciple.
18. What happens at the Last Supper? (Mark or Luke)
19. Why is the Last Supper important to Christians?
20. Using Mark or Luke, make a list of the key events from Jesus' arrest to his moment of death.
21. Describe the morning of the Resurrection (Mark or Luke)
22. How does Jesus ascend to heaven?

Chapter 6
Personal and social relationships

6.1 Christian approaches

Christians believe that moral behaviour and social practices are governed by belief in God and the teachings of Jesus. Everything that Jesus taught about how people should relate to one another is based on Christian beliefs about the nature of the human person.

Genesis 1 tells how God created the world and saw that it was good; and He created humankind to be stewards of the world, to look after His creation. Genesis says that God created man and woman in His own image. Christians accept the scriptural teaching that every human person is unique and special to God. God took human form in the person of Jesus Christ to show His love for His creation. Because of this belief Christians have an obligation to make the love of God the focus which directs their personal relationships.

> So God created man in his own image;
> in the image of God he created him;
> male and female he created them.
> God blessed them and said to them,
> 'Be fruitful and increase, fill the earth …' (Gen. 1:27–28)

> I give you a new commandment: love one another; as I have loved you love one another. (John 13:34)

> 'Every sexual act must be within the framework of marriage.' (Casti conubii Papal Encyclical – Catholic Truth Society)

> 'For this reason a man shall leave his father and mother and be made one with his wife; and the two shall become one flesh. It follows that they are no longer two individuals: they are one flesh.' (Mark 10:5–8)

Relationships between the sexes

Relationships between people of opposite sexes are seen as natural and desirable by all Christians. Young people are encouraged to form friendships and Christian churches often have youth groups and activities to enable the development of natural friendship in a structured environment.

Within the major Christian cultures young people mix freely so they can have friendship without inhibition and be ready to choose their own life partner when the time is right. As adulthood approaches and young people have a growing awareness of their own sexuality, the churches try to give guidelines on the nature of sexual love. To express love through sexual intercourse is recognised as right and natural in Christianity but chastity is encouraged.

The churches try to show young people that the total giving of self in sexual union is a deep and powerful giving which should not be treated casually. People should understand the idea of self respect and honouring their own bodies. Young people are encouraged to be in charge of themselves and to be assertive of their rights over their own bodies. Promiscuity is seen as a sad dishonouring of oneself and a loss of self-respect.

For these reasons Christianity is a monogamous religion. Christians are only allowed one partner. Adultery is wrong. It is against the Ten Commandments and the teachings of Jesus.

Sexual love

The churches teach that ideally full sexual love should be reserved for married couples, while some Christian denominations recognise that for some couples it is appropriate to have a sexual relationship outside marriage. Couples living together without being married are regarded as 'cohabiting' and may become in law 'common law spouses'.

Marriage

Marriage is regarded as a sacrament in the Roman Catholic Church and in some Churches of the Anglo-Catholic tradition. It is therefore an indissoluble bond. Marriage is a lifelong commitment between two people who have vowed to each other before God and witnesses 'to love and cherish

for better for worse,
for richer for poorer
in sickness and health
till death do us part.'

Before marriage a couple should be prepared by the minister to recognise the seriousness of marriage. They should forsake all others and bring integrity, loyalty and fidelity to their union. The purpose of marriage is to find fulfilment with a lifelong partner and to raise children.

The Marriage Vows
I take you to be my husband (wife),
to have and to hold
from this day forward;
for better, for worse,
for richer, for poorer,
in sickness and in health,
to love and to cherish,
till death us do part,
according to God's holy law;
and this is my solemn vow.

The marriage ceremony

There are four basic parts to the marriage service.

1. The minister establishes that the couple are free to marry and no one has any lawful objection.
2. The couple exchange vows.
3. The couple exchange rings as symbols of fidelity.
4. The minister blesses the union in God's name.

Breakdown of marriage

Despite preparation and right intentions, sometimes a marriage does not work. The Christian churches recognise that we do not live in a perfect world and they have developed ways of trying to help people who are faced with the tragedy of a broken marriage. Couples can separate and remain married using any agency, either of the church or another, to try to bring about a reconciliation. The Catholic Marriage Advisory Council (CMAC) and RELATE are two such organisations which welcome people of all or no religious persuasion. Ultimately a couple may decide they must divorce and put an end to their legal status as a married couple. This is done through the legal system but it is not recognised by the Roman Catholic Church or the Church of England.

'What God has joined together, man must not separate.' (Mark 10:9)

Annulment

Occasionally in the Roman Catholic tradition an official appointed by the church can look into the circumstances of a marriage if there is reason to believe it is not a valid one. This is the case if one or other of the marriage partners was not competent to make the vows or if it can be proved that the vows were not meant, e.g. if one partner agreed to accept children of the marriage and later refused to have any or maybe concealed that he or she was not able to have any. For a marriage to be valid it must be consummated: the couple must have sexual intercourse. If any kind of compulsion is discovered behind either partner marrying, the marriage is not valid.

In these cases the marriage is deemed not to have taken place and is declared null. It is annulled. The couple also have a legal divorce and are then completely free to marry as they wish in the same way as any unmarried persons.

Remarriage

'For married people I have a command which is not my own but the Lord's: a wife must not leave her husband; but if she does she must remain single or else be reconciled to her husband; and a husband must not divorce his wife.' (1 Cor. 7:10–11)

The churches regard marital breakdown as a tragedy and believe that the couple should be treated with compassion and understanding by the community and given every help in trying to become reconciled with each other. Sometimes a couple who have been validly married in a church will divorce. Neither partner is then eligible to remarry in church, and if they marry it will be in a civil ceremony in a Registry Office. They are considered to have cut themselves off from the sacraments of the church and are expected not to receive them where it is likely to cause a scandal. In practice this letter of the law is rarely adhered to and people who wish to receive the sacraments are usually deeply troubled by marital breakdown and go to great lengths to avoid causing distress in the local faith community.

Parenthood and family life

One of the main reasons for marriage is to provide a stable and loving environment in which to bring up children; and Christians regard the family as an institution which should be cherished, respected and encouraged. Traditionally the nuclear family of mother, father and children has been regarded as ideal, and also the extended family where different generations share the home and influence decisions in the home.

With soaring divorce rates reaching nearly 50% there has to be acknowledgement that some other types of family are happy and stable and enable children to develop and grow. Such families are single-parent families and restructured families, the latter being families in which two divorced people have come together and bring up their respective children in one joint family home.

The Christian churches try to support family life. Christianity teaches through the commandments that children should honour their parents. Through the New Testament parents are taught not to alienate their children and through the example of Jesus they are taught to regard children as special gifts who are close to God. To provide practical help, many Christian communities run parent and toddler groups and youth groups of different types, and organise family entertainments and social events. In particular, families are encouraged to worship together as churches will have family services with special children's liturgies and youth participation.

'Fathers, do not exasperate your children for fear they grow disheartened ...' (Col. 3:21)

Birth control

Human beings have the power to control their own fertility. They can live in chastity, i.e. without sexual intercourse, or they can utilise natural or artificial methods of contraception.

The Roman Catholic Church says that only natural methods of 'family planning' are acceptable and that ideally couples should always be open to the possibility of children. The natural method involves abstaining from sexual intercourse when the woman is fertile.

The other Christian denominations leave the couple to plan their family in their own way, using any method they choose. Artificial contraceptives include condoms, femidoms, the contraceptive pill, the intra-uterine coil, the cap and the diaphragm.

Most couples today choose to limit their families to two children for social and financial reasons.

'The love of husband and wife in God's plan leads beyond itself and new life is generated, a family is born.' (Pope John Paul)

'It is right and proper for parents to regulate the number of children they have and to space them out in the family, but not by means which artificially make it impossible for sexual intercourse to result in conception.' (Catholic Truth Society)

Diversity of lifestyle

The Christian churches today recognise that every human is unique and all cannot conform to the same lifestyle and pattern. Some people choose other ways of life.

Some people choose celibacy which is the unmarried state. The Roman Catholic Church insists that all priests are celibate. Members of many religious orders also vow to be celibate.

The churches also recognise that some people wish to have a close-partner relationship with a member of the same sex – a homosexual relationship. If this relationship involves sexual acts, those acts are regarded as wrong; but the individuals themselves are not to be ostracised but given the same love and consideration as everyone else.

'Homosexual acts are disordered and can no way be approved of.' (Roman Catholic declaration of Sexual ethics 1975)

You shall not lie down with a man in the same way that you would lie down with a woman. It is an abomination. (Lev. 18:22)

6.2 Focus on Judaism

Personal relationships in Judaism

The human person
In Genesis 1, the beginning of the Torah, it says that God gave man control over everything on earth; Judaism teaches that this power makes human beings special and unique. People have the ability to make moral choices and distinguish between right

Chapter 6 Personal and social relationships

and wrong. When people choose to do right they are justifying God and helping to make a good world.

Over the thousands of years in which Judaism has developed there has grown up a system of laws to guide lifestyle and relationships. There is the **Noahide code** or sheva mitzvot (seven commandments) which command all people to live under God's rule. There are also the Ten Commandments given to Moses in Exodus and altogether 613 commandments throughout the Old Testament which give guidance on all aspects of life.

He gave them:'... control over the fish of the sea and the birds of the sky, over the animals and over the whole earth.' (Gen. 1:26)

Marriage

Marriage, called **kidushin**, is very important in Judaism. It is seen as the natural state for man and woman to be in. In marriage the male and female partners join to become a complete unit, a whole. Jews are encouraged to marry Jews, particularly since Judaism is passed from mother to child. Only two Jews can have a religious wedding. A Jew marrying a Gentile would not be able to marry according to tradition unless the non-Jewish partner converted.

'A man shall leave his father and mother and cleave to his wife, and they shall become one flesh.' (Gen. 2:24)

The naturalness of sexuality is acknowledged; sex outside marriage is considered wrong. Jewish communities try to discourage wrong sexual behaviour by keeping boys and girls separate as far as possible to avoid natural temptation. This separation is more marked in Orthodox Jewish communities. The different approaches of Orthodox, Reform and Liberal Jewish communities will be discussed in later chapters.

Friendly relationships between people of the same sex are encouraged but homosexual relationships are seen as wrong. There are pressures from gay communities for a more tolerant attitude and this is brought to bear in the Reform and Liberal Jewish traditions.

Marriages are monogamous and sometimes (in Orthodox communities) arranged between families. There are three parts to a Jewish marriage.

1. The **Ketubah** is a document, signed before the wedding, in which couples agree to 'cherish, respect and support each other'. In an Orthodox marriage the document might include details of financial arrangements in the event of divorce.

2. The Chuppah and Kidushin. The bride steps under the chuppah (canopy) which represents the marital home and the wedding is made holy by the kidushin, who is usually a **Rabbi**. The couple drink from a cup of wine and are blessed. The groom gives the bride a ring and says, 'By this ring you are married to me in holiness and according to the law of Moses'. The groom throws a glass to the floor and smashes it with his foot. This act is meant to recall the destruction of the temple in the first century – even the happiest of days is tinged with sadness. The congregation shouts 'Mazel Tov' (good luck).

3. The marriage is validated by the couple then living together as man and wife.

Marital breakdown

Provision is made for divorce but the application of that ruling is interpreted differently in different Jewish traditions. When a marriage is considered to have broken down the couple agree to divorce and in a rabbinical court of three rabbis called a **Bet Din** a divorce document called a 'get' is prepared; this must be given by the husband to the wife. Occasionally the wife can apply for divorce, in which case she gives the 'get' to her husband. A wife or husband can refuse to be divorced in the Orthodox tradition but in Israel a man can be imprisoned for refusing to divorce his wife.

A woman must wait three months before remarrying in case she is pregnant. A child of a divorced woman is regarded as illegitimate. Under Jewish law a civil divorce is only recognised in the Reform tradition.

The family

Family life is paramount in the Jewish tradition and the parents have key roles. Living as an extended family with many generations together is seen as a great blessing. In Israel some Jews choose to live in community families on a **Kibbutz** where all the roles are shared.

Contraception is regarded as sometimes necessary but should not be used for the wrong reasons. Couples should not put material wealth above the blessing of children. Family life is to be fostered by gathering together for the Friday night Sabbath meal.

Judaism teaches that parents and children have duties and responsibilities to each other. Parents must provide for their children and teach them what they need for their safety and security and ability to make a living. Where necessary parents should punish children appropriately to correct them, but they should not threaten to punish them. Children must respect their parents and listen to them.

God created the world, he created it not to remain empty; he made it to be populated.' (Isa. 45:18)

'Honour your Father and Mother …' (Exod. 20:12)

6.3 Focus on Islam

Personal relationships

Muslims believe all human life is created by Allah and is a sacred gift.

Relationships between the sexes

Relationships between people of opposite sexes are seen as natural and desirable and the married state is seen as the natural state for humans. Marriage is for the purpose of a stable, loving relationship with profound commitment. Sex is not permitted outside marriage and permissiveness is seen as wrong. Any form of sexual misconduct is regarded as weak in Islam and careful steps are taken before marriage to guard against dishonour.

Before marriage takes place a woman makes it known that marriage is her wish; she is then approached by representatives. A couple will be given the chance to get to know each other but they should always be chaperoned.

If a woman agrees to marriage it is contracted but not immediately consummated. Within marriage fidelity is absolutely essential. Adultery is regarded as a terrible wrong and can be severely punished under Islamic law.

Marriage is by contract which is read out by a qadi (judge) at the mosque. A husband must provide for his wife and agrees to pay her a mahr (dowry) in order to provide her with some security. She retains her property and can have the right to divorce written into the contract.

There are provisions in Islam for polygamy. It is permitted for a man to have more than one wife. The Islamic countries which allow this expect a man to be able to support all his wives. It is recorded in the **Qur'an** because Mohammed showed it was the male duty to look after as many women as possible, especially in time of war when men might be in short supply. A man may also take another wife if his wife is ill, infertile or unable to satisfy his needs sexually.

When a husband and wife share intimacy, it is rewarded and a blessing from Allah. Just as they would be punished if they engaged in illicit sex.' (Hadith)

Relationships between people of the same sex

Friendship is encouraged and because the sexes are often kept apart as young people these friendships are the norm. Social events and schooling are usually single sex as far as possible. Sexual relationships are seen as depraved and against the natural order. There is no tolerance of homosexual practice and some Islamic lawyers believe it merits the death penalty.

'If two men are guilty of lewdness, punish them. If they repent and change their ways, leave them alone.' (Surah 4:16–17)

Marital Breakdown

Divorce is permissible as a last resort when all else has failed. A couple can agree mutually to divorce. A wife can divorce her husband if she has a grievance. She returns the wedding gift and the marriage is dissolved.

'The most detestable act that God has permitted is divorce.' (Hadith)

Chapter 6   Personal and social relationships

For a divorce to be valid both partners must be sane and free from influence of intoxicants or coercion, and the divorce agreement must be clear to all.

A woman can divorce her husband if he mistreats her or cannot maintain her; if he is impotent, insane or has a disease; if he deserts her, is excommunicated or imprisoned; or if he was deceitful at the time of the marriage.

After agreement there is a waiting period of 30 days to 9 months before the divorce is final. This is called iddah. During this time the couple can be reconciled. After iddah they can remarry. They are allowed to remarry each other twice more if they wish.

Normally after a divorce in Islam the father takes responsibility for the children.

'If a wife fears cruelty or desertion on her husband's part, there is no blame on them if they arrange an amicable settlement between themselves.'
(Surah 4:128)

The family

Family life is central to Islam and all Muslims have a duty to one another. All generations who are related to one another by blood are regarded as part of the family. Parents must cherish and nurture their children. They must set them a good example and not overestimate their talents. They must teach them the truths of their faith. Old people must be cared for, respected and honoured and their opinion must take precedence over that of the children as they are the providers of the past.

A great deal of importance is accorded to blood relationships and adoption is not allowed in Islam although families are expected to care for orphans.

Islam permits a degree of birth control but teaches that every life is a gift from Allah and should be welcomed. Family planning should be mutually agreed between man and wife and should only be employed for good and honourable reasons.

'It is He who created you from a single cell with a mate of like nature in order that they might live together.' (Surah 7:189)

An Islamic wedding

Summary

1   Christianity, Judaism and Islam teach that all life is created by God and is sacred. Every human person is unique and humans have power over the earth.
2   Christians believe that God created man in His own image.
3   In all three faiths friendships between the sexes are encouraged and marriage between a man and a woman is seen as the most natural state in which to live your life. In Islam and Judaism marriage is the ideal state. In Christianity it is recognised that for some people celibacy is more appropriate and this is as valid as the married state.

4   The purpose of marriage is to provide lifelong companionship for both partners and a secure, loving environment for children.
5   Sex before marriage and adultery are seen as wrong.
6   Homosexual relationships are seen as unnatural and wrong; they are tolerated in Christianity and the liberal tradition of Judaism, but they are not tolerated in Islam.
7   Divorce and remarriage are allowed in Judaism and Islam but they are not allowed in all denominations of Christianity.
8   Contraception is permitted in all three faiths but the Roman Catholic denomination specifies the use of natural methods and Judaism stipulates that the method should be utilised by the woman.
9   Family life is to be promoted as the ideal for all people and in Judaism and Islam there is a definite duty to care for the extended family.
10 Children are taught to honour and respect their parents and parents are to provide for their children, set them the right example and guide them in the right ways as they grow.

Quick questions

1   Why should the love of God be the guiding factor in all human relationships according to Christian teaching?
2   What type of family groups are: extended; nuclear; and restructured?
3   What is the difference between chastity and celibacy?
4   What is the purpose of marriage?
5   Why do some Christian denominations not allow divorce?
6   What is an annulment?
7   How might faith communities encourage friendship between the sexes?
8   How do Muslims/Christians/Jews regard homosexual relationships?
9   What is the teaching on birth control in Islam/Judaism/Christianity?
10 What is the teaching on child–parent relationships in Judaism/Islam/Christianity?

Chapter 7
Personal and social issues

7.1 Christian approaches

Medical ethics

Abortion

Abortion is the name for a situation in which a pregnancy is ended before the term has been completed. The foetus dies. This can occur naturally or it can be procured by surgical procedure.

Abortion has been legal in Great Britain since 1967. The law was amended in 1990 and it allows for abortion up to the 24th week of pregnancy if two doctors agree that there is a risk to the mental or physical health of the mother or her existing children. The law also allows abortion without time limit if the danger to the mother's health is severe, her life is at risk or the child is likely to be severely handicapped.

Abortion is a complex issue which has always existed. Women have sought abortion because they have felt unable socially, physically, emotionally or financially to take care of a child. The legalisation of abortion was in response to the numbers of deaths and injuries brought about by illegal abortions. Legal abortion was sought by the women's movement who believed that a woman must have the right to choose what she does with her own body. It is still a controversial area and there are strong pro- and anti-abortion groups who constantly lobby governments to have the law made tighter or more liberal.

The Roman Catholic church says that abortion is wrong. Life begins at conception and the foetus' right to life is equal to the mother's. The Church of England says that abortion is permissible if the mother's life is in danger.

> 'From the time that the ovum is fertilised, a life is begun which is neither that of the father nor the mother. It is rather the life of a new human being with its own growth. It would never be made human if it were not human already.'
> (Declaration on procured abortion of the Roman Catholic Church 1974)

> 'Although the foetus is to be specially respected and protected, nonetheless the foetus is not absolutely sacrosanct if it endangers the life of the mother.'
> (Church of England board of social responsibility)

Childlessness

Family life is portrayed as desirable and natural in all cultures and is promoted by Christianity. Therefore infertility leading to childlessness is a cause of great heartache. As medical science has discovered ways to help people to have children the churches have become concerned with the ethics of the situation.

There are six main artificial methods of helping childless couples.

1. AIH is when the husband's sperm is introduced artificially into the woman.
2. AID is when a donor's sperm is used artificially.
3. IVF is when the parents' own sperm and egg are fertilised in a test tube and then transferred to the wife.
4. Egg donation is when the husband's sperm is used to fertilise a donated egg which is then transferred to the wife.
5. Embryo donation is the transfer of an embryo fertilised in a test tube from donated egg and sperm.

6. Surrogacy is when a woman actually has a baby for another couple, becoming pregnant either by sperm donation from the father or another man.

Because it is possible to create an embryo (a potential human being) in a test tube there have to be laws to guard against the abuse of that potential person. The Human Fertilization and Embryology Act 1990 ensures that:

- Donated eggs and semen are anonymous and the woman giving birth is to be regarded as the mother.
- A donor should not provide for more than ten children.
- Embryos should be frozen for up to ten years at which point they become the property of the storing authority rather than the parents.
- Surrogacy is a criminal offence.
- No human embryo can be used for research after 14 days and it is illegal to implant a human embryo in another species.

Those engaging in artificial insemination are involved in a positive affirmation of the family. It is therefore regarded as an acceptable practice. (Church of England Report: Human fertilization and Embryology)

'Artificial insemination violates the dignity of the person and the sanctity of marriage. It is contrary to God's law ... a third party becoming involved in a marriage is like "mechanical adultery."' (John Hardon, Modern Catholic Dictionary. Robert Hall, 1980)

The Roman Catholic church is opposed to all methods of artificial help which remove the creation of the child from the act of union between the married couple. The only method acceptable is the donation of the husband's sperm. The Church of England accepts all the methods and supports the clauses of the above-mentioned Act, agreeing that surrogacy is wrong.

Treatment of the sick, elderly and dying

In Great Britain there are ever-growing numbers of elderly people and also many sick. People are living longer because of better living conditions and advancements in medicine. Christianity teaches that all people should be respected and honoured.

Many old people do not have any relatives to care for them and have to be cared for in nursing or rest homes. Large numbers are also dependent on the state for practical and financial support.

It is now possible to keep people alive who are extremely ill or suffering terminal illness. Euthanasia is a process which leads to a gentle and easy death for such people. Some believe that seriously ill people should have the option of being allowed to die to end their pain and suffering. This is called voluntary euthanasia and it is an active choice. It is illegal in Great Britain for anyone to assist someone to die.

Sometimes it is not clear whether a medical decision is really euthanasia. For example, a decision might be made not to treat an infection in a seriously handicapped baby and that baby might die as a result; or, after a decision not to feed a severely handicapped baby by tube that baby may become weak and die. Medical ethics cannot be absolute in these circumstances. Occasionally relatives may have to make a decision to allow a person to die when there is no hope of his or her recovery. People can be kept breathing by machine but there is controversy about whether this can be described as life when the person has no hope of ever sustaining independent life.

Students should look for examples of ethical dilemmas, which are often in the news.

When someone is suffering from a terminal illness and death is near that person may be able to have care in a hospice for the dying. Here people are offered pain relief and the chance to live fully until the moment of death in an atmosphere of joy, love, caring, gentleness and hope compatible with Christian Gospel values. The hospice movement was begun by Dame Cicely Saunders.

Christian teaching is that the body is a temple of the Holy Spirit and life is sacred. It is against Christian teaching to commit suicide. Many Christians struggle with the idea that a loving God should allow suffering in His creation. Suffering is seen all over the world through such things as hunger, illness and war. Christians believe this suffering is a great mystery about life which is beyond comprehension. They believe man suffers because of original sin, the fall of Adam and Eve. They believe that much suffering is therefore caused by man himself but there are some aspects of suffering which seem to have no cause at all and it is these that Christians offer up to God to show their faith and trust in Him.

Christians are enabled to do this because of their ultimate belief that all will be revealed to them

Chapter 7 Personal and social issues

after their death. Christian teaching is that Christ died on the cross to save man from his sins. If Christians accept the gift of Christ's sacrifice and turn to God, trying to live their lives in Christ, they will be united with God for all eternity after death; all mysteries will be revealed to them and they will know no more suffering.

Christian communities endeavour to care for those in need, for example by working in the hospice movement. Local communities offer a variety of ways of looking after the sick and elderly. These range from fund-raising for basic necessities to other more practical means such as giving food at harvest, organising social events and outings and a programme of visiting. Forward-looking schemes look to integrate the elderly in the community by encouraging them to participate in school life and sit on active church committees.

7.2 Focus on Judaism

Medical ethics

The teaching of Judaism on abortion is similar to that of the Church of England: it is wrong because it is the taking of a life. But Judaism does not give the life of the child the same status as that of the mother, and if the mother's life is in danger, or she may be psychologically harmed by the pregnancy or the child is likely to be severely retarded then abortion is regarded as sad but permissible.

For childless couples artificial insemination with the husband's sperm is permitted. *In vitro* fertilisation is accepted provided the embryos are protected. Other methods are seen as too unnatural and surrogacy is not acceptable. It is seen as an abuse of the body. Judaism teaches that the body should be kept clean and healthy.

Old age, illness and death

Elderly people are an important part of Jewish family life; they should be respected, honoured and cared for within the family. Some Jews see this as a sign that there has been no change in values over the generations. Each generation maintains the teachings of the Jewish faith and is therefore able to tolerate other generations.

Life is God-given and it is against Jewish teaching to commit suicide. Only God has the right to decide the hour of death. Jews are opposed to euthanasia but they do not agree that life support machines should continue to sustain life when there is no independent brain, heart or lung function. It is also acceptable to stop treatment when it would be too painful and not really useful.

'Not to have known suffering is not to be truly human.' (Midrash)

Suffering

In Judaism suffering is part of life. Suffering makes it possible for man to operate his free will to reject God and do evil. Jews believe that God tests the strong with suffering and that suffering helps people to become more human.

'God says, 'If I grant you happiness, give thanks; if I bring you suffering, give thanks.' (Rabbis of the Talmud)

7.3 Focus on Islam

Medical Ethics

Abortion is regarded as wrong in Islam although it is permissible in some situations. It is allowed if the mother's life is in danger. Some Muslims believe that the soul is breathed into the foetus on the 120th day and if an abortion is necessary it should happen before then. It is a very serious matter and the Qur'an teaches that on judgement day the babies will want to know why they were killed.

'Slay not your children, the killing of them is a great sin.' (Surah 17:31)

Infertility

Artificial insemination with the husband's sperm is allowed, as is test-tube fertilisation between husband and wife. Donor sperm and eggs are not acceptable as these are regarded as similar to adultery. Surrogacy is generally seen as unnecessary as (in some countries) a Muslim is permitted to have up to four wives to provide children.

Experiments on the embryo amounting to genetic engineering are seen as wrong as they interfere with God's plan.

Old age, illness and death

It is a duty in Islam to care for the elderly just as they cared for and provided for the younger generations. Muslim communities provide help within the community for the needy. Each person has a duty to help others.

Life is a gift and Allah decides its span. Allah has control over everything and eventually all will be revealed when you finally pass into paradise, which is described as a garden of delights. Euthanasia and suicide are wrong in Islam.

'Your Lord orders that you ... be kind to your parents. If one or both of them attain old age with you, do not say one word of contempt to them, or repel them, but speak to them in terms of honour.' (Surah 17:23–24)

Summary

1. Abortion is the premature expulsion of the foetus from the womb by accident or surgery and it is forbidden in the Roman Catholic Church. It is acceptable in Judaism, Islam and Christianity in general if the life of the mother is at risk.
2. There are several artificial methods of helping childless couples but Judaism and Islam only accept AIH and *in vitro* fertilisation. Roman Catholicism accepts only AIH and the Church of England allows all methods given.
3. In all three named faiths life is seen as a gift from God and is sacred. Suicide and euthanasia are considered wrong.
4. Elderly people are to be respected and honoured. In Judaism and Islam it is a duty to care for the elderly within the family.
5. The hospice movement has grown up to give care to the dying through easing pain and encouraging an atmosphere of joy, hope and peace.
6. Christians believe that some suffering is a result of the 'fall' or original sin and that we will not fully understand its purpose until we are granted eternal life.
7. In Islam the reason for suffering is known only to Allah and everything is controlled by Allah.
8. In Judaism suffering is in God's hands and is a test for the strong, helping them to grow more human.

Quick questions

1. What is abortion?
2. What religious teaching might a believer give to support opposition to abortion?
3. In what circumstances is abortion seen as permissible in Christianity/Judaism/Islam?
4. Why might a religious believer say that suicide is wrong?
5. What is the difference between voluntary and involuntary euthanasia?
6. Why should elderly people be respected and honoured?
7. How does the hospice movement aim to alleviate suffering?
8. What is the purpose of suffering according to your chosen faith?
9. What methods are available to help infertile couples?
10. Why might a particular faith be opposed to infertility treatments?

Chapter 8
Prejudice and discrimination

8.1 Prejudice

Prejudice is shown by someone who pre-judges a situation. For example, a man might believe he knows what another person is like because of what he has heard or been told about that person, rather than basing his opinion on what he discovers on meeting that person face to face.

Prejudices are formed in a variety of ways. Young children pick up prejudices from their home environment initially. Thus, if they hear others voicing opinions about particular groups of people they might form a prejudice. An adult might have had experiences of a person from a particular racial/ethnic or religious group and may then decide all people of that group have similar characteristics, which may of course be pleasant or unpleasant. When that adult continually voices that opinion in the hearing of a child, the child will form a prejudice. This is because the child has no experience of his or her own to form a balanced, informed opinion.

'Every human being created in the image of God is a person for whom Christ died. Racism, which is the use of a person's racial origin to determine a person's value, is an assault on Christ's values and a reflection of his sacrifice.' (World Council of Churches)

Examples

1. A grandmother whose husband had returned, very ill and weak, from one of the Japanese forced labour camps operating during the height of the Second World War might continually speak, in the hearing of children and grandchildren, of the wickedness of the Japanese. In this way a child might build up a prejudice against Japanese people in general.

2. A family living in an area where a large number of immigrant families settle may find the different way of living and cooking difficult to understand and describe the newcomers as 'dirty and smelly'. Simply by absorbing this opinion a child could grow up with the prejudice that a particular group of people is dirty and smelly.

We generally understand prejudice to be a negative thing since in an educated society it is regarded as desirable that children should be educated and able to make informed opinions. They should be discouraged from basing their opinions on prejudices they have picked up while young. Prejudice, because it often stems from ignorance, is frequently accompanied or fed by fear and suspicion. It grows in an environment where exposure to anyone different heightens insecurity. Scapegoating is a feature of prejudice which is likely to happen when countries are at war or suffering serious economic decline characterised by unemployment and poverty.

There are many types of prejudice which are damaging to relationships in society. The very nature of prejudice makes it very difficult to re-educate people once they have an idea fixed in their minds. Prejudice is often reinforced through constant exposure to one-sided opinions at home. In the past prejudices were often strengthened by careless portrayals of particular groups in films, on television and in books. Latterly this practice has been carefully monitored by watchdog groups to try to ensure that every group is fairly represented. Unfortunately some groups are not strong enough or do not have enough political influence to have their case put fairly and still suffer from prejudice in society.

Typical examples of prejudices which people hold and which have been strengthened in the past by the media are gender prejudice and racial prejudice.

Gender prejudice

Women are over-concerned about home and family affairs and not about work and career. The image of women as harassed and preoccupied at work – an image which is fostered in many television series – reinforces prejudices about women. (Some prejudice against women is closely monitored but many advertisements, for example, are still regarded by women as patronising and degrading.)

'I permit no woman to teach or to have authority over men, she is to keep silent.' (1 Tim. 2:12)

Racial prejudice

Black Afro-Caribbeans all listen to reggae music and smoke dope; they have noisy parties and are lazy and stupid. This is the way they are often portrayed in the media and although the music people listen to is an important part of their culture, and having a certain demeanour is also part of belonging, the stereotype does not give a true picture and reinforces negative perceptions.

Surveys show that teachers often have low academic expectations of children of Afro-Caribbean origin. These expectations stem from deeply held prejudices. In theory teachers should be educated and informed yet even when people are informed enough to recognise and acknowledge their own prejudices, they are not always able to *act* objectively – subconscious prejudice may affect their judgement and actions.

All Asians run shops, make lots of money and have large families, living in overcrowded buildings. Asian people in Britain suffer more racial attacks than any other group. Portrayal of Asians in a particular way in the media has caused people to build up a stereotype and pre-judge every Asian before knowing the truth. Many Asians do run shops but like people in most other groups they are also to be found in many other walks of life.

'And if a stranger should live in your country, you must do him no wrong. the stranger who lives with you shall be as the home born among you, and you shall love him like yourself.' (Lev. 19:33–34)

Apartheid

One of the worst examples of racial prejudice was manifest in the apartheid system in South Africa. Each person was categorised by race: white, coloured or black. White children were brought up to see blacks as subhuman, unworthy of education, unworthy of a vote and not needing decent living conditions. Black people had to live in overcrowded townships with poor facilities. They were disenfranchised until 1994.

Apartheid on the beaches

Chapter 8 Prejudice and discrimination

The system meant that blacks had separate schools, transport, hospitals and eating places, and were not allowed to mix with whites. Relationships and marriage between races were forbidden and all blacks and coloureds had to carry a 'pass' which could be examined at any time; this showed where blacks were allowed to travel and work.

Many campaigns were conducted in efforts to end apartheid and many people died in protests and riots. It will also be many years before the prejudices which built up among each group about the other can be overcome.

Archbishop Desmond Tutu campaigned tirelessly through speeches and marches for the ending of apartheid. Nelson Mandela (elected president in 1994) served 25 years in prison for his membership of the ANC (African National Congress) which campaigned for rights for black people in their own country.

Class prejudice

Britain remains a very class-conscious society. Every child is still labelled as belonging to a social group when he or she is registered. The media portrays class in a very prejudiced way. The aristocracy are seen to behave in one way, the middle class in another and the working class in another. Thus we have prejudice about how people might behave depending on their status in life.

During a time of economic depression when the government seeks to cut spending on social services we might find that certain groups are portrayed negatively in the media. A young, single mother might be shown to be living off state benefit in her own home and contributing nothing to society. Little thought will be given to the deserted wife or husband trying to keep the family together in the family home under great personal and financial strain. Similarly, old people might be described as living comfortably at state expense in a nursing home while the greedy family waits for him or her to die so that they can inherit the house.

The class system is still an important factor in the governance of Britain. A great deal of fuss was made about Margaret Thatcher being the daughter of a grocer and John Major being an 'ordinary' man but still the majority of parliamentarians are from public schools and overwhelmingly middle class. Britain still has the upper chamber, The House of Lords, membership of which is open mainly to the aristocracy: a favour usually conferred by birth although sometimes by merit. Given that all people hold prejudices of one kind or another it must be recognised that such a one-sided way of choosing members will have its effect on decisions made by government.

Religious prejudice

Religious prejudice is also reinforced through the media. The idea that all Roman Catholic families have dozens of children can be promoted by showing families with many children in Latin America without explaining the economic realities alongside religious teaching. It is also easily distorted by those who mock the Pope's teaching about contraception and by press reports which take lines from his encyclicals out of context and quote them without giving the whole picture.

Jokes about Roman Catholicism and its stance on contraception can be heard every day. It is testimony to the security of the church that they rarely cause offence. A presenter on daytime TV, while watching a delicious 'diet' recipe full of bananas, rum and sugar, was heard to remark, 'This is like the Pope going for contraception.' An innocent off-the-cuff remark which could be offensive, certainly reinforces prejudice but is unlikely to shake the Vatican.

In popular culture in Britain – comedy and cartoons, for example – Jewish people are often portrayed as mean. Schoolchildren studying Shakespeare are exposed to the character of Shylock who is seen as the epitome of meanness. He is so mean he insists upon a pound of flesh cut from near the heart to compensate for nonpayment of debt. From this play comes the saying, 'He exacted his pound of flesh', which speaks of someone, at work for example, demanding every minute of your time and more effort than is possible. People can be called 'a real Shylock'.

There is a suspicion of religion in secular British culture. Religious people are often portrayed in the media as eccentric or out of touch with reality. There have been several television programmes showing religious ministers as unusual. It is also true that religious broadcasting is marginalised and reserved for late night or brief 'Sunday slots' on television. It is very difficult for presenters to give balanced views of the many different religious groups that are found in Britain today and it is extremely difficult for nonbelievers to convey the faith of believers and probably impossible for nonbelievers to give a sense of faith to other nonbelievers. It is, after all, often difficult for believers to share faith together.

Perceptions about religious believers are distorted by coverage of religious cults. These, and people who use religion for corrupt purposes, are given greater emphasis than legitimate faiths which have been practised quietly for hundreds of years.

Ageism

Ageism is holding prejudices against the elderly – deciding that they cannot think or act rationally and are all physically frail, weak and not able to understand what is going on. It is also easy to see old people as marginalised simply because we are told they have no interest in the future, only in the past. Again there are certain programmes which reinforce this stereotype.

Schoolchildren will often have this prejudice against anyone over the age of thirty! Fortunately they often meet many elderly people who they realise are not senile and sometimes are quite fit but it is a source of great suffering to old people that they are often treated with casual ignorance. It is common practice to dispense with someone's services suddenly when he or she reaches the age of 65 or 70 and yet no one suddenly becomes senile because they are one day older.

Ageism is seen as a disgrace in our society, especially by those of oriental culture who regard elderly people as wise and worthy of respect and honour.

Disability

We often have prejudices against disabled people. A recent advertisement on behalf of cerebral palsy sufferers highlighted how degrees of spasticity cause more problems for the able-bodied than for the disabled. The disabled are under-represented in the workplace and the media, and people are prejudiced that disability is synonymous with stupidity. Because we have little contact with disabled people we act according to prejudice because we are not in a position to be informed.

8.2 Discrimination

Prejudice leads to discrimination. This means treating someone differently because of a judgement we have made about them. Thus we find people disregarding women as serious job candidates because they are pregnant or because it is believed that they might have too many family responsibilities. In fact many men and women have a very deeply-rooted prejudice that mothers should stay at home to look after small children. This prejudice is often very subtly reinforced by advertising, which often shows the mother in the home environment or attending to children's social arrangements. Discrimination can be completely unintentional as people do not recognise their prejudices. It can also be totally, blatantly intentional, and insultingly so.

It is common to see advertisements which require applicants to be within a particular age group – perhaps under 35 – and this is very damaging to the self-confidence of older people. It is against the law to practise discrimination on the grounds of race, colour, religion or ability through advertising job vacancies although in special circumstances the law can be circumvented to allow for special needs. Occasionally, for example, it might be necessary to recruit from an ethnic group for communication or language reasons. Many employers advertise themselves as equal opportunities employers and will sometimes mention groups which are under-represented in their workforce.

Actively seeking to appoint people because of their colour, race, age, gender or ability is called positive discrimination. This is occurring increasingly – and interestingly, as the number of people over 50 years of age increases, some employers are recruiting older workers, regarding them as more reliable and capable. Supermarkets, a traditional area for young recruitment, have increasingly looked to older workers to give stability to a workforce and to improve standards of customer care.

8.3 Freedom of religious practice

Religious freedom is enshrined in law in Britain through custom and practice. The US constitution states people's right to hold and practise religious beliefs but in Britain this freedom has developed and is cherished. Any religious group has the right to worship as they wish. Britain has large numbers of religious faiths. Each major town has a plethora of Christian churches and chapels, a Quaker meeting house and a Salvationist citadel, as well as one or two synagogues (Orthodox and Reform), a mosque and a Hindu or Sikh temple.

Each group holds its own festivals and believers are free to wear traditional clothes and observe feasts as they wish. Muslims keep **Ramadan** and other festivals; Jews observe Channukah and all other festivals, Hindus observe Diwali and other festivals. Children in schools with significant numbers from a variety of faiths are told about the various religious festivals in an effort to promote religious understanding and tolerance and to undermine prejudices.

8.4 Prejudice within the religions

The Christian churches have been widely criticised for what some consider to be sexual discrimination. In 1993 the general synod of the Church of England voted to allow women to be ordained to the priesthood after years of lobbying and pressure-group action. Some members of the church believed this was a great breakthrough for equality.

Supporters of women in the priesthood argue that Jesus chose men for his disciples because he had no choice in the culture of the day and the church subsequently developed in line with tradition so that women had a domestic or secondary role. In the twentieth century women have the vote, the right to work, the ability to control their fertility and equal access to education and social freedom. They can be regarded as intellectually equal, physically empowered and socially more fitted to the ministry of the priesthood.

Opponents of the ordination of women have tended to argue that the synod exceeded its authority. Many members of the Church of England believe that Jesus instituted the priesthood through Peter and the popes and only through the Apostolic succession can women be admitted to the priesthood. The Roman Catholic Church remains opposed to the ordination of women. The Pope wishes to emphasise that men and women are equal but they have different ministries to offer. Pastorally in the Roman Catholic church many argue that women priests would not be readily accepted after a 2000 year tradition of male priests and the understanding that has been promoted that Jesus chose men.

It is, however an undeniable fact that fewer men are being ordained and many RC diocese in Britain have a vocation crisis. Many Catholics wonder how the shortfall will be met.

8.5 The Holocaust

The most poignant and terrible example of prejudice leading to discrimination is the Holocaust known as **Shoah** (whirlwind). Details of this can be found in Chapter 9 because this is also an example of persecution.

8.6 Religious teachings

'So God created man in his own image; in the image of God he created him. Male and female he created them.' (Gen. 1:27)

There should be no coercion in the matter of faith.' (Surah 2:256)

'If anyone walks forth with an oppressor to strengthen him, knowing that he is an oppressor, he has gone forth from Islam.' (Hadith)

'Glory to Allah who created in pairs all things that the earth produces.' (Surah 36:36)

Judaism, Christianity and Islam all teach that every person is made by God and is a unique individual. In Christianity and Judaism there is the belief that God made man in his own image. It is not necessary in Christianity and Judaism for every person to be Christian or Jewish in order to be saved and therefore people are to be allowed to hold their own beliefs.

In Islam believers see life as a gift from Allah which must be lived with certain rights and it is a religious duty to actively protect those rights. Human beings have free minds and can reason for themselves. All religious beliefs should therefore be respected.

All citizens should have equal rights in Islam. No one must be above the law. There is some propaganda that Islam regards women as inferior but this is a distortion which leads to prejudice. Women are considered equal but different. In some Muslim cultures women wear the veil (**Hijab**) and regard this as a liberating thing. It is a sign of modesty and permits women to conduct business as they please.

The wearing of loose clothes thus can easily be equated with the tradition of feminists in Western cultures wearing shapeless clothes to deter others from seeing them as sex objects. Some customs which seemingly discriminate against women, such as purdah (the seclusion of women) and arranged marriages, are based on certain Qur'anic passages. They are, however, thought to be cultural, being used also by Hindus and others.

Ageism is also not part of Islam or Judaism as it is a religious duty that the elderly should be honoured, respected and cared for in the family. Jews and Muslims have a high incidence of living in extended families.

In Judaism men and women are to be regarded as equal. Jews have a particular understanding of prejudice because of the suffering of their race over the centuries. Jews have been persecuted since the diaspora and Hitler utilised this prejudice to his own advantage. As well as Jews, Hitler wanted to exterminate all those he regarded as unworthy, such as the disabled, gypsies, the mentally ill and homosexuals. Judaism teaches tolerance of all people.

Summary

1. To show prejudice is to prejudge an issue – to make up your mind about something without having full knowledge.
2. Prejudice is formed by early influences and generally held beliefs which are gathered from non-objective sources.
3. Prejudice grows in the uneducated mind which is not schooled to study issues from a variety of perspectives.
4. To show discrimination is to treat a person differently because he or she shows characteristics which are perceived as different.
5. To show discrimination is to choose one person above another, ignoring merit and focusing on factors such as gender, sexuality, age, colour, religion or physical appearance.
6. Prejudice and discrimination can be heightened by media presentation.
7. Religious groups can work to overcome prejudice by being together, co-operating in services and social ventures and emphasising their commonality.
8. Christians and Jews teach that man was created by God in his own image and that all men are equal and worthy of equal treatment.
9. Islam teaches man is made by Allah, life is Allah's gift and all should be afforded respect and honour.
10. Christianity, Islam and Judaism all advocate religious freedom and tolerance.
11. British law allows for freedom of religious practice in Britain but some groups are subjected to intolerance in certain areas because of prevailing prejudice.

Chapter 8 Prejudice and discrimination

Quick questions

1. What is prejudice?
2. What is discrimination?
3. How do people become prejudiced?
4. How can someone discriminate against women?
5. Give an example of racial prejudice.
6. Give an example of religious prejudice.
7. How is ageism promoted through the media?
8. How could a company publicise its intention to positively discriminate?
9. What teaching might a believer use to reject discrimination?
10. Why is it sometimes difficult to practise your religious faith when technically you are free to do so?
11. In what way could the Roman Catholic church be regarded as prejudiced against women?
12. Why do some Christians feel women should not be priests?

Chapter 9
Peace and conflict

9.1 Christian approaches

Reasons for war and persecution

All animals compete against one another for food and territory. All creation struggles for survival ultimately to the point of conflict and death. The human animal is no different. Through the centuries mankind has developed methods of engaging in that competition which have grown more sophisticated, efficient and expensive.

Human beings go to war against one another for many reasons and increasingly the causes of wars can be seen to be a complex mixture of several factors.

Some of the more obvious reasons for the outbreak of war between or within nations can be identified:

- the desire for power on the part of an individual or a national government;
- desire for territorial gain;
- desire for (or need of) the natural resources of another country;
- a build-up of armaments disturbing the balance of power;
- to distract the population from domestic difficulties;
- national self-determination by ethnic groups;
- international alliances;
- military strategies or timetables.

> Examples of recent conflict include that in the former Yugoslavia where the individual races – Bosnian, Serbian and Croatian – each wanted their own nation state and fought to claim land for that state. In the war in Rwanda in 1994 the Hutu tribe attempted to wipe out the Tutsis in a bid for control of the country in which they both lived.

Take the opportunity to learn some facts about a current example of war in the world and find out the major cause.

'Where do all the fights and quarrels among you come from? They come from your desires for pleasure, which you are constantly fighting within you. You want things but you cannot have them, so you are ready to kill; you strongly desire things, but you cannot get them, so you quarrel and fight.' (Jas. 4:1–2)

Persecution

Persecution is in operation when a person or group deliberately singles out an individual or individuals and subjects them to *planned cruelties*. Tactics employed can range from name-calling through any manner of physical and mental punishment to genocide (the slaughter of entire races), as seen in the persecution and murder of the Jews in Nazi Germany.

Often people are persecuted simply for being different; thus their persecutors are given a focus for their hatred. Or people may be persecuted simply because they are weak, vulnerable and without allies.

'He created every race of men of one stock, to inhabit the whole earth's surface.' (Acts 17:26)

Hitler had a charismatic personality and by employing propaganda, he made use of natural prejudices against people who were regarded as *different* to scapegoat the Jews for Germany's defeat in the 1914–18 war and her economic problems in the 1920s and 1930s.

Many Germans needed a scapegoat and Hitler was therefore able to embark on his terrible scheme to exterminate 6,000,000 Jews in death camps in Eastern Europe. He called it his *final solution*.

Resolution of conflict

Wars used to finish when one nation or party was seen to have won. This was achieved normally when the weaker side could no longer continue to fight because they did not have enough weapons or supplies for their armies. The winning side would normally make substantial territorial gains. In the twentieth century some wars have ended (or conflict has been avoided altogether) because one side was able to threaten the use of vastly superior weapons which would cause enormous suffering, e.g. the atomic bomb.

The United Nations

'How blessed are the peacemakers, God shall call them His sons.' (Matt. 5:9)

After the Second World War The United Nations was set up to maintain international peace and security, to develop friendly relations among nations and to promote co-operation in solving problems between nations. Most countries have become members of the UN. Decisions are made by the Security Council which has 15 members. Five permanent members are USA, China, France, Great Britain and Russia. Any decision must be sanctioned by these members and any one of these five can veto a decision.

Latterly the world has seen the United Nations increasingly called upon to act to maintain peace and security. Increasingly this has meant that serving members of the armed forces of member states have been sent to areas of conflict in the world to be part of a United Nations peacekeeping force or to help to secure the passage of humanitarian aid (food, medicine and shelter) to the civilians affected by conflict.

The degree to which the UN is successful in this is difficult to assess. Some people feel it is not appropriate for the UN to be involved in civil conflicts. Sometimes the UN appears to have to withdraw without achieving its aims and sometimes it seems that the UN is drawn into a conflict on one side, thus appearing to judge which is the aggressor and which the aggrieved in a conflict which might have very complex causes.

The most powerful member of the UN is the USA which alone has the military resources to enforce any UN resolutions. A criticism of the UN is that it depends heavily on the agreement of the USA to carry out any of its resolutions.

Just war

'It is lawful for Christian men, at the commandment of the magistrate, to wear weapons and serve in the wars.' (Article 37 of the Church of England)

Christians recognise that war is not compatible with the teachings of Jesus, and theologians have looked for ways of reconciling involvement in war with their professed beliefs. In AD 400 St Augustine put forward ideas to support a 'just' war. This theory was developed by Thomas Aquinas in AD 1250. A Christian can look at these principles and use them to decide if a war is justifiable or not.

The 'just' war theory declares that:

- a war must be declared by a properly constituted authority, i.e. a constitutionally elected government, president or a sovereign in a monarchy.

- a war must have a just cause, such as self-defence or the reclaiming of lost territory.

- a war must have a just aim and should stop when that aim is achieved.

- a war must be waged justly, that is without endangering civilians (discrimination).

- a war must be waged without using undue force and without causing more damage than would have ensued from the original issue (proportionality).

Holy war; martyrdom; self-sacrifice

'Declare a Holy War. Call the troops to arms.' (Joel 3:9)

Holy wars are so called because those fighting them believe they have God on their side. Christians waged 'holy' war against the Turks in the crusades of the eleventh and twelfth centuries to free the holy places of Palestine from the muslims. In Islam a holy war is called **jihad**; it is fought for the faith and anyone who fights is guaranteed a place in paradise (see Section 9.3).

Martyrdom

To be a martyr is to give your life for what you believe in, to die for your faith. This total subjugation of self-will is fundamental to Christianity and other faiths. The main period of Christian martyrdom in British history came after the Reformation. As Mary Tudor fought to reinstate Roman Catholicism as the established faith in England, many Protestants were put to death for their refusal to acknowledge the authority of Rome. Under the reign of Elizabeth 1 Catholics suffered martyrdom because of their refusal to acknowledge the Queen as head of the Church in England.

Jesus calls those who would follow Him to take up their cross and put self last. Every day many of the people who preach the Gospel of Jesus across the world put their lives at risk by presenting a challenge to governments. They call for justice for the poor in the name of Jesus. Oscar Romero, the Archbishop of El Salvador was assassinated as he continually spoke out against the government in the name of Jesus.

'There is no greater love than this, that a man should lay down his life for his friends.' (John 15:13)

'Anyone who wishes to be a follower of mine must leave self behind; he must take up his cross, and come with me.' (Mark 8:34)

Non-violent protest and pacifism

Mahatma Gandhi demonstrated the efficacy of non-violent protest. He encouraged Indians to resist the rule of the British by passive resistance, by quietly ignoring instructions and laws and by not fighting back when attacked. He personally used to go on hunger strike to draw attention to a particular cause.

Many Christians base their belief in non-violent protest on the teachings and actions of Jesus. A pacifist is someone who is against all war and physical violence under any circumstances. The Quakers are a group of Christians utterly opposed to war.

'Violence is the policy of barbarians, non-violence is the policy of men.' (Mahatma Gandhi)

'You have learned that they were told "eye for eye, tooth for tooth". But what I tell you is this: do not set yourself against the man who wrongs you. If someone slaps you on the right cheek turn and offer him your left.' (Matt. 5:38–39)

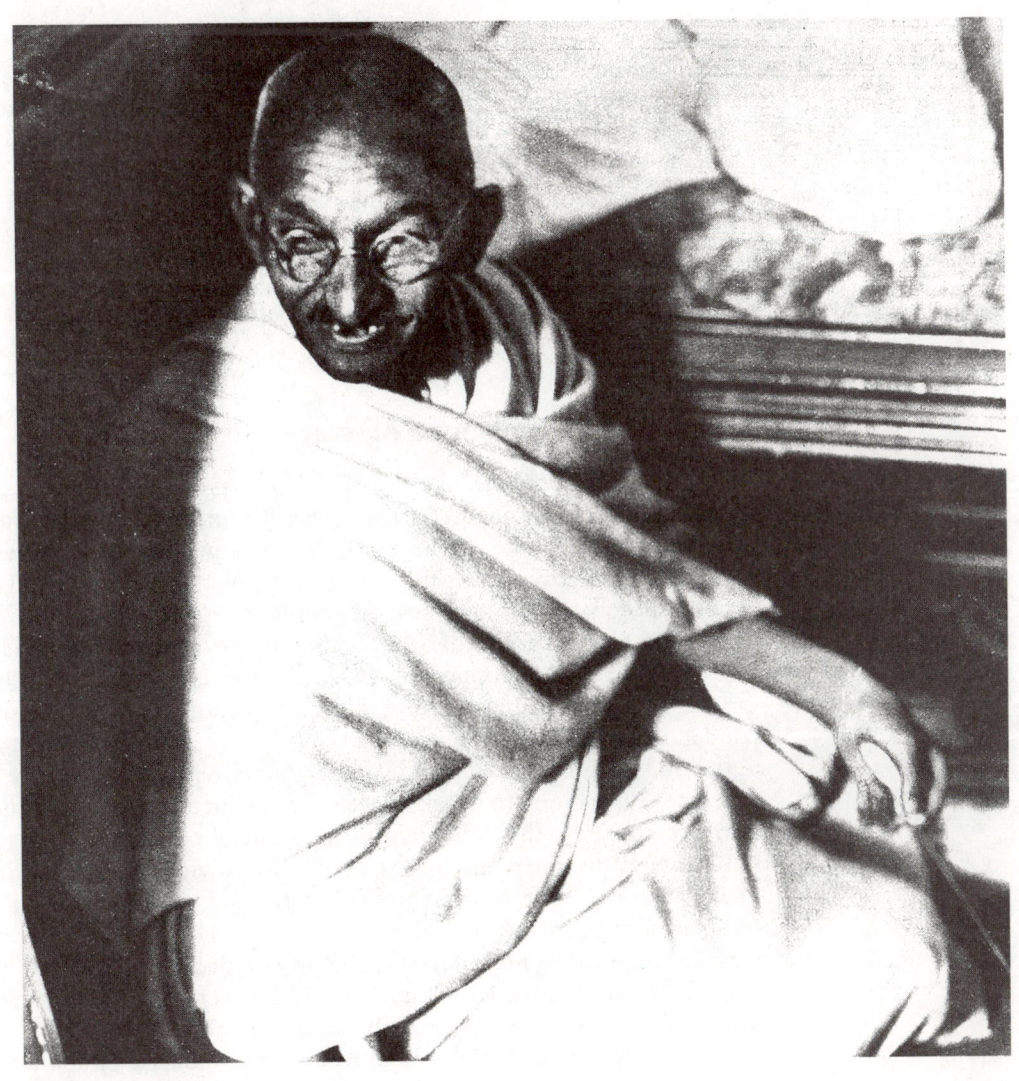

Mahatma Gandhi

Chapter 9 Peace and conflict

Prisoners of conscience

All over the world there are people in prison because they have refused to fight in a war they disagree with or they have spoken out against the actions of their government. These are prisoners of conscience.

In Britain there were pacifists who refused to fight in either of the world wars and others who simply didn't agree with the British cause during these wars. These men went to prison and were known as conscientious objectors or 'conchies'. They suffered terrible humiliation in prison and later in the community. Amnesty International campaigns on behalf of prisoners of conscience by writing to prisoners and also writing to governments known to be (or suspected of) violating the human rights of their citizens by not allowing them freedom of speech.

Human Rights

'Each individual is truly a person with a nature that is endowed with intelligence and free will, and rights and duties ... these rights and duties are universal and inviolable.' (Encyclical letter, Pope John XXIII)

'No rights are possible without the basic guarantees for life, including the right to adequate food, to guaranteed health care, to decent housing ...' (World Council of Churches)

The United Nations produced its Universal Declaration of Human Rights in December 1948. All the member nations agreed a basic code aimed at guaranteeing the quality of life for all their citizens. There are 25 clauses and the most important ones state that: all human beings are born free and equal; everyone has the right to life, liberty and freedom from fear and violence; and no-one shall be subjected to arbitrary arrest, detention or exile.

It is on the basis of the above-mentioned Declaration that groups campaign for the freedom and rights of prisoners of conscience throughout the world. You can find evidence of these campaigns in the national daily newspapers in Britain and should always look for current examples. For example, you could scan these newspapers for headlines under which there is likely to be direct or indirect information on prisoners of conscience.

Violent protest

Terrorism is an example of violent protest. Terrorism is a form of war which is not open warfare because the terrorists do not have a large and well-equipped army. Terrorists aim at any target, building or person that they believe will draw attention to their cause. Terrorism is seen all over the world. For people in Britain the terrorist campaigns waged by Republican and Loyalist terrorists in Northern Ireland and on the mainland between 1969 and 1994 are the most obvious examples. Unfortunately terrorists have now perpetrated so many atrocities that the unthinkable has become unexceptional.

Look for examples of terrorism in the news. One terrorist group, for example, terrorised the Japanese people by using a poison gas called Sarin in the subway; killing 6 people but panicking the whole of Tokyo in March 1995.

Nuclear war/the cost of war

'The monstrous power of nuclear weapons will have fatal consequences for life on earth. Justice, right reason and humanity therefore urgently demand that the arms race should cease ... nuclear weapons should be banned.' (Pacem in Terris, Roman Catholic Statement, 1965)

All Christian denominations recognise that, even if a war can be called a 'just' war, the cost of that war is a tragedy for the globe. The money spent on modern warfare would, if directed instead towards the poor, feed many hungry people and set up many life-giving schemes to improve the life chances of the disadvantaged in the Third World. Schools, hospitals, roads and factories could be built.

The world has lived under the shadow of the threat from nuclear weapons since the atomic bombs were dropped on Nagasaki and Hiroshima in 1945. That threat grows greater as more nations acquire nuclear weapons. All the Christian denominations condemn the use of nuclear weapons.

In 1983 a Church of England working party report entitled *The Church and the Bomb*, called for all nations to work together to reduce nuclear armaments; the report did, however, recognise the difficulty of the unilateral option.

Unilateral disarmament means that one individual country chooses to give up its nuclear weapons. This was the policy supported by the Labour Party for many years and publicised by CND (Campaign for Nuclear Disarmament). Broadly speaking, the argument was that if no one began the process disarmament could not happen.

Multilateral disarmament is understood by everyone. The idea is that all sides should give up their nuclear weapons at the same time. The thinking is that this method would not leave any countries vulnerable to attack by nuclear weapons while stockpiles were being dimished.

Christian views of peace and forgiveness

Christians campaign against war and violence in various ways and to varying degrees. Some Christians accept some wars as justifiable and some accept violent punishment as the only means of dealing with certain criminals. These Christians use different examples from Scripture to explain their position and different church teachings.

Christians can go to the Old Testament and find words to justify war as well as words to support opposition to war. Here are two well-known passages calling for an end to war:

- 'They shall beat their swords into mattocks and their spears into pruning knives; nation shall not lift sword against nation nor ever again be trained for war.' (Mic. 4:3–4);

- 'Is not this what I require of you as a fast: to loose the fetters of injustice, to untie the knots of the yoke, to snap every yoke and set free those who have been crushed?' (Isa. 58:6–7).

'I remitted the whole of your debt when you appealed to me; were you not bound to show your fellow-servant the same pity as I showed you?' (Matt. 18:32–34)

'Your brother here was dead and has come back to life, was lost and is found.' (Luke 15:32 – The Prodigal Son)

Overwhelmingly in the Gospels, Jesus' message is one of peace and forgiveness. In the Great Commandments Jesus says, 'You must love your neighbour as yourself.' (Mark 12:31). The Parable of the Good Samaritan in Luke makes it clear that everyone is a neighbour.

On the subject of physical violence, Jesus says, 'Put your sword back in its place. All who take the sword will die by the sword.' (Matt. 26:52). Jesus tells his followers to forgive. Peter came up and asked Him 'Lord, How often am I to forgive my brother if he goes on wronging me?' Jesus replied, 'I do not say seven times; I say seventy times seven.'

All Christians believe that Jesus has secured absolute and ultimate peace for them by the supreme sacrifice of His death on the cross. Because the death of Christ assured salvation and His resurrection promised eternal life, Christians place their faith in the world to come. St Paul wrote, 'On the cross, Christ stripped the spiritual rulers and authorities of their power.'

9.2 Focus on Judaism

'The world stands on three things, on justice, on truth and on peace.' (Ethics of the Fathers)

Jews greet each other with the word shalom (peace); and they believe you should go to great lengths to avoid war. Jews are not pacifists and see some wars as necessary. The war to establish themselves in the promised land (Palestine) was a *milchemet mitzvah* – an obligatory war, one which the Israelites were commanded to fight by God. An optional war is called a *milchemet reshut*.

'If your enemy is hungry, give him bread to eat; if he is thirsty, give him water to drink.' (Prov. 25:21)

Obligatory wars must be fought if you are attacked or to save yourself from being attacked. An optional war can be fought if other methods of reconciliation have failed. It is not acceptable to fight a war for revenge or in order to colonise a land or build an empire.

While there was no Jewish state, there was no Jewish military tradition. Since the foundation of Israel in 1948 the Jewish state has had an army and has been engaged in wars with her immediate neighbours to defend that state. An example of such a war was the Six Days War in 1967 when Israeli forces attacked Egyptian and Syrian aircraft on the ground in order to avert a prospective attack.

'The generals are regarded as clever men. They commission powerful weapons and calculate how to kill thousands of people. Can there be any greater foolishness than this?' (Rabbi Nachman of Breslov, 1772–1810)

Not all Jews recognise the legitimacy of the state of Israel and some would therefore not accept that action – especially military action – by Israel is always in line with Jewish teaching.

9.3 Focus on Islam

Muslims believe that war is sometimes necessary. War is called **Jihad** (striving) and a Jihad is a holy war. The great Jihad is the struggle with oneself against evil. A military

Chapter 9 Peace and conflict

'O Lord! I seek Thy protection against creeping sloth and cowardice and miserliness, and I seek Thy protection from oppressive debt and the tyranny of people.' (Prayer of Mohammed)

'The person who struggles so that Allah's word is supreme is the one serving Allah's cause.' (Hadith)

'Hate your enemy mildly; he may become your friend one day.' (Haddith)

Jihad or 'Holy War' can be justified in self-defence; in defence of family, tribe or country; when fought against oppression; or when fought to right injustice.

Rules for Jihad are the same as those for a 'Just War' in Christianity. Because the rules are the same, the use of nuclear weapons is unacceptable as they cause indiscriminate killing.

Islam aims to bring about peace but not in a pacifist sense. Muslims believe there cannot be peace where there is injustice or oppression and Muslims regard it as an honour to protect the faith and the community even if they have to suffer.

A Muslim can become a martyr if he gives his life for his religious beliefs. Not all soldiers killed in war are martyrs – defending the country is not regarded in the same way as dying for the faith. A true martyr is forgiven all his sins and taken straight to paradise.

Summary

1. Human beings have always had conflicts arising out of rivalry and greed.
2. There is not usually one single identifiable cause of a war. Wars begin for many reasons and sometimes a series of complex reasons.
3. The United Nations exists to try and resolve conflicts and maintain peace.
4. Christians and Muslims have a series of criteria which must be met before a war can be called a 'Just' war or a Jihad.
5. A 'Holy War' is a war in which the combatants on at least one side believe that God is with them.
6. A martyr is someone who dies for his or her faith.
7. A pacifist is someone who opposes and refuses to take part in all war and violence.
8. Terrorism is literally terrorising communities by perpetrating murders and bombings against any target which might be imagined to advance or bring attention to the terrorists' cause.
9. A prisoner of conscience is someone who is prepared to go to prison rather than deny what he or she believes in.
10. Human rights are those basic conditions which every human being has a right to enjoy. They are proclaimed in the 1948 United Nations Declaration on Human Rights.

Quick questions

1. Name two main causes of conflict between nations today.
2. Why might a group or person be a likely subject for persecution?
3. Explain the work of an organisation whose cause is to resolve conflict in the world today.
4. Describe two important reasons why a Christian might say a war is 'just'.
5. What is a martyr?
6. What religious justification would a Christian use to explain martyrdom?
7. What methods could be used in non-violent resistance?
8. Where would you find prisoners of conscience today?
9. Why would a Christian say a nuclear war could never be 'just'?
10. Why could a nuclear war not be called a **Jihad**?
11. What are the differences between an 'obligatory' war and an 'optional' war for Jews?
12. What Old Testament sources might you use to justify *and* condemn war?

Chapter 10
Law and order in society

10.1 State responsibilities and Christian teaching

'Pay Caesar what is due to Caesar and pay God what is due to God.' (Mark 12:17).

Laws have been established by human society to govern conduct. The type and nature of law depends on the type and nature of government. An elected government in a culturally Christian country might be expected to have different laws from those of a non-elective dictatorship in a totalitarian state. In Great Britain the elected parliament proposes and passes laws and in theory these laws arise out of a fundamentally Christian culture.

Many laws exist to establish 'a rule of law' under which all members of society are protected and are entitled to equal treatment. Laws are designed to protect the vulnerable so that human society is raised above a basic situation in which the 'law of the jungle' applies and the rule is 'survival of the fittest'.

Thus in Great Britain there exist a series of statutory laws which have been passed by parliament and written into the statute books. These laws are enforced by the police and interpreted by the judiciary (the system of courts and judges).

Religious law and state law

'... you must obey the authorities – not just because of God's punishment, but also as a matter of conscience.' (Rom. 13:5).

'For sin pays its wage – death; but God's free gift is eternal life in union with Christ our Lord.' (Rom. 6:23).

Although Britain is a state with an established church, The Church of England, it is not true to say that religious law is state law. Many state laws are based on Christian principles but the two are separate. It is possible to sin without committing a crime. A crime is deemed to have been committed when someone transgresses the state law.

Religious laws are a facet of each particular religion. Christian laws are commandments of Jesus. Christians are obliged to follow the rules Jesus has set out for them, particularly the Ten Commandments and the two great commandments. Each denomination has clarified certain transgressions which are regarded as sins. To sin is to ignore the laws of Jesus and in effect to turn away from Him by one's own actions.

In the Roman Catholic tradition sin can be either 'venial' (less serious) or 'mortal', which is extremely serious and involves 'grave matter, full knowledge and full consent'.

Reasons why people commit crime

'A person will reap exactly what he sows.' (Gal. 6:7).

The reasons why people commit crimes are very complex. Some people believe that human nature is naturally selfish and greedy and people will always compete with one another; they will always want to have more and be more powerful than others. Sigmund Freud was of this view and held that people had to be schooled therefore to live together in an amicable way in society. Others, e.g. Karl Marx, believed strongly that people are formed by the circumstances in which they live. Thus if one belongs to an environment in which some members are much better off than others and material possessions are held up as the most worthwhile criteria on which to judge people then inevitably many of the disadvantaged will take whatever steps they see as necessary to finding a place in such a society. If the underprivileged have a lack of education and have grown up in an environment that is brutal and violent then they have very few means other than criminal ones of trying to grasp a place in the sun for themselves.

The balanced view is that crime is the result of a combination of factors which probably include the natural predisposition of a person to react against the negative aspects of his or her environment. Certainly within the Christian tradition it is understood that people have original sin. They are naturally disposed to sin and transgress law and must be trained through Christianity to reject these feelings and try to do good to others.

Control of criminals

Because people live so closely together in society, those who do not conform to the laws present a problem as they threaten the lifestyle of the rest of society and sometimes the physical well-being of others. The laws are enforced by the police and those who are suspected of breaking the law are tried by the courts and, if found guilty, can be punished by the courts. One of the purposes of punishment is to make a person understand the serious nature of his or her crime. The nature of the punishment depends on the seriousness of the crime.

Punishments include:

- fines;

- probation orders;

- community service orders;

- custodial sentences in an appropriate institution for a particular length of time.

'Then everyone will hear of it and be afraid and no one else will dare to act in such a way.' (Deut. 17:7,13).

Punishing people for crimes enables society to exact retribution and to control the offenders, if necessary placing them in positions in which they cannot offend again. The criminal can also be made to go some way to making reparation for the crime. Sometimes he or she is asked to pay financial compensation or is given community service to compensate the community, perhaps for an act of vandalism.

Punishment is exacted on behalf of the victim and the perpetrator is not usually regarded as the one in need of consideration. Those who favour this method of control believe that the prospect of punishment deters likely criminals.

Forgiveness and reconciliation

'If anyone slaps you on the right cheek, let him slap you on the left cheek too.' (Matt. 5:38–39).

Within Christianity there exists the belief that reconciliation between criminal and victim and society should always be sought and that punishment should be designed to rehabilitate the offender. Attempts should be made to understand the circumstances which led to his or her criminality and then efforts should be made to amend those circumstances, helping the offender to become a law-abiding member of society.

Corporal and capital punishment

'Whoever sheds the blood of man by man shall his blood be shed.' (Gen. 9:6).

'And that is how my father will deal with you unless you each forgive your brother from your hearts.' (Matt. 18:35).

It is against the law in Britain for teachers to inflict corporal (i.e. bodily physical punishment) on students and there is a strong lobby campaigning to stop all physical punishment. Recent judgements in the courts have mainly upheld the right of parents to use reasonable physical force when chastising their own children.

Capital punishment is the death penalty. In Britain this was always by hanging; it was abolished in 1970. Hanging is a subject of great debate and is seen as the ultimate retributive punishment. Opponents argue that in places where it exists (e.g. certain American states) there are more murders than in places where it doesn't exist.

There are about 5000 people awaiting execution in various states across the USA. Gradually (as violent crime increases) more states opt for this punishment which is believed to be deterrent and retributive. In the USA it costs more to execute someone than to keep them in prison because of the appeals process – lawyer's fees etc. Many people wait for years before the sentence is carried out. This is done by hanging, shooting, gassing, the electric chair or lethal injection.

Try to look for examples of capital punishment in the news; apart from the USA it also occurs in many eastern countries — and for crimes such as drug smuggling as well as violence.

Forgiveness in the Gospel

Christianity teaches that wrongs should be forgiven countless times and that while the sin is condemned the sinner should be forgiven. Christians are taught that sin is forgiven when the sinner repents the sin, does all he or she can to make amends and is determined not to sin again. This does not preclude punishment, and a truly repentant sinner accepts punishment as a penance to make reparation for sin.

In the Roman Catholic and Anglo-Catholic traditions believers can receive the sacrament of reconciliation (through confession). He or she confesses the sin to a priest, makes an act of contrition, is granted absolution and accepts a penance – usually a shorter or longer period of prayer.

'I tell you this: whatever you forbid on earth shall be forbidden in heaven, and whatever you allow on earth shall be allowed in heaven.' (Matt. 18:18).

10.2 Focus on Judaism

According to Jewish tradition Law comes from God. Human beings are not capable of distinguishing right from wrong. A code of Law has been handed down by God and can be found in the Torah. Jews are found in almost every country in the world; each Jew is obliged to follow the laws of the state in which he or she lives. Jews are also obliged to follow the **mitzvot** (commandments) set out in the Torah (see Chapter 14, Jewish beliefs).

The mitzvot help Jews to realise their purpose in life which is to grow closer to God through changing and developing as a person.

Jews would only be permitted to transgress the laws of the land if they were being persecuted or forced to change their religion.

There is a national Jewish state, Israel, in which Jewish law has an important role. In other countries there are **Bet Din** (courts) of three rabbis who make judgement in religious matters and other issues of conflict between Jews, perhaps in business or commerce. They do not replace the courts of the land.

Jews have a special time of the year, **Yom Kippur**, when they fast and show repentance for their sins; they ask forgiveness of each other for any wrongs. This is a time of purification and enables believers to focus with a clear conscience on trying to follow the Torah more closely in the following year.

Jewish Law allows for capital punishment in certain circumstances but decrees that it should be carried out in a humane way. It is permissible as a punishment for murder if it can be established that the murderer understood the consequences of his act and if there are two independent witnesses to the murder. The death penalty exists as a deterrent to others and to enable the murderer to atone for the wrong.

'You must do according to the instruction which they give you and the judgement which they tell you. Do not turn aside from it.' (Deut. 17:11).

'You shall appoint judges and officers in all your towns … and they shall judge the people righteously.' (Deut. 16:18).

'If anyone takes the life of a human being, he must be put to death …' (Lev. 24:17).

10.3 Focus on Islam

Islam lays down very clear and detailed laws for believers. Muslims in non-Islamic countries must follow state law while keeping Islamic law. There are some Islamic countries, including Saudi Arabia, in which religious law is state law. Islamic Law is called **Shar'iah**, which means 'clear path', and it shows Muslims how to follow the rules in the **Qur'an** and the **Sunnah** of the **Hadith** (sayings of Mohammed). There are five grades of rules or duties called **Fique**:
(1) binding – **fard** or wajib
(2) recommended – mandub
(3) permissible – mubah

'If the enemy starts leaning towards peace, then you also start leaning towards peace.' (Surah 8:61).

(4) disapproved of – makruh
(5) forbidden – **haram**

Of these duties the first four are permissible (halal) and the last forbidden (haram).

Islam teaches forgiveness and reconciliation. Muslims believe that Allah will always forgive a truly repentant sinner although that does not mean the sinner is able to escape punishment for his crime. In Islam the basis of law is the good of the community, not the individual. This is because of the institution of **ummah** which is the understanding of the Muslim community throughout the world.

Everyone is equal before the law but all efforts must be made to ensure that law is just and no one is ever condemned without a fair hearing before an unbiased court of law. It is also important to have hearings and punishment in public so that everything is open and not subject to corruption or excess brutality. Ultimately every person will be judged by **Allah** and all evil is seen by Allah. Even if an innocent person is mistakenly punished he or she knows Allah has seen the truth.

Islam is very clear about which acts constitute major sins against society.

- **Shirk** is to regard anything as comparable to or partner to Allah. There must be no other idols. Muslims discourage adulation of idols of modern society such as sports personalities, pop stars or film stars.

- Sihr means magic; it is wrong to give false authority to the spirits (**Jinn**) as this raises false hopes and causes misinterpretation of the will of Allah.

- **Qatl** is murder – a serious sin and crime as all life is sacred and a gift from Allah.

- **Riba** (usury). Under Islamic law lending money for profit is usury. Anyone who is rich enough is obliged to help his fellow men.

- **Sariqah** (theft) is a sin and in many Islamic countries persistent thieves who do not have dire economic need can have their hands cut off. Islam aims to support people so that such crime should not be necessary.

- Jubn means cowardice. It is a sin to desert the battlefield. All Muslims are obliged to fight **Jihad** if necessary as a responsibility to society.

- Qadhf (slander) is also a sin. It is wrong to gossip maliciously and defame someone's character or to use bad language.

In Islam adultery is a crime as well as a sin. It is forbidden in Islamic law and is punishable in Islamic states. Punishment can vary but in the Qur'an one hundred lashes are to be given for flagrant and witnessed adultery. Adultery is seen as dishonourable.

It is also forbidden under Islamic law to consume intoxicating substances as the Qur'an condemns the man who has no control of his faculties. Some Islamic countries punish abuses severely and non-Muslims are requested not to corrupt the people if they live in a Muslim state.

Capital punishment is permissible in Islam for murder and for threatening Islam if the threat is issued by a once-believing Muslim. Some Islamic countries have severe penalties for once-believing people who speak against Islam.

The Shari'ah guides every part of life and provides a code upon which laws should be based. Thus Islamic law encompasses rules for living that dictate how man should treat his environment and care for Allah's creation, human and animal.

Summary

1 Laws are made by parliament, enforced by the police and interpreted by the courts.
2 To sin is to go against the law of your faith, to turn away from God.
3 It is possible to sin without committing a crime (breaking the law).
4 Christians believe that all humans have the capacity to sin. This is because of the presence of original sin.

5 One branch of sociology teaches that people commit crimes because their environment has taught them no other way to cope with life.
6 Punishment can be retributive; reparative; rehabilitative; deterrent.
7 Corporal punishment is physical; beating and flogging are examples of it.
8 Capital punishment is the death penalty.
9 In Jewish tradition law comes from God and can be found in the Torah.
10 **Yom Kippur** is the time when Jews repent of their sins and try to forgive one another.
11 Islamic law is called **Shari'ah** (clear path).
12 All three faith traditions teach the importance of forgiveness and reconciliation.

Quick questions

1 What are statutory laws?
2 What are sins?
3 How is it possible to sin but not commit a crime in Britain?
4 On what are Christian laws based?
5 What does original sin mean?
6 Why do some people feel obliged to break the law?
7 For what kind of reasons would it be permissible for a Christian to break the law of the land?
8 What sort of punishments are available to the courts?
9 What purposes do punishments have?
10 What is capital punishment and why is it sometimes permissible in Judaism/Islam?
11 What is the purpose of **Yom Kippur**?
12 What function do **Bet Din** have in Britain?
13 Why did God hand the Law to Moses?
14 What is Islamic law called?
15 Why should the law be applied publicly in Islam?
16 Which acts constitute major sins against society in Islam?

Chapter 11
Poverty and environmental issues

11.1 Causes of poverty

Poverty means to be poor and it is now recognised that people perceive their own poorness in relation to those around them. So poverty becomes relative. To be truly poor is to have no food, shelter or security. This is the situation for millions of people in the world.

In Great Britain the government has established a certain standard of living which people expect. Those who do not have the means to reach this standard are said to be living below the poverty line. In Britain a poor person might have enough to eat, a home and even a car and many consumer durables; he or she could, on the other hand, be homeless and begging for money for food. In each case the person is poor relative to those around, and according to life expectations and chances.

The Third World

In the developing world many people have no shelter or food and little prospect of either. Nor do people have access to education or health care. They have a very short life expectancy and that life is often characterised by suffering through hunger and disease. Such conditions exist in much of what is called the Third World. This sort of poverty is seen as absolute rather than relative.

The Brandt Report

The Brandt Report (1980) identified that the Northern Hemisphere, together with Australia, contained 25% of the world's population and received 80% of the world's income.

In the north people have access to education and healthcare and can expect to live for 70–80 years. These countries dominate world politics, economics, business and industry.

The developing world has 75% of the world population and 20% of the income. People have little or no access to education, healthcare, business, commerce, politics or any economic influence and can expect to live to 50.

Reasons for inequality

The reasons for this divide are complex and any discussion of ways in which the peoples of the world might be made more equal generates great controversy. Several causes of poverty in the Third World are generally acknowledged:

- the purchase of armaments which they can ill afford by poor nations from rich ones;
- populations growing out of control;

- trading conditions which make Third World countries depend on selling raw materials at a low price;
- international banking which lends money at high rates of interest;
- reducing levels of aid from rich countries to poor ones.

The developed or 'First' world cannot ignore the Third World. The world is shrinking as a result of easier travel. Industries in the developed world depend on the Third World for raw materials and as a market for manufactured goods. Therefore developed countries are closely involved in Third World politics and economics. Many of the aid programmes are reciprocal so that money is leant in return for contracts being awarded to the lender country for other development projects.

11.2 Christian responses to world poverty

'For when I was hungry you gave me food; when thirsty you gave me drink; when I was a stranger you took me into your home, when naked you clothed me; when I was ill you came to my help ... I tell you this, anything you did for one of my brothers here, however humble, you did for me.' (Matt. 25:35–38;40)

'Go, sell everything you have and give to the poor and you will have riches in heaven.' (Mark 10:21)

Christians are closely involved with efforts to alleviate suffering in the Third World and efforts to create a more equal world. The motivation for this is to be found in the Gospel teachings, particularly the commandment to love your neighbour. Jesus is unequivocal in describing people's duties to the poor. He tells the rich man to sell everything and give it to the poor (Mark 10:21). He condemns the rich man for ignoring the beggar at his door (Luke 16:19–31). In the Parable of the Good Samaritan He demonstrates it is important to have a care for all people (Luke 10:25-37). In 1 John 3:17–18 we read, 'If a rich person sees his brother in need, yet closes his heart against his brother, how can he claim that he loves God? My children, our love should not be just words and talk; it must be true love, which shows itself in action.'

Christians recognise that they have a duty to bring Christ into the world through working amongst the disadvantaged. Jesus was always found with those on the margins of society: the lepers, tax-collectors, sinners and the mentally ill. Jesus was insistent that the well did not need a doctor, only the sick (Mark). Christians are called to minister to the sick and poor.

Christian organisations alleviating poverty

For the above-mentioned reasons several Christian organisations were founded. These work to relieve poverty in the Third World. The Roman Catholic church has CAFOD (Catholic Fund for Overseas Development), which collects money from churches, schools and other groups and uses most of that money to fund development projects helping countries to build an infrastructure which will improve chances for the people. Similar work is undertaken by Christian Aid, which collects nationwide in May each year. Other agencies with a Christian foundation which collect and assist in the developing world are Tear Fund and Trocaire. It is also usual for individual Christian groups to raise money to fund projects or even send workers out to schemes and projects in the Third World. There is a growing tradition in which Christian churches adopt a parish in the Third World just as towns are often 'twinned' with towns in another country. This is very effective if a member of the parish has worked abroad or the minister has personal contacts.

'I tell you this, this poor widow has given more than any of the others; for those others who have given had more than enough, but she with less than enough has given all she had to live on.' (Mark 12:43–44)

Christians are also obligated to help others by Jesus' teaching about wealth. Jesus taught that people could not serve God and money. It is wrong to devote life to making money and acquiring possessions and wealth. In the Gospels Jesus frequently demonstrates how He has come to be with the poor and how difficult it is for a rich man to enter heaven. The widow who gives more than she can afford to the poor is greatly blessed, more so than the rich man who gives plenty but has plenty to spare (Mark).

Stewardship of the Earth

Christianity teaches that all that is on this earth is lent to the inhabitants for the brief duration of their lives. It is a Christian duty to care for the earth in the manner of a

Chapter 11 Poverty and environmental issues

'Be fruitful and increase, fill the earth and subdue it, rule over the fish in the sea, the birds of heaven and every living thing that moves upon the earth.' (Gen. 1:28)

steward. Each person has a responsibility to help to cherish the earth so that it is fruitful for the next generation. Many of the problems leading to the destruction of the planet can be seen to result from mismanagement of the earth and man's failure to act as a careful steward. In fact man acts irresponsibly, destroying trees and stripping raw materials which can never be replaced purely for monetary gain. This is unjust to those who suffer as a result of greed.

Dangers to the planet

It is possible to identify several major problems which are of universal concern regarding the destruction of the planet.

- The greenhouse effect which causes gases to be trapped in the earth's atmosphere is causing average temperatures to rise and thus sea levels rise as polar ice melts. Rising sea levels cause flooding. Warmer seas can lead to an increase in pressure, causing hurricanes and typhoons.

- Environmentalists are also concerned about *deforestation* which means there are fewer trees to absorb CO_2 (a greenhouse gas) and which also causes *desertification* as water is not held by roots and topsoil is simply washed away so nothing can grow.

- The industrialised nations *pollute* the atmosphere with by-products of industry which contaminate the rivers, sea and land and cause the rain to become acid, which in turn poisons the land on which it falls.

Man needs the planet to sustain him and all nations try to work together to agree strategies. Unfortunately not many of the wealthy want to simplify their lifestyles and forego resources; so the poor need to take whatever chance they can to improve their standard of living. Thus there is often a conflict of interest between governments, environmentalists, businessmen and the indigenous people.

Governments are always seeking to strengthen their economies so they need to make money. They encourage businessmen to speculate and invest and this sometimes leads to destruction of the environment rather than its preservation. In this way governments and businessmen are often in conflict with those who live in the area they wish to exploit, the original inhabitants.

Christians believe there is enough for everyone provided it is managed properly but those who have plenty need to understand that they do not have the right to more than a fair share; they must sacrifice some of what they believe to be a right even though they have worked hard and see others having many practical benefits from a working life in the form of consumer durables. Christians should not live a life directed by profit motive and materialism.

11.3 Focus on Judaism

'Regard the needy as members of your household.' (Ethics of the Fathers)

According to Jewish teaching God made the earth; and He made man to be in charge of the earth. Humans are special and have greater rights than all other life on earth. As God's will is worked out man has a duty to protect and guard his creation. Traditionally, following the guidance and direction set down in the **Talmud**, every person should have access to green land to enjoy at leisure. It is wrong for factories which pollute the neighbourhood to be near to towns. Jews have a religious obligation to protect the planet and people from pollution.

Zedakah

'Just as I am righteous, says the Lord, so you too, be righteous. Just as I visit the sick, feed the hungry and clothe the naked, so you do the same.'(The Talmud)

In Judaism it is taught that every person must care for others: helping the poor is an obligation. Charity is called Zedakah (justice) and in theory a tithe of income (10%) is the correct amount to give to charity. The more that is given anonymously and cheerfully the better. The best way for a Jew to help is to use his money to help a poor person to become self-supporting.

'If ... there is a fellow Israelite in need ... do not be selfish and refuse to help him ... be generous and lend him as much as he needs ... Give to him freely and unselfishly.' (From Deut. 15:7–8,10)

Children are brought up to recognise that a certain portion of their money belongs to the poor and *not to give it* is to steal from the poor. Families may have collection boxes called pushke. The accumulation of wealth is not seen as wrong in Judaism – only a pre-occupation with wealth and materialism. The only sin is not to share that wealth.

'Man lives always in tension between his power and the limits set by his conscience.' (Jewish Declaration on Nature.)

11.4 Focus on Islam

Helping the poor and giving to charity are an absolute duty in Islam. Zakah is one fortieth of a Muslim's income after he has cared for his dependants and a sum is usually collected and sent to the poor at **Ramadan**. A Muslim may also make small voluntary gifts called **sadaqah**.

Zakah

Zakah at Ramadan is the equivalent of the cost of two meals and is given on the feast of Eid-ul-Fitr before the Feast Prayer so the poor can join the festival.

On the feast of Eid-ul-Adha during the **Hajj** pilgrims pay for an animal to be slaughtered and given to the poor as part of the duty to give.

Because giving is part of Islamic witness to the work of Allah in the world and devotion to the will of Allah there are Muslim aid agencies founded on Islamic teaching. These include Islamic Relief, Muslim Aid and the Red Crescent, as well as many less-well-known agencies and work carried out by individuals and local groups for relief of poverty locally and nationally. It is not wrong in Islam to make money or acquire material goods but it is wrong to make these things above Allah and not to use wealth to help others.

Man as vice-regent

'He who eats and drinks while his brother goes hungry is not one of us.' (Hadith)

'The earth is green and beautiful and Allah has appointed you stewards over it.' (Hadith)

'It is He who has made you custodians, inheritors of the earth.' (Surah 6:165)

Muslims believe that Allah created the world and that he created man to have responsibility for the care of the world. Therefore it is wrong to abuse the natural resources of the planet and it is a duty to care for the earth. Many Muslims are severely affected by problems in the environment such as the desertification of many parts of Africa and flooding in Bangladesh which can be seen as caused by the greenhouse effect and global warming. Muslims are charged to participate in and support measures to conserve resources and protect nature.

'For the Muslim, mankind's role on earth is that of **khalifa** (caliph), vice-regent or trustee of God ... Earth belongs to God and we must answer to Him for the way in which we use or abuse that trust.' (Taken from Muslim declaration on Nature).

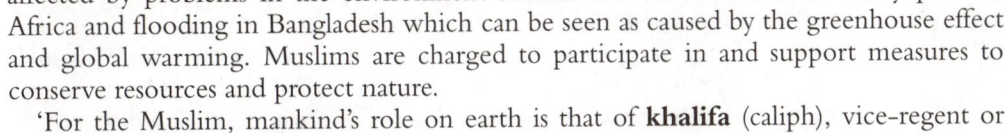

Pollution from a coke works

Chapter 11 Poverty and environmental issues

Summary

1. Poverty can be absolute or relative.
2. Relative poverty is characterised in the Third World by lack of food, shelter, education and health-care, and short life expectancy.
3. In Great Britain poverty is relative and perceived according to the standard of living of those around a person.
4. The world population in the Northern Hemisphere accounts for 25% of people and uses 80% of resources, leaving the rest of the world 20%.
5. The developed world depends on the developing world for raw materials and as a market for manufactured goods.
6. Christians are directed to care for the poor by Jesus through teaching and example.
7. Christians give aid to the Third World through official organisations such as CAFOD, Christian Aid, Trocaire and Tear Fund.
8. Christianity, Judaism and Islam all teach that the planet was created by God and all humans have dominion over the earth and all living things; they have the role of vice-regent or steward of the earth.
9. It is a duty in Judaism to give Zedakah (justice) or charity to the poor and 10% of income is recommended.
10. It is a duty in Islam to give **Zakah** to the poor.

Quick questions

1. What is the difference between absolute and relative poverty?
2. How is absolute poverty characterised in the Third World?
3. How is poverty relative in Great Britain?
4. What is the inequality between the Northern and Southern hemispheres according to the Brandt Report?
5. How does the developed world depend on the Third World?
6. What Scriptural evidence do Christians use as motivation for helping the poor?
7. Why are Christians, Jews and Muslims all obligated to care for the earth in the role of steward/vice-regent?
8. What are the main environmental problems which threaten the planet?
9. Explain the nature of Zedakah in Judaism
10. Explain the nature of **Zakah** in Islam.

Chapter 12
Work and leisure

12.1 Christian approaches

What is work?

Work is an essential part of life. For many people work is what they get paid for but work can also be unpaid, e.g. looking after children at home or voluntary work. A basic Christian traditional belief is that work is a means of taking part in the creative work of God. In the book of Genesis Adam and Eve are given the garden of Eden and told to till it and care for it. Pope John Paul II explains that work helps mankind transform nature, adapting it to his own needs; and that it helps people to achieve their potential. St Paul told the Christians of Ephesus that they should work hard and with gladness all the time, as though working for Christ.

Sometimes, however, work can be tiring or painful. In the Marxist tradition work is regarded as something which dehumanises the worker. It is not seen as a means to fulfilment but rather a means of control.

The right to work

According to Christian teaching every human being has the right to become a fulfilled person. The loss of a job often leads to poverty for the worker and the whole family is affected. Work brings people into relationships with others and lends a sense of community by giving people a place and status in society; work enables people to provide for their families. Christian teaching is opposed to discrimination on grounds of race, age, gender, religion or colour in employment.

Leisure

The importance of using leisure time properly is central to the Christian tradition. The Genesis creation story tells of God resting on the seventh day after his six-day work of creating the world. This is the origin of the Sabbath being a day of rest.

Sensible use of leisure time enables a person to become re-created and more human, thus sharing in the creative work of God in the world. A Christian might use his or her leisure time to develop intellectually through reading or studying; physically through sport or dance; spiritually through spending more time in prayer or service to others.

Christians believe that leisure time can be used to help an individual develop as a person – grow more human. Ultimately the Christian ideal that each individual grows more into Christ can be applied to each day. Christians are obliged to make everything they do a contribution to God's Kingdom. Thus Christians must recognise their gifts, give thanks for their abilities and use each day to work for the Lord even in a leisure activity. Through social clubs and contacts Christians can bring kindness to others and thus be witness to the love of God for His creation.

Vocation and career

A vocation is a call. Christians believe that everyone is specially called by God for some work. Each person has a particular talent and should try to discern the particular work

---

'Our brothers, we command you in the name of Our Lord Jesus Christ to keep away from all brothers who are living a lazy life ... We were not lazy when we were with you. We kept working day and night so as not to be an expense to any of you.' (2 Thess. 3:6-8)

'Work is a good thing for man – a good thing for his humanity – because through work man not only transforms nature, adapting it to his own needs, but he also achieves fulfilment as a human being and, indeed, in a sense becomes a "more human being".' (The teachings of John Paul 11 – Human Work, *The Catholic Truth Society*, 1982)

'I have come in order that you might have life – life in its fullness.' (John 10:10)

'Let us go off by ourselves to some place where we will be alone and you can rest for a while.' (Mark 6:31)

Chapter 12 Work and leisure

'A sense of vocation means that we see what we do as an expression of our faith and a response to God's love for us. Ideally it should be possible to have a sense of vocation about the whole of life ...' (What does Methodism Think, 1980)

that God has set aside. This usually means finding paid employment in order to be financially secure and yet doing work which is suited to one's talents and beneficial to the family and community and in keeping with Christian ethics.

In modern society people are encouraged to have a 'career'. This means choosing an area in which to work and aiming to be a successful achiever in that area. Having a career does not necessarily mean not following a vocation. Indeed, many people follow careers to which they feel specially called. Having a career is distinguished from just working, which is seen as unfulfilling and unsatisfying. Yet some people with very simple jobs can feel called to their work because of the contribution they make to their own family and the community in general.

Acceptable and unacceptable professions

For some Christians some areas of work are unacceptable because they feel those areas are not compatible with a Christian life. Many Christians would, for example, object to working in the arms trade or in a job associated with pornography. Christians might find working in family planning difficult, especially if it involved an abortion option. A Christian would feel challenged by any work which openly exploited others. Any work which is demeaning, degrading, evil or exploitative would be unacceptable to a Christian.

Christians are often called to work in service, in teaching, medicine and social work; most work is acceptable, especially if the primary purpose is good, i.e. service to others. Working in industry, commerce or banking services is acceptable as it benefits the community. Christians have responsibility to remember that neither money, status or power must become a false god.

Contemplative life

Some people find that, for them, an appropriate way of life is to withdraw from society and spend life in silent prayer. There are Religious Orders which are contemplative. The Carmelite nuns enter convents and devote themselves to constant prayer as an interpretation of complete submission to the will of God. They usually work to support themselves by farming or producing goods for sale for the Christian communities. The life is regulated by strict rule and a rigid routine of prayer.

Responsibilities of employers and employees

'Do not hold back the wages of someone you have hired, not even for one night ... Each day before sunset pay him for that day's work; he needs the money and has counted on getting it.' (Lev. 19:13. Deut. 24:15)

Christianity is against cheating and profiteering through exploitation. Christians believe that employers have a duty to behave justly so they should pay fair wages and make sure their employees have healthy working conditions. According to Christian ethics, employers have a duty to protect the legal employment rights of their workers. All forms of discrimination are against Christian teaching.

Christians believe that employees have an obligation to work hard, by using their time and talents to the full. St Paul told the Christians at Ephesus that they should remember they serve God through their work, not only their employer. The Bible contains many warnings against laziness.

Christian teaching reminds both employers and employees that they should not make love of money and material things the prime motivation of work as this can lead to greed and exploitation.

Unemployment

Unemployment is one of the major problems of modern times, caused mainly by technological and economic changes. In areas of high unemployment poverty and crime often increase.

People who become unemployed can often feel cut off from society. The psychological shock of losing a job can lead to physical illness. Christians regard unemployment as a social evil because of the loss of dignity suffered by the unemployed. It is sometimes possible for people who have become unemployed to regard this as an opportunity to retrain for a new job. Christians might also regard unemployment as an opportunity to reflect on whether God is calling them to new work.

12.2 Focus on Judaism

'Great is work. God's presence only rested upon the Jewish people when they began occupying themselves with useful work.' (Midrash)

Jewish teaching on work and leisure generally is similar to that of Christianity since they both come from the same route in Genesis. Judaism teaches that work is desirable and idleness is not good for people as it can lead them into bad ways and ultimately it leads to a corrupt or criminalised society.

It is important in Judaism that work should be productive, providing for people and for generations to come. Those who wish to withdraw from society in order to pray (like the contemplative religious in Christianity) are not found in Judaism. However, there are certain, very religious groups of Jews whose men spend much of their time studying and learning about all aspects of the religion. Jews believe that it is through action and work that God's will is brought about on earth.

'You shall do no unrighteousness in measurement, neither in land measure, in weight nor in liquid measure.' (Lev. 19:35)

A Jew is always aware that God sees everything and therefore there are certain jobs which would not be acceptable, particularly anything that involved cheating or exploitation. A Jew would not be expected to work at anything contrary to Jewish moral codes. It is acceptable to work in business and commerce but God sees everything and a Jew is obliged to conduct business fairly, to charge a fair price for goods and be honest about their quality, and not to use enticements to persuade people to enter a shop.

'When God stopped work on the Sabbath he created contentment, peace of mind and rest.' (Midrash)

The main understanding in Judaism with regard to leisure stems from the obligation to rest on the Sabbath which establishes a pattern and is kept with varying degrees of rigidity. Leisure is important to a full life as it enables a person to develop the whole self.

12.3 Focus on Islam

It is expected in Islam that everyone should work to provide for dependants. This work may be paid or it may be practical such as raising children or caring for the elderly. Only the infirm are expected not to work and there is no tradition of contemplative religious life. Each community should have enough imams to allow the latter to do additional gainful work. Some communities do support full-time priests.

'No one eats better food than that which they have earned by their own labours.' (Hadith)

It is expected in Islam that each person will have sufficient skill to support self, and it is dishonourable to be a burden to others and society. It is not acceptable to beg unless in dire need; this should not arise in a good Muslim community. All work is to be regarded as of equal status as society needs workers to fulfil every need.

'He who begs without need is like a person holding a burning coal in his hand.' (Hadith)

It is permitted in Islam to work in business but usury (called **Riba**) is forbidden. Money in Islam is to be used and not bought and sold or hoarded. In Islamic states a tax is levied on money not in circulation. Betting is forbidden in Islam.

'On the day of Resurrection Allah will not look on the person who swears to the truth while lying about his merchandise.' (Hadith)

It is a duty (**fard**) in Islam to develop the skills necessary to have a thriving community. Thus, each community encourages the training and education of teachers, doctors, engineers, politicians, scientists and so on. If there is a shortage of the necessary skills the community is at fault as it has a duty to ensure the well-being of everyone.

It is very much against Islamic teaching to work in areas regarded as unsuitable, such as those which are seen as immoral. For example, no Muslim must have anything to do with pornography, indecency, prostitution, intoxicants, injustice or anything which is hostile to Islam.

It is important for employers to treat their employees fairly and for employees to work honestly and honourably. It is not acceptable to exploit or cheat employees or for employees to steal from or cheat the employer.

Leisure time should be used wisely to worship Allah, to be with the family and to build the community. It is necessary to relax to be a whole person and it is a duty to keep the body healthy by regular exercise.

Chapter 12   Work and leisure

Summary

1 Work is vital; it can be creative, painful, healthy and good.
2 Work is a means by which humans fulfil their purpose. It is necessary for survival and growth into personhood.
3 All people should have leisure time and use it well to keep healthy – spiritually, physically and intellectually – and to grow closer to family.
4 A vocation is the life that a Christian feels called to live.
5 Work which is clearly incompatible with a Christian life is not acceptable. Work which harms or exploits others or is demeaning in its association with indecency or obscenity must be avoided.
6 Employers must treat employees justly, pay them fairly and not exploit them.
7 Employees must work honestly and give a fair day's work for a fair day's pay.
8 Unemployment is a great evil which can rob a person of an identity in modern society.
9 In Judaism work provides for future generations and all have a duty to work.
10 In Islam all must work in order to contribute to society and each community must ensure enough workers to sustain a balance of roles.
11 In Islam each person must work to provide for self.
12 Usury (**Riba**) is strictly forbidden in Islam.

Quick questions

1 What Scriptural teaching might a Christian use to justify the need to work?
2 How does working help a person to become more human?
3 How can a Christian use leisure time beneficially?
4 What is a vocation?
5 What kind of work is unsuitable for a Christian?
6 What responsibilities do employers have to their employees?
7 Why is unemployment regarded as evil?
8 What evidence from the **Torah** might a Jew use to explain the duty to be honest in business?
9 What duty does an Islamic community have to train workers?
10 Why is usury forbidden in Islam?
11 How will a business cheat be regarded by **Allah** at the last judgement?
12 Which areas of work are forbidden by Islam?

Chapter 13
Religion and the State

13.1 Christianity in England

Church and State

There is an Established Church in England called the Church of England. This Church was founded at the time of the Reformation when Henry VIII wanted a divorce from Katherine of Aragon. When the Pope refused to allow this Henry VIII declared himself head of the church in England and annulled his own marriage.

The Church of England was Established in 1558 when Elizabeth I declared herself to be head of Church and State. Since that time England has been governed on the basis of Christian teachings and culture. In practice this means that parliament has prayers at the beginning of the day and the reigning monarch is crowned in Westminster Abbey and has the title Defender of the Faith. Prince Charles caused controversy in 1994 when he suggested he would like to be Defender of Faith, rather than *the* Faith, thus recognising the many faiths which are practised in England today. Protestant churches which do not conform to the established church are known as nonconformist.

Christianity is at the root of English culture. Recent education legislation (1988 Education Reform Act) instructs that each pupil in school should: 'Unless exemption has been obtained, experience an Act of Collective Worship which shall be wholly or mainly of a broadly Christian character.' The majority of public schools and old universities in England had Christian foundations and policy makers mainly come from that background. Education was for most of the nineteenth and twentieth centuries dictated by the churches, which established and supported schools. Either explicitly or implicitly there is a Christian influence on society. English law makes allowance for the celebration of Christian festivals with statutory holidays given for Good Friday and Christmas Day.

Religion and society

Today it is recognised that established religion plays little part in most people's lives. Numbers attending the Church of England are in steady decline and while baptisms in Roman Catholicism continue to grow the numbers attending church are also slowly declining. There is a growth in evangelical churches but on the whole only a small proportion of people in England are active members of a church community. That does not mean that people do not believe in a 'transcendent power' such as a religious believer might call God. In surveys a high proportion of people will acknowledge experiencing some power beyond themselves.

Co-operation and conflict between church and state

Although England is nominally a Christian country there are many legislators who do not regard Christian ethics as the guide to their work; as a result conflict sometimes

Chapter 13 Religion and the State

'God blessed the seventh day and made it holy, because on that day he ceased from all the work he had set himself to do.' (Gen. 1:3)

arises between organised Christianity and the state legislature. Such conflict arose during 1992–1994 concerning Sunday trading laws. Organised Christianity sought to 'Keep Sunday Special' with a campaign aimed at keeping shops closed on Sundays, allowing time for worship and family life for both consumers and shoppers. Legislators argued that the Sunday trading laws were unclear and legislated for limited trading on Sundays. Businesses with strong religious traditions were reluctant to open on Sundays. Marks and Spencer accepted a degree of flexibility but John Lewis stores remained closed. In the world of commerce it is often difficult to reconcile religious teachings with profit-making business practice. (Students should monitor the situation on Sunday trading as it unfolds.)

Another area in which organised Christianity has been in conflict with the state is that of legislation on abortion. Many Christians feel very strongly that abortion is never acceptable and yet the state sanctions 175,000 abortions each year. Church groups of all denominations protest against this and there have been a number of amendments since 1967, brought about by the anti-abortion lobby. (See Chapter 7 for details.)

The 1988 Education Reform Act stated that every student should take part in an act of collective worship which was mainly Christian. Since then some areas of society have examined what is meant by the idea that Britain is mainly Christian. Some church representatives have suggested that worship should be less frequent, of a higher quality, and perhaps involve more ministers; that it should be more like worship which is shared by the Christian believers who attend church. Since the law allows both students and teachers the right to opt out of collective worship it seems not to really support itself and would be difficult to uphold if ever put to the test.

Individual conscience and church authority

Sometimes individuals find themselves unable to follow a teaching of their church and feel obliged to follow their own consciences. Such situations may arise when a divorcée wishes to remarry in church. This is forbidden in the Roman Catholic and Anglican churches. In the Anglican church clergy have the right to exercise individual discretion to conduct remarriages.

Sometimes Roman Catholic divorcées remarry in a Registry Office or another Christian church. By doing this they officially deny themselves the right to the sacraments of the church but many refer to their individual conscience and continue to receive the sacraments, especially if they believe that doing so will not cause a scandal.

Similarly many Roman Catholics exercise choice regarding the use of artificial means of contraception by following the dictates of their own conscience.

A Christian woman or couple might also find themselves faced with a pregnancy which they believe should be terminated even though church law states that this should not happen. In these cases Christians do sometimes choose to follow their own consciences rather than the letter of church law.

In many ethical issues church teaching can seem harsh and unfeeling. Roman Catholicism is very strict about fertility treatments yet a childless couple will feel prepared to do anything to have their own family and the urge to follow conscience and not accept church law is very strong amongst a well-informed and educated people.

Making decisions

In making major life choices and decisions many Christians are guided by church law and cannot easily detach themselves from the teachings which have formed their very identity. The major guiding forces for Christians are the commandments to 'love God and love your neighbour' and the Beatitudes (see page 55) which stress certain attitudes to life.

Christians are taught to have a strong sense of duty to those in need and an obligation to make Christ's Kingdom come on earth. Christian churches charge all parents to bring their children up with knowledge of their faith and an understanding of right and wrong. Christians believe in a conscience which is like a safety guard which develops as a person grows and learns. A Christian is taught to follow that conscience and through prayer try to discern the will of God in order to make important decisions. Thus Christians use situation ethics to understand how they must act in particular circumstances.

13.1 Christianity in England

'May Christ's sacrifice give us the courage to offer our own bodies for justice and peace.'
(Oscar Romero's last words)

Liberation theology

In the Gospel of Luke Jesus says, '… he has sent me:

- to give the Good News to the poor;
- to proclaim release for prisoners and recovery of sight for the blind;
- to let the broken victims go free' (Luke 4:18).

'When I give food to the poor they call me a saint. When I ask why the poor have no food, they call me a communist.' (Helder Camera)

Christians have taken this as a directive, but while many see their role as one of praying and raising money to try to help the poor and oppressed, some Christians feel they need to be more proactive. Liberation theology teaches that Christians can work to set people free either by:

1. personally giving aid in the form of charity and donations;
2. influencing the infrastructure by working in education, medicine, government or engineering, *or*
3. helping the oppressed to rise up against their persecutors in political or physical combat.

'In many places in Latin America there is a situation of injustice that must be recognised as institutionalised violence, because the existing structures violate people's basic rights: a situation which calls for far-reaching urgent action.' (Bishops of Latin America, 1968)

This is the theology of liberation and it is taught by some priests and bishops in the Third World and others who work in the Third World. Some Christians have been prepared to lay down their lives to set people free. Oscar Romero said if he was killed his spirit would rise up again in the people of El Salvador. Since his death in 1982 he is a recognised martyr of the church. Desmond Tutu in South Africa has also spoken out bravely for justice for the poor in South Africa.

Church and community

Christians work in their own communities to witness to Christ's love for all people. Each church has its own schemes such as lunch clubs, day centres, church transport schemes, youth clubs and various outreach projects. The Salvation Army was founded to take Christ to the poor and it runs hostels for the homeless and provides care on the streets. Members of the Salvation Army wear a uniform as a reminder they are soldiers for Christ and lay themselves open to abuse by collecting in public houses and on the streets. Local church communities will also staff hospices voluntarily as well as working to raise money for many humanitarian projects.

It is important that you carry out research enabling you to gain, for example, a better idea of any humanitarian projects that a church close to you may be engaged in. Find out which clubs are organised and which groups in the community benefit from local church action.

Members of the Salvation Army providing soup

13.2 Focus on Judaism

Judaism and the state

For over a thousand years Jews did not have a nation state. After the diaspora in AD 70 Jews lived in communities all over the world and their very uniqueness made them easy and obvious prey to bullying and scapegoating. This scapegoating was profoundly manifest in the Holocaust when Hitler decided that Jews could be blamed for many of Germany's problems and that Jews were a threat to his mission to create a pure Aryan master race of tall, fair, strong and intelligent people. He undertook a massive programme of extermination and murdered over six million European Jews in death camps between 1933 and 1945. All thinking people in the world have asked why and how this could have been allowed to happen.

The Jewish response to the suffering of the Holocaust is generally that it is a tragedy and a mystery which cannot be understood and it has to be seen as part of God working his purpose out.

As a result of the events of the Holocaust, which was the most terrible culmination of years of persecution and pogroms against European Jews, the pressure to create a Jewish nation state was intensified. The Zionist movement which campaigned for such a state was formed in Switzerland in 1897 by Theodore Herzl. It was supported by Britain in the Balfour Declaration in 1917. After the Second World War Britain had control of Palestine and, with the approval of the United Nations, a nation state of Israel was formed in Palestine in 1948 and Jewish law was established.

When Jews live in Israel they obey Jewish law. When they live outside Israel they must obey state law but not break the commandments. A Jew must follow his informed conscience when deciding what is right or wrong.

The synagogue in the community

For Jews the synagogue means a faith community (**kehilla**) not simply a building. It is where people meet and discuss and learn. It will be the focal meeting point for Jews in a community.

Humanitarian work in the community

There are specific Jewish organisations which are involved in caring work in the Community. For example:

- Norwood Child Care began as an orphanage in South London in 1795 and now provides social services to Jewish children and their families. It provides help for children who need counselling about abuse, drug dependency or simply support.
- The Jews' Temporary Shelter provides shelter for refugees, runs a day centre for the elderly and organises meals on wheels for the housebound.
- Jewish Care runs housing schemes for the elderly and disabled.

Jews are obliged to support charity (Zakadah) and as well as giving to Jewish concerns they also give to other local charities.

13.3 Focus on Islam

Religion and the state

In Islam the main focus is to submit to **Allah** (the word Muslim means submit). It is the duty of every Muslim to search for the way (**shari'ah**) in every situation. The will of

Allah is found in the **Qur'an** as revealed to the Prophet Mohammed and thus in Islamic states the whole infrastructure is based on Islamic teachings and no Muslim can take issue with the law.

There is, however, a division in Islam which sometimes leads to disagreement about the interpretation of the Qur'an. After Mohammed there were a series of right-minded prophets (**al-Khulafa-ur-Rashidun**) who interpreted the **Qur'an**. The last of these was **Ali-Al Murtada**, who was assassinated in AD 660. Leadership in Islam was then in control of Mu'awiya, governor of Syria.

Most Muslims today are called **Sunni** Muslims because they follow the Sunnah, the way of the prophet, and believed originally that any good Muslim could lead the community as Caliph. Some Muslims close to Ali believed that the leader should be a blood relative of the prophet and formed a sect called Shi'i after Shi'at Ali. Only 10% of Muslims are **Shi'ah** and mainly they follow the way of the Sunni but there is a greater emphasis on suffering and martyrdom.

Some Muslims take issue with the way the Qur'an is interpreted and, because it is a worldwide religion, Islam is practised amongst many cultures. Thus a Muslim living in a particular culture might find it difficult to accept religious restrictions on his or her traditional lifestyle. Occasionally there is conflict which focuses on the cultural attitude towards women in some Islamic states; some educated Muslim women say this is not law in the Qur'an but a cultural imposition.

Islam, like all faiths, is sometimes interpreted through the actions of the believers but in fact Islam teaches that it is a divine revelation which stands forever revealed to Mohammed in the Qur'an.

Summary

1 The Church of England is Christian and the Established church in England.
2 English culture and law is based on Christian principles.
3 Most people in England are christened, married and buried by the rites of the Christian Church although relatively few people attend church regularly.
4 Sometimes the law of the land seems to transgress Christian teaching such as in the case of Sunday trading laws.
5 A Christian's own conscience can cause him to reject the law of the church.
6 Liberation theology is the philosophy that says people must be set free from oppression in the name of Christ, that justice must be brought to the poor.
7 The oppressed can be liberated through prayer, work and aid or if necessary through armed struggle.
8 It is part of Christian witness to work in the community to bring Christ's message of hope, joy and love to all people.
9 Israel is the only state which is governed by Jewish law.
10 Observation of the Sabbath and all Jewish festivals are part of life in Israel.
11 Jews are involved in good works in the community as part of their obligation to give to charity.
12 There are a number of countries in the world in which Islam is the established faith and state law is Islamic law.
13 There is sometimes conflict between Muslims as a result of different interpretations concerning the right person to be leader of the community.
14 A Muslim might have difficulty following Islamic law when the culture in the country in which he lives and grows is radically different.

Quick questions

1. What do Christians understand by the Established Church of England?
2. How is the culture and law of England Christian?
3. What involvement do most Christians in England have with church?
4. In what circumstances might a Christian find that his conscience contradicts the teaching of the Church?
5. What is liberation theology?
6. How can liberation theology be used?
7. How is Israel a Jewish nation state?
8. What is the difference between a **Shi'ah** and a **Sunni** Muslim?
9. In what circumstances might a Muslim find it hard to follow religious laws?
10. What is the essential truth about Islam that affects the way Muslims believe?

Contemporary issues in society

(Recommended passages for study by Exam Syllabus)

Syllabus / Issues	MEG Papers 1 & 2	ULEAC Units 1, 2 and 5	NEAB Syllabus B: 2A and 2B	NEAB Syllabus C, General	SEG Syllabus A, Option 2	SEG Syllabus B, Section B	SEG Syllabus C, Unit 2(b) Unit 5	WJEC, Unit 1	SCE
Family life / Marriage	Matt. 5:31–32 Mark 10:2–12 1 Tim. 5:8 1 John 1:9		Gen. 1–3:3 Matt. 5:27–32 1 Cor. 6:18–20 Eph. 5:21–33 Luke 12:4–7	Mark 10:1–12 Eph. 5:21–23 Mark 10:13–16 1 Cor. 3:12–17 1 Pet. 3:1–9		Matt. 3:11–17; 5–7 John 2:1–11; 6:45–49 Rom. 12–14 1 Cor. 3:16–17; 6:13,19 Gal. 3:26–29; 5:16	Mark 10:2–12 1 Cor. 13:1–13 Eph. 5:25–33		
Social issues/ethics abortion, euthanasia, old age, illness/death	Gen. 1:26–27 Ps 139:13 Job 1:21 1 Cor. 3:16–17	Mark 4,5,6,9 Matt. 5–7		Matt. 25:14–46 1 Cor. 15:1–58 2 Cor. 11:16; 12:10					
Prejudice and discrimination	Deut. 24:14–22 Amos 8:4–6 Luke 10:30–37 Col. 3:8–11 Jas. 2:1–7		Mark 14:3–9 Luke 7:1–10 Luke 10:25–36 Acts 11:1–18						
War and peace	Isa. 58:6–10 Mic. 4:1–4 Matt. 26:47–52 Matt. 25:32–46 Rom. 12:17–21	Matt. 5–7			Mic. 5:2–4 Exod. 13:1–3 Deut. 19:15–21 Mic. 4:1–3 Luke 10:27 Luke 22:35–53 John 5:1–15 Acts 2:37–39 Eph. 4:25–32	Luke 10:27; 22:35–53 John 5:1–15 Acts 37–39 Eph. 4:25–32			
Law and order in society		Mark 2:23–28 Mark 6,7,9,10 Mark 12:28–34 Mark 14,15 Matt. 5–7 Exod. 20	Matt. 5:38–48 Matt. 18:23–35 Matt. 26:47–53 Mark 11:15–18 Luke 15:11–32 Luke 23:32–43 John 8:1–1 Rom. 13:1–7	Luke 15:11–32 Matt. 18:1–35 Eph. 2:11–22	Exod. 20:1–17		Isa. 58:6–10 Amos 8:4–7 Luke 10:25–30 Jas. 2:1–4 Luke 10:25–30; 16:19–31 Matt. 25:31–46 Matt. 5:43–48 18:21–35	Matt. 5:21–26; 38–42;43–48; 18:15–17 Luke 15:11–32 Matt. 5:17–20; 22:15–22; 7:1–5 Luke 10:29–37 Matt. 18:21–35	
Work and leisure		Mark 1;2;3;8; 10:17–45; 11; 12;14;15;16 Matt. 5–7			Prov. 6:6–11 1 Tim. 6:6–10 2 Thess. 3:6–13 Luke 20:1–26 Mark 10:17–31		Gen. 26–31 Matt. 25:14–30 Luke 12:13–54		
Poverty and environmental issues	Gen. 1:26–31 Ps. 19:1–10	Mark 4;5;6;9 Matt. 5–7	Matt. 25:31–46 Luke 12:21–31 Luke 16:19–31 Acts 4:32–37	Luke 14:12–24 Jas. 2:1–13	Jas. 2:14–19 Gen. 1–3 Gen. 8:22–9, 17 1 Kgs. 21 Job 38–9 Luke 3:1–14 Matt. 25:31–46 John 6:1–15	Matt. 25:31–46 Luke 3:1–14 John 6: 1–15		Matt. 6:19–21; 6:24 Mark 10:17–27 Luke 12:13–21; 16:19–31	
Church and State		Mark 1;2;3;8; 10:17–45 11;12;14;15;16 Matt. 5–7			Acts 2:43–47			Matt. 5:13–16; 13:33	
General moral guidance	1 John 4:7–21 Luke 15:11–32 Mark 12:28–34 Matt. 5:17–20 Matt. 5:43–48 Mark 10: 17–25 1 Cor. 13:1–8a 1 Cor. 17:23–26 Lev. 19:18 Deut. 6:4,5 Matt. 5:17–26 Matt. 7:1–6 Matt. 22:21 Mark 12:28–31	Gen. 1 & 2 Matt. 16:13–20 Mark 14–16 Luke 10:25–37 John 1:1–18 1 Cor. 10:23; 12;13;15 Unit 2 Matt. 16:17–19; 25–40; 28:18–20 John 15:5 (i) Dei Verbum (ii) Lumen Gentium (iii) Sacrosanctum Concillium (iv) Gaudium et spes	2B in particular Luke 5:1–11; 27–32 Matt. 28:18–20 Matt. 19:16–30 Luke 10:25–37 Mark 6:7–13 Matt. 13 Mark 8:34–38 Matt. 20:24–28 Mark 12:41–44 Mark 12:28–31 Mark 2:1–12 Luke 15:11–32 Luke 7:1–10 Philem. James 2:1–9 Matt. 25:14–46 Luke 15:1–10 Jas. 5:13–15 Matt. 10:23–35	Matt. 5:13–16 1 Cor. 6:12–20 1 Pet. 4:7–11 Acts 2:1–13 Rom. 7:18–25; 8:1–4 John 14:5–7; 15:1–8 1 Cor. 12:13; 13:10 1 John 4:7–14	Matt. 5–7 Rom. 12–14 1 Cor. 13 Hos. 3:1 Matt. 3:11–17 John 2:1–11 John 6:45–59 1 Cor. 3:16–17 1 Cor. 6:19 Gal. 3:26–29; 5:16 Philem. Eph. 5 Lev. 19:33–34	Jas. 2:14–19	Exod. 20:1–17 Matt. 6:21–23 Luke 10:25–37 Rom. 13:8–10 Jas. 2:14–17 1 John 3:11–18; 4:7–12; 20–21 Phil. 2:3–11 Luke 1:46–55; 18:9–14 Gen. 1:26–27 Luke 10:27	Exod. 20:1–17 Matt. 5:3–12; 21–48; 6:25–34; 7:1–5 Rom. 13:1–14; 14:13–23 1 Cor. 13 Gal. 3:27–28 Matt. 5:3–12; 5:33–37; 6:1–4 Mark 9:33–37; 38–41 Luke 14:7–14 Mark 7:1–8; 11–23 Luke 17:7–10 Matt. 16:21–26 Mark 12:41–44 Matt. 7:13–14; 24–29	No texts prescribed. Look at general guidance on lifestyle and behaviour

Issues / Syllabus	ULEAC Unit 3, Section 2 Unit 6	Issues / Syllabus	SEG Syllabus B Section 8	Issues / Syllabus	ULEAC Unit 4, Section 2 Unit 7	Issues / Syllabus	SEG Syllabus B, Section B
Self and society	Qur'an 1, 2:1–39, 2:153–188 2:211–221, 2:254–266 2:274–281, 2:284–286 3:21–30, 7:40–47, 22:1–10, 24:35–40 36:68–83; 96:1–5 103,108,112,113,114	Marriage and family	Qur'an 2:223, 233 4:2,4,21,35,125–30 5:5 57:27	Personal relationships Personal and social issues	Gen. 1:27 Mishnah peah 1:1 Prayer Book 14ff/6 Amos 5:4–25	Marriage and family	Exod. 20:1–17 Deut. 32:39 2 Kgs 4:14–16 Isa. 45:18
Wealth, work and leisure	Qur'an 2:183–188, 2:217–221 2:261–266, 3:21–30 8:70–75, 17:23–40, 22:26–33, 107	Peace and conflict Punishment Equality Law and order War and peace	Qur'an 2:178,190 4:15,30,92 5:38,48 6:151 8:39,61 24:26 25:52	Freedom and choice Wealth and poverty Suffering Messianism Zionism	Exod. 20 Deut. 30 1 Kgs. 21 Isa. 5:8–23; 52:13–53; 12 Jer. 31:29–34 Ezek. 37 Pirkei Not 2:1; 3; 19 Authorised daily prayer book (154/93) Aleinu prayer (134/79/41)	Peace and conflict Punishment Equality Law and order War and peace	Exod. 17:8–13 Lev. 19:33–35 Deut. 16:18 Judg. 11:12–33 Hos. 3:1 Mic. 4:3, 5:2–4 Mal. 2:10 Ps. 34:15, 146;7–9
The State, Sin and crime, forgiveness, justice	Qur'an 2:1–39, 2:211–216 2:258–260, 3:1–9 3:31–63, 4:34–42 4:153–172, 5:100–115 12; 18:1–31, 18:60–82 19:1–40; 97	Humankind and nature Health Drug abuse Animal rights	2:219 4:43,140 5:2,93–4,98 6:165 16:67 24:41 45:12–13 55:7			Humankind and nature Health Drug abuse Animal rights	Gen. 1–3; 8:22–9,17 Deut. 20:19 1 Kgs. 22 Ps. 24:1 Prov. 12:10; 23:20 Job. 38–39
Law and order Medical ethics Ecology Poverty and suffering	Qur'an 2:1–39, 2:168–176 2:183–188, 2:217–221 2:274–281, 5:87–93 24:1–10, 24:27–43			Ecology Punishment Crime Forgiveness Law and order Work ethics The State	Exod. 16:23–30 Decalogue 3:12–17 Lev. 23 Deut. 15/16; Ruth 1,2 Neh. 13,15–22 Pirkei avot 2:18 Prayer book pp 76–90/45ff Evening service prayer book pp 190–2/116–117/33 Exod. 32 Num. 27:12–32 Deut. 20:19–20, 25:13–16 Jer. 29:1–15 Pirkei avot 1:1 1:12–13, 2:2, 2:20–21 3:1–2		
General guidance	Unit 3 Qur'an 1: 2:285 3:83 3:145 18:47–49 32:13 35:1 36:51–67, 112				General Unit 4 Tenakh Gen. 1:27; 2:1–3; 12:1–19 Exod. 19:1–15; 16–24; 20; 24:1–11; 12–18; 31:16–17 Lev. 19:1–4; 9–19, 23–27 Deut. 6:4–9 2 Sam. 12:1–13 1 Kgs. 19 Isa. 2:1–4; 11:1–10 Amos 5:4–25; 7:1–10 Zech. 8:18–20		

NICCEA syllabuses A, B and C

The following passages are recommended for looking at the issues of war and peace:
Exod. 20:13
Deut. 7:1–16, 24
Amos 1:3–8; 2:4–16
Matt. 26:52
Rom. 12:17–21
Col. 5:12–17

Chapter 14
Jewish beliefs

14.1 The Torah

Jews do not have a set creed of beliefs which they recite and which unites them all. Judaism has developed over thousands of years. Jews live their life according to the understanding of God which can be found in the **Torah**. The Torah is the first five books of the **Tenakh** (Old Testament): Genesis, Exodus, Numbers, Leviticus and Deuteronomy.

Deuteronomy 6:4–5 provides the nearest thing to basic Jewish belief: the Shema, 'Hear O Israel the Lord is our God, the Lord is One …'.

> Hear O Israel, the Lord is Our God, one Lord, and you must love the Lord your God with all your heart and soul and strength. (Deut. 6:4–6, The opening lines of the Shema prayer)

14.2 Covenant with Abraham

The Torah is a description of how Jews understand God. Central to this understanding is the Covenant which Jews believe God made with Abraham (Gen. 12:1–19). The story of Abraham is contained in Genesis. Abraham represents the first man to believe in one God and he showed absolute faith and trust by moving from Ur to Canaan with his family because he believed this is what God wanted him to do. He was even prepared to sacrifice his only son, Isaac, because he believed that it was God's will. When God saw Abraham's faith he sent a message via an angel and promised that Abraham would have many descendants and they would be abundantly blessed.

> The time came when God put Abraham to the test. 'Abraham', he called and Abraham replied, 'Here I am'. God said, 'Take your Son, Isaac, your only son, whom you love, and go to the land of Moriah. There you shall offer him as a sacrifice on one of the hills I shall show you.' (Gen. 22:1–3)

14.3 Jacob called Israel

In Genesis 32 Abraham's grandson, Jacob, wrestles with a man who asks his name and then says, 'I will call you Israel because you strove with God; in Genesis 35 God appears to Jacob and calls him Israel again and blesses him, giving him the land of Canaan for all his descendants. Jews have interpreted the stories of Abraham, Isaac and Jacob as a sign that they are God's 'chosen people'. The believed promise of land is a theme throughout the Old Testament.

14.4 A 'Kingdom of priests, a holy nation' (Exod. 19:1–15)

The book of Exodus is also central to Jewish understanding of their history and culture. The Jews were enslaved in Egypt for 400 years; Moses was sent by God to free them from slavery and lead them back to the promised land of Canaan. On the journey the Israelites kept losing

Chapter 14 Jewish beliefs

faith in God and reverted to worshipping false gods such as the Golden Calf which they made when Moses was up on Mount Sinai. It was on the mountain that God revealed to Moses the ten commandments (the decalogue) by which the Israelites should live their lives.

Because of their constant doubting of God the Israelites were condemned to roam the wilderness for 40 years. During this period, the generation which had doubted God died, as did Moses. A new generation, led by Joshua went in and took possession of Canaan. During the wandering period the Lord had given the Israelites many laws. According to tradition the Torah gives 613 mitzvot known as 'Taryag' which is a word formed from the initials of the words 613. There are 248 positive commandments and 365 things a Jew should not do. This number is the number of days in the year and allows the Jewish people to remember God with the whole self every day.

1. There is only one God 2. You shall have no false Gods 3. Do not misuse the name of God 4. Keep the Sabbath holy 5. Honour your Father and Mother 6. You shall not murder 7. You shall not commit adultery 8. You shall not steal 9. You shall not bear false witness against your neighbour (lie) 10. You shall not covet (want) what belongs to anyone else	1. I am the Lord your God who brought you out of the Land of Egypt, out of the land of slavery. You shall have no other God to set against me. 2. You shall not make a carved image for yourself nor the likeness of anything in the heavens above, or on the earth below or in the waters under the earth. You shall not bow down to them nor worship them, for I, the Lord your God am a jealous God. I punish the children for the sins of the fathers to the third and fourth generations of those who hate me. But I keep faith with thousands of those who love me and keep my commandments. 3. You shall not make wrong use of the Lord your God; the Lord will not leave unpunished the man who misuses his name. 4. Remember to keep the Sabbath day holy. You have six days to labour and do all your work but the seventh day is the Sabbath day of the Lord your God; that day you shall not do any work, you, your son or your daughter, your slave, or your slave girl, your cattle or the alien within your gates;	for in six days the Lord made heaven and earth, the sea and all that is in them, and on the seventh day he rested. Therefore the Lord blessed the Sabbath day and made it holy. 5. Honour your father and mother that you may live long in the land which the Lord your God is giving you. 6. You shall not commit murder. 7. You shall not commit adultery. 8. You shall not steal. 9. You shall not give false evidence against your neighbour. 10. You shall not covet your neighbour's house; you shall not covet your neighbour's wife, his slave, his slave-girl, his ox, his ass, or anything that belongs to him. (Exod. 20:1–17)

Primarily a Jew must uphold and live by the ten commandments; the laws reflect the nature of God who is creator, sustainer, law-giver, judge, redeemer and sanctifier. Jews believe that the world is a place in which God is working his purpose out and that He has everything under control. One must, therefore, have absolute faith in God and obedience to His will. Following on from the Shema and the teaching that *God is one* is the commandment to love God and love your neighbour as yourself.

The second part of the Tenakh contains the books of the prophets Joshua, Samuel, Amos, Hosea, Isaiah, Jeremiah and Ezekiel. Amos taught that God would judge people by how they behaved and they could not appease Him with sacrifices – the God of justice. Hosea taught that God would forgive if sinners repented – the God of mercy. Jeremiah taught that every individual was precious to God – each person is holy. Ezekiel taught that each individual was responsible for his own actions. (In the book of Samuel (2 Samuel 1–13) the prophecy of Nathan had been that the son of David would die because of David's behaviour; this illustrated Jewish belief in the idea that the sins of the fathers are visited on generations which follow.)

Ezekiel gives a new version of the passage in Samuel and the idea that new generations will be punished for others' sins is replaced with the idea that each individual is responsible. Individual Jews subscribe to whichever view suits them. Sometimes it seems as if children suffer the sins and follies of their ancestors yet some young people are able to survive adversity better than others, thus taking a burden from the past and making it a blessing.

14.5 The Messianic Age

There were two prophets called Isaiah. The first taught that the ancestors' sins would be visited upon the next generation but a human messiah-king would deliver them.

14.5 The Messianic Age

The second Isaiah taught that God was great and gentle and introduced the idea that someone could suffer for another's sins. This is the prophecy of the Messianic Age. Isaiah foretold that a servant of the Lord would extend God's covenant to all nations. Later on came the idea that there would be a Messiah (Anointed One, Saviour) who would rule over the people just before the end. Jews had different ideas of this Messiah. Many expected him to be a military leader and were not clear about whether he would be human or more than human. There is no tradition in Jewish understanding that the Messiah would be divine.

Jews believe that people were created by God with free wills and are able to make the choice to do good or evil. At the end God will be the judge. For Jews, the 10 days between **Rosh Hashanah** (the New Year) and **Yom Kippur** (the Day of Atonement) are a period of fasting and repentance. Prayers are offered to God, asking Him to judge each person fairly and to bestow the blessing of a long and healthy life. Jews ask forgiveness for wrongs they have done only after they have done all in their own power to make reparation for those wrongs. Jews fast to show sincerity; to encourage self-discipline; to concentrate the spirit and to become more sympathetic.

Jews believe that death is only part of life and that in the next world the good will be rewarded. Jews used to speak of Sheol where the dead would await judgement but they do not describe a 'heaven' except very loosely as something like the Garden of Eden. Some Jews believe that paradise will exist after the Messiah has come. In Judaism paradise is available for all who live good lives.

Summary

1. To be Jewish is to adopt a way of life which is based on an understanding which has developed over thousands of years.
2. Jewish beliefs are a reflection of the **Tenakh** and especially the **Torah**.
3. Central to Jewish belief is God's covenant with Abraham – a promise of blessings and land.
4. Jews have a sense of being the 'chosen people' because of the Torah stories.
5. Following the Exodus from Egypt the Jews wandered for 40 years, during which time God gave them many laws including the Ten Commandments.
6. A principal Jewish precept is expressed in the **Shema**.
7. From the books of the prophets Jews gain further understanding of the nature of God.
8. By the Messianic Age the Jews look forward to a time when a saviour will rule over the people – either a military leader or a good and gentle one.
9. Jews have free will to choose between good and evil and God is the judge.
10. After death life is continued for those who love God in some sort of paradise.

Quick questions

1. What is the **Tenakh**?
2. What is the **Torah**?
3. What do Jews believe to be God's covenant with Abraham?
4. What does Israel mean?
5. Why are Jews often referred to as 'The chosen people'?
6. Why did the Jews have to wander for 40 years?
7. How do Jews understand God from the writings of the prophets?
8. What is the Messianic Age?
9. What does atonement mean for Jews?
10. What do Jews believe about death?

Chapter 15
Sources of authority in Judaism

15.1 The Tenakh

The **Tenakh** is the Jewish Bible; it is the Old Testament of the Christian Bible arranged differently. The most sacred part is the **Torah**, which is the first five books: Genesis, Exodus, Leviticus, Numbers and Deuteronomy. Torah means law and Jews spend a lifetime trying to understand and live by the Torah.

15.2 The Torah

The Torah is written out by hand by a scribe and this process takes about a year. It is divided into 54 sidrot (weekly portions) and an orthodox synagogue will read all the sidra each week while a progressive one may only read a third and take three years to read through the entire amount. It is a great honour to read the Torah to the congregation. The people are called up by their Hebrew name and this is called aliyah – going up.

- Genesis is the Jewish interpretation of creation and the universe.
- Exodus is the escape from Egypt with Moses.
- Leviticus gives rules for priests and about sacrificing and leprosy.
- Numbers is about the wanderings of the Jews with Moses from Mt Sinai to Canaan.
- Deuteronomy is a summary of the foregoing and instructions on how Jews should live, including a reiteration of the ten commandments.

15.3 The Noahide code

As well as the ten commandments, which occur in Exodus and Deuteronomy, Jews recognise the authority of the sheva mitzvot (seven commandments) given to Noah after the flood and which dictate moral behaviour. They are known as the Noahide Code. God said; man must not:

1. Worship any God but Him.
2. He must not blaspheme.
3. He must not murder
4. He must not steal
5. He must not commit sexual misdemeanours.
6. He must not be cruel to animals.
7. Man must establish a rule of law to live in harmony.

15.4 Nevi'im – books of the prophets

The books of the prophets are the **Nevi'im**; they include the books of Joshua, Samuel, Amos, Isaiah, Jeremiah and Ezekiel and they tell the story of the Jews from the time of Joshua. The prophets reveal different ways of looking at God, all of which have become part of Jewish understanding.

15.5 Ketubim (writings)

The remainder of the Tenakh is taken up with the writings (**Ketuvim**). This section discusses human problems and gives advice on life matters and social behaviour. Widely read are the psalms which consider all aspects of human behaviour. Some books are particularly important to Jewish understanding, especially Ecclesiastes, which sets out that wealth is not important and cannot last; life is transitory and beyond human understanding.

The Book of Job, too, is essential to Jewish understanding of the purpose of life because it concludes that there is no answer to human suffering – it is a great mystery.

The Greek word for the Tenakh is the Septuagint because it was translated by 70 people in 270 BC. The Torah is handwritten on parchment scrolls and kept in a special ark in the synagogue. It is held in total reverence and reading from it is the most important part of Jewish worship. Its authority comes from the fact that it is the Jewish understanding of the revelation of God.

15.6 The Talmud

The **Talmud** is the **Mishnah** and the **Gemara** collected together. The Mishnah is the Oral Law as it was first written down; the Gemara is a collection of commentaries on those oral laws. It has three million words on six thousand pages and is a collection of stories, discussions, parables, history and legal rulings. The Talmud is a rule book which Jews can refer to for social and religious laws.

15.7 The Mishnah

Mishnah are laws featured in the Talmud. The laws were interpreted by **rabbis** and sometimes different opinions are included. Two rabbis, Hillel and Shammai, had different opinions but both were considered acceptable. There are six orders covering six topics in the Mishnah. The orders are the Shisha sedarim (Shas) and each has several divisions called masekhtot.

Sometimes these mishnah are explained by rabbis and these explanations are called **gemara**.

15.8 Maimonides

Maimonides was a twelfth century talmudist (one who studies the Talmud and is an authority on it) who thought up thirteen principles of faith which were the nearest thing to a Jewish creed. Each one began, 'I believe with perfect faith …'

1. God has, does and will create everything.
2. God is one.
3. God is not and does not have a body.
4. God is the first and the last.
5. It is wrong to pray to anyone or anything apart from God.
6. The words of a prophet are true.
7. The prophecy of Moses is true and he is the greatest of the prophets.
8. The Torah was given to Moses.
9. The Torah will never be changed.
10. God knows everything, everyone's thoughts and acts.
11. God rewards those who keep his commandments and punishes those who break them.
12. The Messiah will come.
13. There will be a resurrection of the dead.

15.9 Midrash

Midrash is a way of looking at the inner meaning in the Bible stories. It means 'to search out, expound'. The midrash includes stories to explain stories as well as many parables, puns and myths.

15.10 Authority from people

As well as turning to written guidance for authority on how to live in the Jewish tradition, Jews also recognise people as a source of authority. The commandment to honour your father and mother is an essential part of Judaism and old people are regarded with respect, not least for the experiences they can offer on living according to the teachings in the Torah and applying Jewish laws in a world which is not always sympathetic. Old people are an important part of the family and the family is the primary vehicle for educating a child in the ways of Judaism. Thus a child regards his or her elders as a source of authority in religious matters.

A personal problem of a particular nature is called a she'eylah and can be given or sent to a rabbi. The rabbi will respond with a ruling or guidance on the matter. Many of these responses are on computer in Israel together with the Talmud and codes (brief explanations of the Talmud). They are called responsa and Jews can access them to get advice on a problem.

15.10 Authority from people

The rabbi is a leader in the community and source of authority. A rabbi is literally a teacher. Today a rabbi has many roles. He leads prayers and advises the Jewish and non-Jewish community on Jewish affairs. He officiates at weddings and funerals. Sometimes a group will get together to form a beth din (court) which can act with authority to issue divorce documents (known as a get) and also to license kosher butchers. The rabbi can issue **Agadah**, which are teachings on the moral code.

Jewish children are encouraged to learn about their faith among their people. In some areas there are separate Jewish schools where learning Jewish teaching and tradition is passed on to the children by teachers who understand the nature of Judaism. Where this is not possible children can attend Hebrew school organised by a rabbi in the evening or at a weekend. Here they will study the Torah and the laws and learn to read some Hebrew.

Rabbi helping a boy put on tefillin

Summary

1. The **Tenakh** is the Jewish Bible; it consists of three parts: the **Torah** (laws); **Nevi'im** (prophets); **Ketuvim** (writings).
2. The Torah is the most important source of authority as, through stories, it explains for Jews the nature of God.
3. The Prophets all reveal different aspects of God.
4. The Writings are concerned with human problems; most widely looked to for authority are the psalms and the books of Job and Ecclesiastes.
5. The reading from the Torah is the most important part of a religious service and the Torah scrolls are regarded with deep respect.
6. The **Talmud** is the second source of authority; it gives the oral laws and a collection of interpretations of the Torah from thousands of contributors.
7. The **mishnah** are legal rulings in the Talmud and explanations of these rulings are called **gemara**.

Chapter 15 Sources of authority in Judaism

8. The family, especially the elders, are a source of authority for younger Jews.
9. The **rabbi** (teacher) is the religious leader of the Jewish community and a guide on religious matters and human problems.
10. The beth din is a court of rabbis who can issue divorce documents (get) and licences for **kosher** butchers.

Quick questions

1. What is the **Tenakh**?
2. Why is the **Torah** so important to Jews?
3. How do Jews show reverence for the **Torah**?
4. Who are the prophets and what did each one reveal?
5. Why are the books of Job and Ecclesiastes seen as important sources of authority?
6. What is the **Talmud**?
7. What are the **mishnah** and **gemara**?
8. How are family members regarded as a source of authority?
9. What is the role of the **rabbi**?
10. What authority is exercised by the beth din?

Chapter 16
Practice and organisation in Judaism

16.1 Different traditions

Because Judaism is an ancient religion, inevitably different traditions have developed.

Orthodox Jews believe God revealed all that was necessary to his chosen people in the **Torah** and that Jews must follow the instructions contained in the **Talmud**. Some orthodox Jews believe that the state of Israel should not have been established until the Messiah came.

The Liberal Jewish tradition (which began in Germany with David Friedlander, 1756–1834) regards the Torah as a document open to interpretation as times change. They see it as representative of Jewish understanding of God and especially believe that rituals such as Sabbath observance are not divine. They do not regard God in the same 'all-powerful' light as the orthodox and see some miracles as legends, not literal happenings.

Reform Jews (formed in Germany under Zachariah Frankel, 1801–1875) have views somewhere between those of Orthodox and Liberal. They try to apply rituals in a modern way and do not believe the whole of the Torah to be divine. Reform Jews are not waiting for a Messiah and although many support Zionism, they do not regard it as necessary to emigrate to Israel.

16.2 Differing cultures

Jews have formed communities all over the world since the diaspora. Therefore different cultural backgrounds can be identified.

The **Sephardi** Jews can be identified as developing in Spain. When Spain was conquered by Muslims in 714 CE they found Jews, and the two cultures mixed. Jews held high positions in languages, diplomacy and trade. Out of the Sephardi culture come the writings of **Maimonaides**, a scholar of the Talmud who set out the Jewish beliefs and also wrote the Mishneh Torah.

The **Ashkenazi** Jews lived in Northern Europe and suffered persecution for their refusal to be baptised. They were ordered to wear a hat or badge of identity by Pope Gregory X in 1240, and he also ordered all copies of the Talmud to be burned. This was terrible religious persecution as the Jews honoured the Talmud and treated all copies with deep respect as the Law.

The **Hasidic** Jews, a sub-group within the Ashkenazi Jews, emerged in Poland as Jews moved East, looking for security. In 1648 the Polish Jews were tortured and massacred by

CE refers to the Christian Era and is used by non-Christian people to refer to time after the birth of Christ where Christians use the phrase AD (Anno Domini – The Year of Our Lord).

Chapter 16 Practice and organisation in Judaism

the Ukrainian Chmielenicki. The Polish Jews had a great leader called Baal Shem Tov (Besht) who propounded the idea that prayer could be active and enjoyable.

16.3 Worship

'Magnified and sanctified be His great name in the world which he hath created according to his will. May He establish His Kingdom during your life....' (The beginning of the Kaddish – prayer of Sanctification – spoken as the Torah is returned to the Ark)

To pray is to be in interaction with God; prayer is regarded as essential if the relationship between man and God is to grow. For Jews it is essential to feel at one with God; therefore acts of prayer are vital, preferably daily. Jews regard prayer as particularly effective when form (kavah) and feeling (kavanah) are in harmony, for this means the intention of the prayer fits in with the words.

For Jews who are able there is a pattern of daily worship with prayer three times a day: evening (ma'ariv); morning (sharit); afternoon (minha).

Each service has a form which includes the standing prayer (**Amidah**) followed by the **Aleinu** (it is our duty to praise God) and finally the **kaddish** (from the word holy).

Essential to worship is the observance of the Sabbath. This is central to all Jewish traditions. It begins on Friday evening at sundown when the mother lights the candles and says, 'You are Our light, O Lord and our Salvation. In your name we kindle these Sabbath lights. May they bring into our household the beauty of truth and the radiance of love's understanding.' The father blesses bread (**challah**), which represents manna, and recites the **Kiddush** (blessing) over a cup of wine as well as verses about creation and the Sabbath. It is then part of Jewish life that no work is done (according to individual tradition) until sundown on Saturday when Sabbath is officially ended with a service called Havdalah.

The **Shema**: 'Hear, O Israel: the Lord is Our God, one Lord; and you must love the Lord your God with all your heart and soul and strength ...' (Deut. 6:4–6)

'You shall take these words of mine to heart and keep them in mind; you shall bind them as a sign on the hand and wear them as a phylactery on the forehead.' (Deut. 11:18)

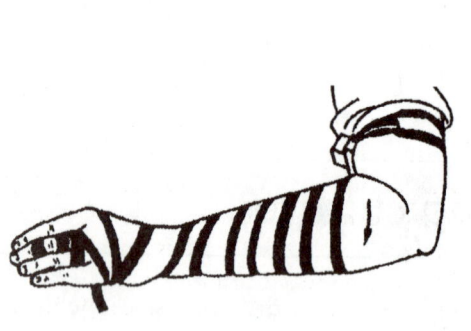

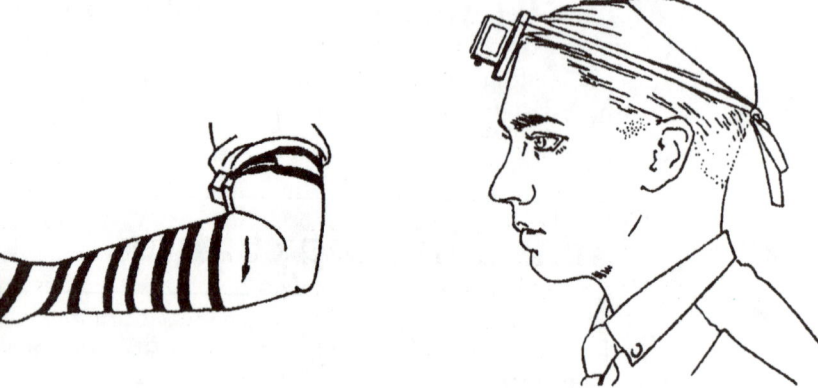

For Orthodox and Reform Jews there is a service on Saturday; for liberal Jews there is one on Friday. Orthodox and Reform Jews practise certain rituals when praying at the synagogue as well as in daily prayer. A man will put on a small round cap called a cappel or yarmulke and strap on phylacteries which contain Scripture verses (Exod. 13:1–10; 11–16; Deut. 6:4–9; 11:13–21), one on his forehead to remind him to think of his faith and another on his arm to remind him to act on his faith. These phylacteries are called **tefillin**. While praying, a Jew also wears a prayer shawl called a **tallit** made of silk or wool. This is usually blue and white and has tassels all around.

Phylacteries are strapped to the forehead and arm

'This is the Law of Moses set before the children of Israel...It is the tree of life for them that grasp it ...' (Spoken as the Torah is taken from the Ark)

The heart of the Jewish services is when the Sefer Torah is taken from the ark where it is kept. This happens on Monday, Thursday and Saturday mornings and during many festivals. It is carried around the congregation cradled in one arm and supported by the other. There is a ritual of unrolling the Torah and then it is lifted up as words of praise are said together with the affirmation of the belief that the Torah is the way of God, as revealed to Moses.

A Jew might use the **Siddur** to pray. This is an official prayer book which contains the main 'set' prayers and which develops as new prayers are added.

An important part of Jewish witness is the **Mezuzah**. This is a small decorated container which is fixed to the door post and contains the verses of the **Shema**. It is a reminder that therein Jewish values can be shared and occupants will touch it on their way in and out to remind themselves of this.

16.4 Festivals

Jewish festivals occur at different times each year because the Jewish calendar is a lunar calendar. There is a cycle of twelve months of 354 days in contrast to the Roman calendar which was adapted by the Christian world with 365 days. In the Jewish calendar the year begins with the seventh month (Tishri) and the new year is always celebrated by Jews all over the world. The calendar (called luach) then dictates the timing of all the following festivals which must follow each other as they are decreed in the Old Testament.

Jews have many feasts and festivals to unite them, to share and enjoy together. These occasions unite Jews with all generations past and present and with Jews everywhere. They focus on Jewish faith and on family and community life.

Pesach

Pesach is the feast of the Passover or 'unleavened bread'. It is held in order to remember the time when the Israelites were led out of Egypt by Moses. On this night they ate a special meal of roasted lamb. They had to smear blood from the lamb on the lintel of the door so the Angel would pass over that house and spare the first born. The lamb was accompanied by special herbs and unleavened bread because there was no time to allow the bread to rise. Thus at Pesach Orthodox Jews have no food containing leaven for a week. They also keep special utensils which never have contact with leaven. The special, symbolic meal is called the Seder and consists of:

- Three matzoth (unleavened bread) – bread of affliction;
- Roast lamb;
- Roasted egg as a symbol of new life;
- Horseradish to represent bitter slavery in Egypt;
- Parsley which was used to mark the doors;
- A bowl of salt water for the slaves' tears.
- Haroseth, a special paste of apples, nuts and cinnamon to remember the mortar of slavery and the sweetness of freedom.
- A wine glass for everyone;
- One extra glass of wine for Elijah, who will come before the Messiah.

Eating the meal is very ritualised. The father recites the Kiddush and everyone takes parsley dipped in salt water. He breaks the matzah and hides a half. The book of Haggadah (Passover story) is read and the youngest child asks questions about what is happening, the answers to which are contained in the reading. The first part is a reminder of the bitter times. Wine is drunk and spilt to remember those who still suffer. When the meal is over the hidden **matzah** is searched for and the door is opened to let in Elijah. Traditionally Jews make a toast to holding Pesach 'next year in Jerusalem!'

Shavuoth

Shavuoth takes place seven weeks after Pesach to remember the ten commandments. It is one of the Pilgrim festivals and also known as the feast of weeks. (Pesach, Shavuoth and Sukkot are the three 'Pilgrim' festivals. In the days of the Old Testament, Jews made pilgrimages to the temple to offer sacrifices on the occasion of these festivals.) The temple is decorated with flowers as this is a harvest festival. Readings of the giving of the ten commandments are read and also readings from the Book of Ruth connected with the harvest. In the prayer book this festival is called 'The Season of the giving of our Torah.' In some traditions those who have made good progress in education are honoured by being allowed to join in the procession of the Torah Scroll.

Rosh hashanah

This is the Jewish new year, occurring in September or October. It marks the birthdays of

A mezuzah

Speak to the Israelites in these words: in the seventh month you shall keep the first day as a sacred rest; a day of remembrance and acclamation, a day of sacred assembly. (Lev. 23:23–24)

Chapter 16 Practice and organisation in Judaism

Rosh Hashanah readings
The birth of Isaac (Gen. 21–22)

The birth of Samuel (1 Sam. 1–2)

The Lord's love for Israel (Jeremiah 31:2–20)

Yom Kippur
The Lord gives instructions to Moses (Lev. 16). 'The tenth day of this seventh month is the day of Atonement. There shall be a sacred assembly; you shall mortify yourselves and make a food offering to the Lord ...' (Lev. 23:26–32)

Sukkot
'On the fifteenth day of the seventh month the Lord's pilgrim's feast of Tabernacles begins and it lasts for seven days ...' (Lev. 23:33–43)

Abraham, Isaac and Jacob, of creation and also the Day of Judgement. The day is heralded by the sound of the Ram's horn (**shofar**). It is a time for reflection and Jews may greet each other with the words, 'May you be inscribed in the book of life'. Special bread is baked in the shape of a ladder or crown as a reminder of God's Kingship; and apples dipped in honey and other sweet things are eaten in the hope of a sweet year to come. Following Rosh Hashanah are ten days of return – a time of penitence when Jews ask forgiveness.

Yom Kippur

Yom Kippur is the Day of Atonement and is on the tenth day after Rosh hashanah. It is the holiest of festivals and calls for an at-one-ness with God, so all except the sick and children under 13 fast. The ark is draped in white and the solemn prayer (**Kol Nidrei**) is sung in memory of persecuted Jews. There is a reading of the account of the ritual of the temple in Jerusalem. The rabbi wears white as a sign of purity and symbolic of a death shroud. At Yom Kippur families beg forgiveness of each other and the Book of Jonah is read which tells of God's forgiveness for those who repent. At the close of day the service is called Neilah and the shema is read and the **shofar** blown before the open Ark.

Sukkot

Sukkot is the Feast of Tabernacles which marks the time when Jews lived in rough dwellings (tabernacles) in the wilderness. It is held five days after Yom Kippur; and shelters are built in the garden and decorated with flowers and fruit and used for eating meals. The congregation process around the synagogue carrying a citrus fruit (known as the Etrog), palms, myrtle and willow branches (together called the lulav) to represent the heart, spine, eyes and lips respectively to remind worshippers that God must be honoured with all your being.

This festival lasts for seven days (Tishri) and is a rejoicing in the harvest.

At the end of the seven days, each of which is marked by a synagogue service, a willow branch is shaken until defoliated and prayers are said for rain.

Simchath Torah

Simchath Torah (rejoicing in the Torah) comes at the end of **Sukkot** and marks the end of the weekly Torah readings and the beginning of the new cycle of readings. The scrolls are carried seven times around the synagogue while the people rejoice with singing and dancing. The procession passes under a chuppah (a canopy used in marriage ceremonies). The last reader is called the bridegroom of the Torah and the first new reader the Bridegroom of the beginning. This ceremony symbolises the fact that the reading of the Torah is constant and unbroken.

In Jerusalem Jews gather at the Western Wall for this feast and carry small scrolls under hand-held canopies.

Chanukah

Chanukah
(Apocrypha: 1 Macc. 4:36–59)

Chanukah is the festival of lights which takes place in the dark months of November or December (25th Kislev). It lasts eight days and on each day a candle is lit in the eight-branch candlestick – the menorah. This is to remind all that Judas Maccabeus lit a lamp containing a day's oil and it shone for eight days during the time he led his men to cleanse the temple after it had been defiled with idols by Antiochus Epiphanes. At chanukah Jews exchange presents. This is a different and separate custom to the Christian tradition at Christmas.

Purim

Purim is held to remember the Persian Queen Esther who prevented the prime minister Haman from destroying the Jews in Persia. Purim means 'lots' and Hamam is supposed to have cast lots to decide the best day for killing the Jews. At Purim the Book of Esther is read in the synagogue and drums are banged when the name of Hamam is read. After Purim it is traditional to have fancy dress parties and Jews are expected to give to the poor.

Shabbat

Shabbat is the celebration of the Sabbath which is important every week (see Unit 16.3 Worship). Apart from the ritual worship that occurs each week Jews also observe the rule that no work should be done on the Sabbath. Basically this means no cooking, writing, making clothes, carrying in public or building. How these rules are applied depends upon the extent to which a person (or family) is Orthodox. Shabbat is special to all Jews: the house is prepared, meals are planned to avoid cooking on the Sabbath and many Jews will dress in their best clothes.

16.5 Rites of passage

Birth is a symbol for Jews that life is purposeful and continuous. A new baby is introduced to the community at the synagogue as soon as possible.

All baby boys are circumcised and this is called **brit milah**. It is a requirement of the law that a boy should be physically marked as a member of the community and the operation of removing the foreskin is carried out when the child is eight days old by a specially designated person **(mohel)**. Only men are present at this ritual.

The rite of passage which marks passage into adulthood in Judaism is called the **bar mitzvah** (boys) or **bat mitzvah/bat chayil** (girls). It takes place when the young person is thirteen years old. Some young people choose to follow a programme of instruction for two years with the rabbi. In Liberal communities the service is held for 15- or 16-year-old children. Thirteen is seen as too young.

At the actual ceremony the bar or bat mitzvah recites a prayer asking God's help for faith and mature understanding. He or she then reads from the Torah a specially prepared passage. The whole family will celebrate afterwards as this is a major milestone on the journey of life. (Girls only read from the Torah in the Reform or Liberal synagogue.)

It is regarded as desirable and a duty for a Jew to marry and have a family to continue the community (marriage is explained in Chapter 6, Unit 6.2).

Death is regarded as part of life in Judaism and is talked about freely and openly. The body is washed and wrapped in a white shroud and placed in a coffin. It is taken to the funeral hall (bet olam-house of eternity) which is sited in the Jewish cemetery. It is essential for Jews to be buried in a consecrated Jewish cemetery. When the mourners arrive the rabbi makes a small ritual cut in their clothing which they then tear. They recite a psalm and then the deceased is buried with the closest relatives throwing dirt onto the coffin. On returning to the hall they all say the **kaddish**. The family will then sit **shiva** (mourning) for seven days at home. They sit on low stools wearing slippers and their torn clothes, and receive guests who have come to sympathise. It is traditional to take food to those sitting shiva. During the following year the family is in mourning and on the first anniversary of the funeral they will erect a headstone over the grave and each year after remember to recite the kaddish and light a memorial candle.

16.6 Pilgrimage

The wailing wall in Jerusalem is the most popular destination for Jews wanting to make a pilgrimage. This is not a requirement as with some religions but Jews regard it as a place of special prayer as it is the remains of the temple built by Herod the Great on the site of Solomon's temple. Jews pray there, kiss the stones and push written prayers between the cracks in the wall.

Since the Second World War and the events of the Holocaust some Jews make a point of making a pilgrimage to Yad Vashem (i.e. *a place and a name*). This is a bare room lit by a candle with the names of the concentration camps on the floor. It is a memorial to those who were killed.

16.7 Kashrut (food laws)

The rules governing the correct preparation and consumption of food are found in Leviticus, Chapter 11. Mainly Jews are required to eat meat that has been killed by a **kosher** butcher, who is trained to drain all the blood from the dead animal. Certain foods are forbidden (treyfah), most noticeably pork or the meat from the hindquarters of any animal. It is also forbidden to eat meat and dairy products together or for some time after consuming either one or the other. Most Jewish kitchens should have separate utensils for preparation of milk and meat products. How rigidly these rules are applied depends on the degree of orthodoxy and while they might be strictly kept in the home, many Jews will conform to the food culture in which they live in public.

16.8 The synagogue

The **synagogue** is the nearest equivalent to the old temple and it is really a community (kehilla) of people. In Hebrew the synagogue is called three things:

- Bet t'filah (house of prayer);
- Bet hamidrash (house of study); many Jews spend more time in the synagogue studying and discussing than they do attending specific prayer services or praying;
- **Bet ha Knesset** (house of assembly). This refers to the synagogue as a casual meeting place for the community.

The synagogue is a simple building designed with the prayer services in mind. Sometimes there are special seats for the rabbis and the chosen leaders of the community. In Orthodox synagogues men and women sit separately but in the Reform and Liberal traditions they sit together and take equal parts in the service. In the Orthodox tradition it is necessary to have eight men present for a service to take place.

Because the Torah teaches about false images and because God cannot be pictured, there are no pictures or statues in a synagogue. The focal point is the Ark **(aron hakodesh)**, a cupboard in the wall which is ornate and houses the Torah scrolls. The doors of the cupboard may be decorated with images of a **menorah** or Star of David or perhaps replicas of the stone tablets. The presence of the Ark is indicated by a light (**ner tamid**), an eternal light which symbolises the infinite presence of God. It is these features that make the building a synagogue. There is a raised platform (**bimah**) in front of the Ark which is in the wall facing Jerusalem. From here the Torah is read.

The interior of a synagogue

Summary

1. There are three main Jewish traditions: Orthodox; Liberal and Reform.
2. Prayer is essential to forming a relationship with God.
3. The observance of the Sabbath is an essential part of Jewish practice and worship.
4. While praying, an Orthodox or Reform Jew will wear a yarmulke, **tallit** and phyllacteries.
5. The **Torah** is revered in Jewish worship and is the focus of the service.
6. The Torah scrolls are kept in the Ark which is indicated by a light called a **ner tamid**.
7. Jews have a **mezuzah** on the doorpost. It is a small container for the words of the Shema.
8. **Pesach** is an important festival commemorating the Exodus from Egypt when the Angel of the Lord passed over all the houses in Egypt and spared the first born in the houses of the Israelites.
9. Jews also hold festivals on:
   - **Shavuot** (pentecost) to remember the Ten Commandments.
   - **Rosh Hashanah** (New Year).
   - **Yom Kippur** (Day of Atonement).
   - **Sukkot** (Feast of Tabernacles) to remember the days in the wilderness
   - **Chanukah** (Feast of Lights) to remember the light that shone for eight days in the temple
   - **Purim** to remember the Jews' deliverance from Hamam, Prime minister of Persia, through the work of Queen Esther.
10. All Jewish baby boys are circumcised (**Brit Milah**) when 8 days old as a sign of their belonging.
11. Jewish boys and girls become adult members of the community through the ceremonies Bar/Bat Mitzvah.
12. It is a duty for Jews to marry and have children.
13. Sitting Shiva for seven days is traditional mourning for the dead after burial.
14. Jews make pilgrimages as they wish to the Wailing Wall in Jerusalem and sometimes to Yad Vashem, the memorial to those killed in the Holocaust.
15. Food Laws are given in Leviticus and are important to Jewish family life.
16. The Synagogue is an assembly house and general meeting place where the community can learn, talk and pray together.

Quick questions

1. What are the main differences between the three Jewish traditions?
2. Why is prayer important to a Jew?
3. What prayers are said by the mother and father on Friday evening **Shabbat**?
4. What do Orthodox and Reform Jews wear to pray?
5. Why is the **Torah** held in so much reverence?
6. How do Jews show their reverence for the **Torah** in the synagogue?
7. What is the purpose of the **Mezuzah**?
8. What do the Jews celebrate at **Pesach**?
9. What are the main rites of passage for Jews?
10. Make a list of the main Jewish festivals and summarise what each one is for.

Chapter 16 Practice and organisation in Judaism

11 Why do Jews visit the Wailing Wall?
12 What is Yad Vashem?
13 What does **Kosher** mean?
14 What foods are forbidden to Jews?
15 How do Jews keep meat and milk products separate in their diet?
16 Why are synagogues mainly very simple?
17 What function does the synagogue have in the community?

Chapter 17
Islamic beliefs

Islam means 'submission' and Muslim means 'a surrendered man'.
Muslims have a statement of seven basic beliefs called **Al-Imanul-Mufassal**:

- I believe in Allah;
- in his angels;
- in his books;
- in his messengers;
- in the last day;
- in the fact that everything good or bad is decided by Allah, the Almighty;
- and in life after death.

These beliefs are often thought of as having three separate parts.

17.1 Tawhid

Tawhid is the first part of Muslim belief; it is belief in the oneness of Allah. For Muslims there is only one God and He is creator of all and Lord of all. Allah is, was and always has been. He is infinite, He has no human dimension and cannot be imagined by man. He is at one with nature as creator.

The **Shahada** (Kalimah) (statement of belief) says 'There is no God but Allah.' Yet in the Qur'an Allah is named in 99 different ways. This is thought to be a measure of his greatness and the diversity of His nature. According to Islamic belief perfection is represented by 100, a perfect decimal number – and the one hundredth number is a secret of the universe and our not knowing it symbolises our imperfection.

Muslims believe in predestination – this is known as Al-Qadr – and will say 'inshe Allah' (If God is willing) to indicate they have free will but cannot do anything they want. God is in control. Muslims believe they are God's agents on earth (**khalifa**) and must try to do God's will although they will not be forced to.

'In the name of Allah, the Merciful, the Compassionate.
Praise be to Allah, the Lord of the worlds;
The Merciful One, the Compassionate
Master of the day of doom.
Thee alone we serve, to Thee alone we cry for help!
Guide us in the straight path,
The path of them that Thou hast blessed,
Not of those with whom thou art angry,
Nor those who go astray.'
(Surah 1)

17.2 Rusulullah

The second part of Islamic belief is called Rusulullah (prophethood) and refers to the part of the Shahada which says '... and Mohammed is the Prophet of God'. The prophet's role is to give guidance to the people. There are 124,000 prophets but only 25 are mentioned in the Qur'an and they are mainly common to the Muslim/Jewish and Christian traditions.

Chapter 17 Islamic beliefs

Mala'ikah

Belief in angels (Mala'ikah) is important in Islam. They were created from light (nur), not from clay like Adam or from fire like jinn (spirits). Angels exist to help humans exercise free will and they will never be judged. Only occasionally angels appear as humans, as did Jibreel (Gabriel) who appeared to a some companions of Mohammed to teach them about Islam. The angel Izrail is believed to be the angel of death who will trumpet the last day, the day of judgement.

Kutubullah

Belief in the books of Allah is called Kutubullah. The books which Muslims declare belief in are the **Tawrah** of Musa (Torah of Moses); **Zabur** (psalms); and **Injil** (Gospel). These books are regarded as having been mistaken and changed over the years and the Qur'an was revealed to Mohammed to make things right.

17.3 Akhirah

'When my day comes no one can help me, until my day comes no one can hurt me.' (Sayings of the Prophet)

'Such are they that shall be brought near to their Lord in the gardens of delight. They shall recline on jewelled couches face to face … As for those on the left hand, they shall dwell amidst scorching winds and boiling water.'(Surah 56:42)

The third part of Islamic belief is **Akhirah**, or life after death. Muslims believe there will be a final day of judgement called Yawmuddin; this will be held in the court of Allah. A Muslim must live his life according to God's will and he will be judged and rewarded for good deeds and punished for bad deeds. A Muslim's reward for a good life is to be with Allah in paradise. Punishment for a bad deed is to be cast into eternal suffering and endless fire.

Summary

1. Al-Imanul-Mufassal is the statement of seven basic Islamic beliefs.
2. The seven beliefs are regarded as having three parts.
3. The first part of Islamic belief is **Tawhid** – the oneness of Allah.
4. **Rusulullah** is the second part of Islamic belief. It is belief in Mohammed as the Prophet of God.
5. Akirah is the third part of belief. It is belief in life after death.
6. Muslims also believe in angels, such as the angel Jibreel who revealed the **Qur'an**.
7. Kutubullah is belief in the books of Allah.
8. Muslims believe mankind has free will to choose to follow God's will.
9. Muslims believe that on the last day everyone will be judged according to how he or she has lived life.
10. Judgement day is called Yawmuddin.

Quick questions

1. What is the seven-part statement of Islamic belief called?
2. What are the seven basic Islamic beliefs?
3. The seven basic beliefs are thought of as being in three parts. What are these parts?
4. What do Muslims believe about life after death?
5. Which books do Muslims believe in?

Chapter 18
Sources of authority in Islam

18.1 The Qur'an

The **Qur'an** (Koran) is the foundation of Islam. It is a book which was revealed to the Prophet Mohammed by Allah through the Angel Gabriel (Jibreel) over a period of 30 years from AD 610. The words of the Qur'an are absolutely sacred to Muslims as the Word of God which they say He has carved on a tablet next to Him in heaven.

> 'He has revealed to you (Mohammed) the Book with the truth, confirming the Scriptures which preceded it. (e.g the Torah and the Gospel) ... Those that deny Allah's revelations shall be sternly punished. Allah is mighty and capable of revenge. Nothing on earth or heaven is hidden from Him ... It is He who has revealed to you the Qur'an.' (Surah 3:3–6)

Surah

The Qur'an has 114 **surah** (chapters); each surah is shorter than the one before, the first having 286 verses and the last only six verses. The shortest chapters describe the earliest events so the Qur'an is in reverse order as later events and advice occur in the longer chapters.

Mohammed could not write; he is said to have memorised the words and dictated them to scribes. After his death Abu Bakr ordered Said to write it all down. It is written in Arabic rhyming prose. Arabic is always used in the mosque although people use translations in private. As it is regarded as the Word of God no criticism is allowed. All chapters except one begin, 'In the name of God, the Compassionate, the Merciful'.

The Qur'an shows that Islam arose from the same basis as Judaism and Christianity as it acknowledges Abraham and Moses – and Jesus, the Prophet who gave the golden rule to 'love your neighbour as yourself.' In Surah 3:3–7 the Qur'an shows how the Old Testament and Torah were given for the guidance of men and to Mohammed has been revealed the book with the truth.

The message of the Qur'an is the greatness of Allah and His nature which is beyond human comprehension – almighty, creator, judge, compassionate one. Man is Allah's creation and man's soul lives forever to be judged on judgement day. The Qur'an gives advice on living, on worship, marriage, divorce, the role of women, fasting, almsgiving and pilgrimage. It is used in prayer and as a basis for Friday sermons. Many Muslims learn the Qur'an by heart and receive the title **Hafiz**.

The Hadith

Hadith means 'saying', and the sayings record the **Sunnah** which are the rules for life and are based on a saying, action, practice or tacit approval of another's action by Mohammed.

Sunnah can be classified as **Sahih** (sound), Hasan (good), Da'if (weak) or Saqim (infirm) depending on how likely they seem after they have been checked by scholars.

There are several Hadith collections and they elaborate on the simple rules given in the Qur'an on all aspects of life. One of the largest collections is that of Bukhari which fills 97 books. The Hadith are open to criticism as they are not the Word of God. **Sunni** Muslims have six collections of the Hadith and **Shi'ah** Muslims only five.

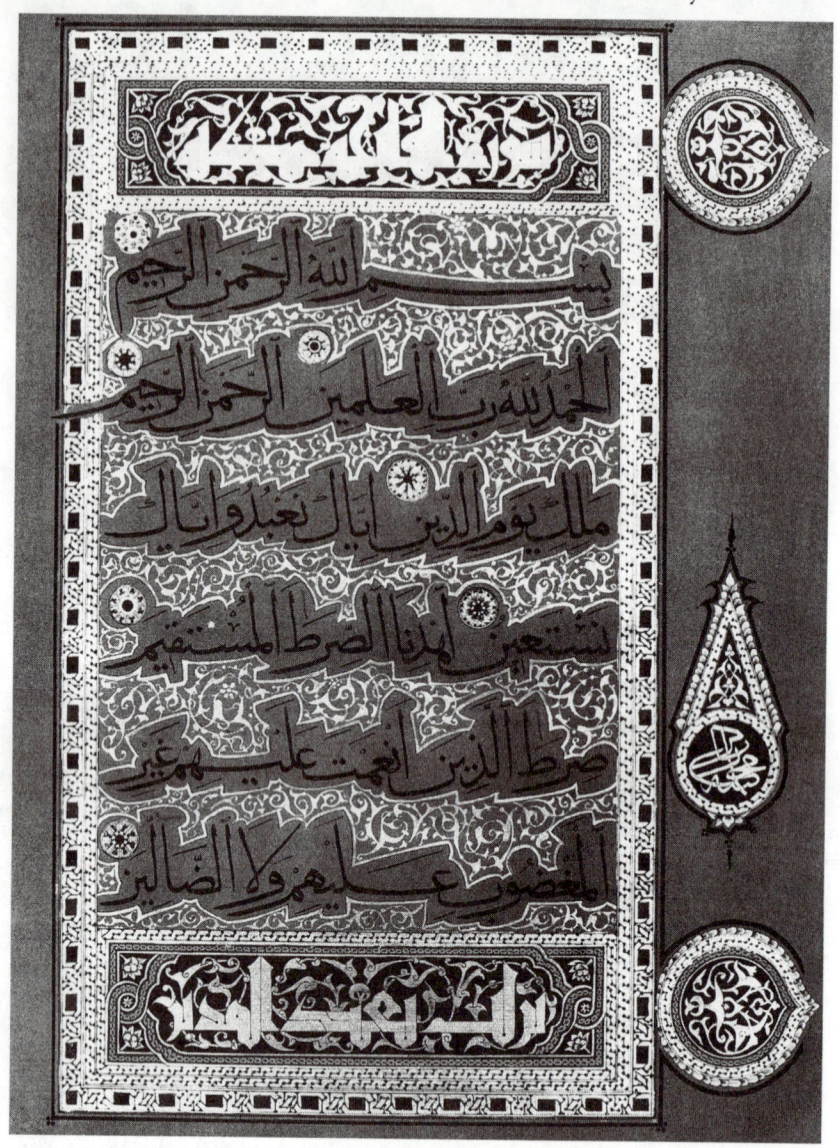

The opening page of the Qur'an

18.2 The Prophet Mohammed

Mohammed was born in Mecca on August 20th AD 570. He was an orphan by the age of six. At the age of 25 he married his widowed employer Khadija, who was 40. He was renowned as being honest and trustworthy; he was disturbed by the immorality he saw around him. He used to keep vigil all night in caves or the wilderness and on one such night the angel Gabriel came to him and told him to recite in the name of the Lord and when he woke he saw Gabriel on the horizon who told him he was an apostle of God. His wife believed he was a prophet. This revelation is called **Laylat-ul-Qadr** and is remembered during **Ramadan**.

Mohammed continued to receive revelations in his own language for the next 10 years and on the basis of them he preached in Mecca. He told people to turn away from idolatry and warned people they would suffer for their actions on the day of judgement. His revelation that all were equal in the eyes of God was very ill-received and his followers were pelted with stones.

The Makkan period
In AD 622 Mohammed had a few loyal followers and was asked to go to Medina to help the faithful. His departure from Mecca (Makka) is called Hegira. The Muslim calendar dates from that time; AH 1 means Anno Hegira 1.

The Madinan period
In Medina Mohammed came to be respected as he preached against alcoholism, idolatry and immorality. He was given many positions: teacher, judge and community leader. He issued a charter granting religious freedom to Jews and Christians.

Mohammed was married several times in his life but never had more than four wives at once. When he married the wife of his friend, who was divorced, he showed that divorced women are not disgraced and thus gave women greater status in society.

Conquest of Mecca

Mohammed believed he had to establish a new state to bring about Allah's rule on earth and he waged war against Mecca, finally capturing it in AD 630. He destroyed any idols and circled the **Ka'ba**, which he then rededicated to Allah. This was a holy war, a **Jihad**.

Mohammed died two years after conquering Mecca, in AH 10. He spent his last years persuading people to convert to Islam and the religion spread rapidly throughout the region.

Mecca

Summary

1. The **Qur'an** was revealed to Mohammed during the years AD 610 to 640
2. The **Qur'an** was revealed by the angel Jibreel, who ordered Mohammed to recite verses when he was alone.
3. The verses of the **Qur'an** were compiled by Said on the instruction of Abu Bakr after Mohammed's death.

Chapter 18 Sources of authority in Islam

4 The basic message of the **Qur'an** is the greatness of Allah, so far beyond human understanding.
5 The **Qur'an** is regarded as the Word of God and is not to be criticised.
6 The **Sunnah** is the way of the Prophet.
7 The **Hadith** are a series of sayings from the mouth or actions of Mohammed.
8 **Sunni** Muslims recognise six collections of Hadith whereas **Shi'ah** Muslims recognise five.
9 The Hadith can be questioned because they are not regarded as the Word of God.
10 Mohammed was highly regarded as upright and trustworthy.
11 The Hegira was Mohammed's journey to Medina from Mecca.
12 Mohammed attacked Mecca to establish an Islamic state.
13 When Mohammed conquered Mecca he destroyed the idols and circled the **Ka'bah**.
14 Mohammed spent his last two years in Mecca teaching people to change and turn away from immorality.

Quick questions

1 When was the **Qur'an** revealed?
2 How was the **Qur'an** revealed?
3 When were all the verses of the **Qur'an** compiled, and by whom?
4 What is the basic message of the **Qu'ran**?
5 Why is the **Qur'an** regarded as infallible?
6 What is the **Sunnah**?
7 What is the **Hadith**?
8 How many **Hadith** do Muslims recognise?
9 Why was the **Qur'an** revealed to Mohammed in particular?
10 What is the significance of Hegira?
11 What did Mohammed do in Medina?
12 Why did Mohammed feel the need to conquer Mecca?
13 When did Mohammed conquer Mecca?
14 What was Mohammed's first act after conquering Mecca?
15 How did Mohammed utilise the final two years of his life in Mecca?

Chapter 19
Islamic practices

19.1 The five pillars

Islam is a faith which emphasises clearly the duties of followers. Every Muslim must adhere to the five pillars: **Shahada**; **Salah**; **Zakat**; **Sawm** and **Hajj**.

Shahada
Shahada or (Kalimah) is the declaration of truth. Every Muslim declares there is no God but Allah, and Mohammed is His prophet.

Salah
Salah refers to regular worship. Each Muslim must pray **rak'ahs** (prayer sequences) five times a day.

- two rakats at daybreak (**fajr**)
- four rakats at midday (**zuhr**)
- four rakats in the afternoon (**asr**)
- three rakats in the evening (**maghrib**)
- four rakats at night (**isha**).

'... so the first thing you will call on them to do is to profess the Oneness of God ... When they have learned that, inform them that God has prescribed ... five ritual prayers a day.' (Hadith)

The method of prayer is very formally ritualised. The purpose is to bring Muslims closer to Allah and make each person aware of the mercy, power and glory of the Almighty.

Muslims are called to prayer by the muezzin calling from the top of the Mosque 'God is the greatest. I bear witness that there is no God but Allah; come to prayer, come to security. God is the greatest.'

Before praying the Muslim must perform **wudu**, a ritual washing which purifies. First the hands are washed, then the mouth and nose, followed by the whole face. Next the right hand and forearm are washed, then the left hand and the head are wiped. Finally the ears and feet are washed and this is all repeated three times.

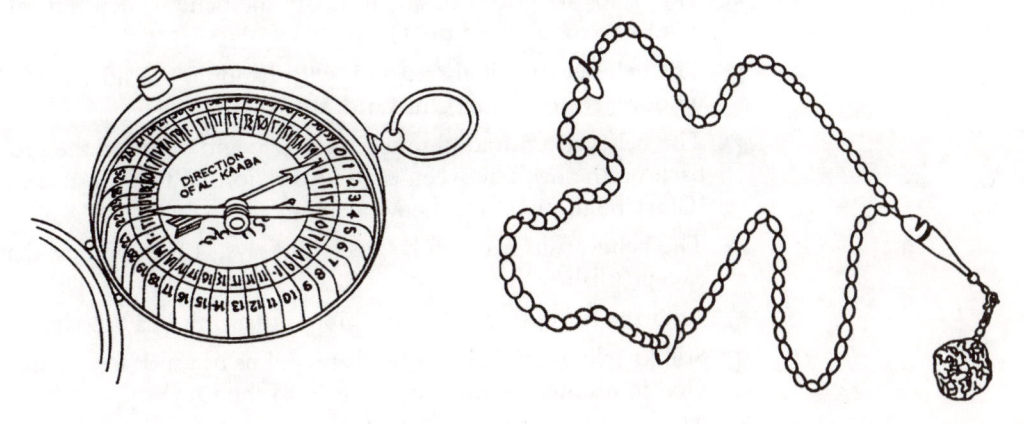

A compass (so that Muslims can always face Mecca for prayer)

Prayer beads

Chapter 19 Islamic practices

The Muslim then faces Mecca. He finds the correct direction by looking for the niche (**mihrab**) on the direction wall (**qiblah**) of the mosque. Alternatively special compasses are available to point the way. The prayer routine follows a distinct ritual. A Muslim prays with his heart and mind and body and all follow the same way all over the world as a reminder that there is a world community of Muslims.

A prayer mat

1. The prayer mat is laid out.
2. The hands are raised to the face as the words '**Allahu Akbar**' (God is Great), are intoned. This is a statement of intent (**niyyah**).
3. The right hand is placed over the left hand at waist level and part of the Qur'an is recited, the **Fatihah**, 'You alone we worship, you alone we ask for help …' (Surah 1)
4. The hands are raised to the face again and 'Allahu Akbar' is intoned.
5. The hands are placed on the hips and the believer bends from the waist, saying, 'Glory be to my Lord the Great'.
6. The believer straightens up and, with hands at the side, says, 'Allah listens to whoever thanks Him. Our Lord, thanks be to thee.'
7. The believer prostrates himself with face and palms to the ground twice and sits back on the heels between each prostration. When prostrate, he says (three times): 'Glory be to my Lord, the Most High'.
8. The believer sits back on his heels and says, 'I bear witness that there is no God except Allah.'
9. After the final prayers the worshipper turns his head to right and left.
10. Still kneeling, the believer holds his palms upwards level with his chin and petitions God in his own words and words from the Qur'an.
11. The sequence ends when the believer wipes his hands over his face to show himself to be in receipt of God's blessing.

This ritual, which is performed anywhere in a clean space after removing the shoes, takes only about one minute to perform.

An individual Muslim can also pray where, when and how he wants to and this is called **du'a**.

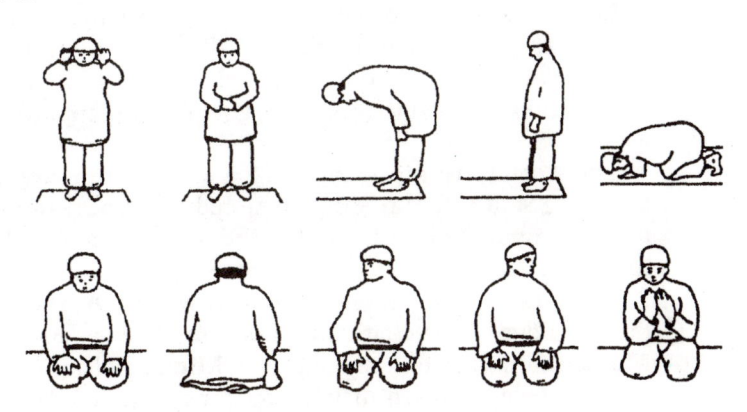

The positions adopted by Muslims when they carry out Salah (prayer).

Prayer beads

Some Muslims use beads as an aid to prayer. These are loosely strung beads in collections of 33 or 99. The beads can be called misbaha, tasbih or soubha and are moved along as the Muslim holds one at a time and recites the names of Allah, calling his strength into his life. The beads are used to praise Allah by saying 33 times each:

Subhan Allah (Glory to God)

Alhamdu Lilah (all praises be to God)

Allah Akbar (God is great)

Zakat

Zakat is the third pillar of Islam; it means purification. Muslims gain purification from giving charitably. Zakat is calculated at 2½% (one fortieth) of income after deductions have been made for clothes, travel, debts, household goods and rent from houses let. Muslims can give **Zakat** to the poor, to relatives or through an Islamic charity but each Muslim is honour bound to account for his actions on the day of judgement.

'Sadaqa (alms) shall be used only for the advancement of Allah's cause, for the ransom of captives, debtors and for distribution among the poor, destitute, the wayfarer, those that are employed in collecting alms and those that are converted to the faith.' (Surah 9:60)

Sawm

Sawm, the fourth pillar of Islam, is fasting. Fasting is observed during **Ramadan**, which falls in the ninth month of the Islamic calendar (twelve lunar months). All adult Muslims (i.e. over the age of 12) except pregnant women must fast for the entire month from sunrise to sunset. It is a discipline, not a starvation, since the believer rises early to eat a large breakfast and can have a substantial meal after sunset. No food at all is allowed in daylight hours, nor inhaled tobacco smoke nor toothpaste.

Ramadam marks the revelation of the **Qur'an** to Mohammed; Muslims are expected to behave well and not to speak vulgarly at this time of renewal.

Hajj

Hajj means pilgrimage. Every Muslim who can afford to do so is obliged to make a once-in-a-lifetime pilgrimage to Mecca in the twelfth month of the year. The purpose of the pilgrimage is to remind every Muslim that everyone will be equal at the day of judgement so pride and prejudice are earthly and futile feelings. This is re-enforced by the ritual of wearing special clothing so that all are alike. The special clothes are to indicate a consecrated state (**ihram**) of self-sacrifice and submission to Allah.

When within 16 miles of Mecca men shave their heads and put on two sheet-like white garments, one around the waist and the other over the left shoulder. Women also wear an all-covering white garment and may only journey on a pilgrimage if accompanied by a male relative.

'Make the pilgrimage and visit the Sacred House for His sake ... Make the pilgrimage in the appointed months.' (Surah 2:196)

Pilgrims call out 'Labbayk' (I am here (God) at your service) as they approach Mecca; then they camp in an enormous pilgrim camp. On arrival at Mecca a pilgrim does **tawaf** which means walking around the **Ka'bah** three times quickly and four times slowly in a clockwise direction.

The Ka'bah is a cube about 15 metres long and 10 metres wide and 14 metres high. It is also known as the Bait-ul-lah (The House of God). The Ka'bah is said to be the first man-made structure dedicated to one God and is covered with black cloth embroidered with the Qur'an.

In the south east corner is a black stone which is believed to have been given to Abraham's son, Ishmael, by the Angel Gabriel (Jibreel) when it was white. It is said it turned black because of the sins of believers. The cloth is renewed each year and the old one cut up and given to honoured guests. Only important visitors are allowed inside the Ka'bah once a year.

The second part of the pilgrim's ritual is to run seven times the 366 metres between two hills, **Safa** and **Marwah**. These hills are where Ishmael's mother, Hagar, is believed to have searched for water and found, on returning to her son, that he had discovered the Well of Zamzam by digging his toes in the sand.

The pilgrim then travels 21 km to Mount **Arafat** (The Mount of Mercy) where there is a duty to meditate from noon until sunset and the night is spent in the open at **Muzdalifah**. Pilgrims then return to **Mina**, a village to the east of Mecca, collecting en route 49 pebbles which they use to stone the devil (Jamrat) who is represented by three stone pillars at the place where Ishmael is reputed to have been tempted to defy his father and to have thrown stones himself.

The pilgrimage ritual is followed by celebration of the festival of Eid-ul-Adha (Great festival of Sacrifice) which lasts four days.

The last part of the Hajj is to walk around the Ka'bah seven times.

Some pilgrims dye their beards red as a sign they have made the Hajj and are called Hajjis. If a Muslim cannot afford to go he can contribute towards one of his community making the Hajj and receive merit for helping to make another's Hajj possible.

19.2 Festivals

Eid-ul-Fitr
Eid means festivity or happiness, and for Muslims festival days are important times for prayer and gathering together. Eid-ul-Fitr is the festival of fast-breaking and comes at the end of Ramadan on the first day of the tenth month.

Eid-ul-Adha
Eid-ul-Adha is the festival to celebrate the end of the Hajj and begins on the tenth day of the twelfth month. It is celebrated by all Muslims because those who cannot themselves make the Hajj become part of it by sending a representative.

Eid days
On Eid days Muslims celebrate the victory of the spiritual person over the physical one, as shown through fasting or pilgrimage. Eid days are days of recollection and prayer for the ill and the dead. Money is collected to distribute to the poor and Muslims participate in reconciliation by forgiving each other and gathering in prayer to ask the forgiveness of Allah.

Eid festivals are usually held in an open space and Muslims are expected to attend well-dressed and open-minded. The following things take place:

- They say **Takbir**, a selection of praises to Allah.

- There are two parts to prayer and the **imam** says the Fatihah plus another Qur'anic verse whilst making the upper body prayer movements.

- The imam gives a two-part sermon and intones Allahu Akbar.

- The imam tells believers to lead better lives

- Muslims are reminded that they should share a meal with the poor.

- On Eid-ul-Fitr the imam reminds Muslims they must give the value of a full meal to charity; this is sadaqat-ul-fitr, and the money is usually given before the feast so that all can eat well on the feast day.

19.3 Rites of passage

A child cannot be a Muslim until he is old enough to choose to be at about the age of ten but parents are expected to bring up their children in knowledge of the faith; and the call to prayer (**Adhan**) is whispered to the baby so that he or she hears the words *God is great* at the beginning of life.

Aqiqa

Aqiqa is a ritual tradition which, the Prophet Mohammed said, saved babies from trouble in later life. On the seventh day the head is shaved and the weight of hair matched in gold or silver and given to charity. Then goats or sheep are sacrificed (two for a boy and one for a girl). The meet is then sweetened and divided – one-third to relatives and two-thirds to the poor. The child is given one of Mohammed's names or one of his family names or one of Allah's 99 names, with the word **Abd** (servant) added.

Sometimes parents ask the imam to choose a name for the baby, as Abu Musa asked Mohammed for a name for his son.

Boys are circumcised because the **sunnah** says it is a practice of all prophets; this can happen at aqiqa but it can also be done at any time up to the age of ten.

Aqd Nikah

Marriage (Aqd Nikah) is the estate in which sexual relations are permissible; it is a public commitment between two people who must be willing to marry. The woman's willingness must be stated by her father. In Muslim countries marriage can take place anywhere but in Britain they usually take place in a mosque and the woman must be free to marry and under no duress. Otherwise in British law the marriage is not valid.

The marriage ceremony includes readings from the Qur'an, and there is a written and spoken contract. Three copies of this are made, one each for the couple and one for the officials. According to the Qur'an, the husband must give his wife money or property (mahr) which she may keep.

Death

When near to death, a Muslim and his or her family pray for forgiveness. The Shahadah is said and the Qur'an is read, especially Surahs 36 and 55. On hearing of death Muslims say, 'To Allah we belong and to Allah we return.'

The burial rite is a serious ritual.

1. The body is washed as before prayer and the mouth and nostrils perfumed.
2. The body is wrapped in a new white shirt without seams which is secured in three places with ties.
3. As soon as possible the coffin is carried to the mosque or cemetery as prayers are said, including the Fatihah.
4. The coffin is placed in front of the imam who is facing the **qibla**.
5. The coffin is lowered into the ground; the corpse has been placed on its side facing Mecca. The mourners recite, 'From the earth we did create you and into it we shall return you and from it shall we bring you out once again' (Surah 20:25)
6. The ground is left raised but without monuments.
7. Mourning lasts between seven days and three months, depending on local custom.

Graves are visited as they remind Muslims of their ultimate destiny. The Prophet Mohammed said that all a person can leave is charity given, knowledge passed on and pious children to pray for them.

Chapter 19 Islamic practices

Summary

1. All Muslims must follow the five pillars of Islam.
2. The five pillars are:
   - **Shahada** – the declaration of truth
   - **Salah** – regular worship
   - **Zakat** – charitable giving
   - **Sawm** – fasting
   - **Hajj** – pilgrimage to Mecca.
3. All Muslims all over the world observe these five pillars, so all are united through practice in belief.
4. Eid-ul-Fitr is the Muslim festival celebrating the end of the fast.
5. Eid-ul-Adha is a festival to celebrate the end of the Hajj.
6. All Eid days are characterised by prayer, alms-giving, reconciliation and forgiveness.
7. Aqiqa is the first ritual observed for a baby and shows that the child is a member of the community.
8. Marriage (Aqd Nikah) is an agreement between a couple which can take place anywhere, though usually in a mosque in Britain.
9. At death Muslims return to Allah and a special funeral ritual is observed.

Quick questions

1. What is **Shahada**?
2. What are the **rak'ahs** of Salat?
3. What is the purpose of **Zakat**?
4. Why do Muslims observe **Ramadan** so strictly?
5. What must a Muslim do who cannot make the **Hajj**?
6. Why are the five pillars so important?
7. How are Eid days characterised?
8. What does Eid-ul-Fitr celebrate?
9. What does Eid-ul-Adha celebrate?
10. What happens at the Aqiqa ceremony?
11. How does a marriage take place in Islam?
12. What are the main rituals of an Islamic funeral?

Chapter 20
Organisation in Islam

20.1 The caliphs

Abu Bakr

The organisation of Islam followed the death of Mohammed. **Abu Bakr** was Mohammed's best friend and had accepted Islam quickly. He was repected in the community for his wisdom and compassion. He had freed slaves, including Bilal, who called people to prayer at the mosque and became the first Muezzin. He was also recognised as firm because the story is told that when his own son, who had fought against him in the battle of Badr, told him that he had twice had the chance to kill his own father, Abu Bakr is believed to have told his son that if the roles had been reversed he would have killed his son. This showed his commitment to **Jihad** for Islam. Abu Bakr was Mohammed's first successor but died after only two years as Caliph.

Umar

Abu Bakr nominated **Umar** as the next caliph. Umar had come to Islam in an unusual way. While journeying to attack Mohammed he had visited his sister Fatima and her husband Said, who were Muslims. When Umar came to the house he heard them reciting the **Qur'an** and wondered what it was; he attacked Said and when Fatima tried to protect her husband she was hurt. Seeing her blood spilt Umar calmed down and when they showed him the Qur'an he fell in love with it and became a Muslim. It was he who wanted the whole of the Qur'an to be in one volume.

Umar led the expansion of Islam into Persia, Damascus and Jerusalem. Jerusalem was beloved of Islam because Mohammed dreamt that Jibreel had taken him there and he had met all the prophets, past and future, and had seen hell and heaven and the glory of Allah working in the universe. After Umar's death a mosque was built in Jerusalem on the site of the Jewish temple and called the Dome of the Rock or The Mosque of Umar.

Uthman

Umar was succeeded as caliph by **Uthman** (the rich) who was one of a committee of six appointed by Umar to elect his successor. Uthman had been close to Abu Bakr and had married Mohammed's daughter Ruqaiyyah. He presided over the distribution of the Qur'an but could not keep the Muslim state together and was assassinated after six years.

Ali-al-Murtada

The fourth caliph was Ali-al Murtada. Since the age of ten, when already a Muslim, he had felt destined to lead but he was not able to heal the rifts amongst Muslims. He was married to Mohammed's daughter Fatima, and they had two sons, Hasan and Hussein. He too was assassinated and the **Ummah** was split.

Organisation after Ali

After Ali, Islam was organised in different ways. Some Muslims followed the relatives of the prophets, regarding them as rightful caliphs. They became the **Shi'ah** sect (20% of all Muslims) and are mainly found in Iraq, Iran and the Lebanon. The remainder recognised any good Muslim as a caliph and are called **Sunni** because they follow the **Sunnah** or Way of the Prophet.

20.2 The Shari'ah

The **Shari'ah** is the way that Muslim's must follow. It is the teachings of the Qur'an and the **Hadith**. Occasionally these sources do not answer all problems raised as new difficulties arise out of progress. At such times Muslims must consider alternative ways of arriving at decisions.

20.3 Alternative ways

Ijma
Ijma is one of the alternatives Muslims must consider. It is a system begun by the caliphs and is a consensus of opinion arrived at by scholars of the Qur'an and Hadith.

Qiyas
Muslims can also use a process called Qiyas, which enables different possibilities to be weighed against one another. Thus Muslims can examine teachings given at the time of the Prophet Mohammed and see how they might be applied in today's world. For example, forbidding drugs now would be regarded as a modern-day equivalent of Mohammed's decision to forbid alcohol. Alcohol is still forbidden in Islam and, as drugs are also considered intoxicating, they must be treated in the same way.

Summary

1. **Abu Bakr** was the first caliph of Islam; he was the Prophet's Mohammed's friend.
2. Abu Bakr was regarded as fair, compassionate and firm.
3. The first muezzin was Bilal.
4. The second caliph was **Umar** who had fallen in love with the **Qur'an** for its beauty.
5. **Umar** had been converted by his sister Fatima and her husband Said.
6. **Umar** presided over great expansion in Islam.
7. The third caliph, **Uthman**, was not able to hold Islam together and there were divisions.
8. Ali-al-Murtada, the fourth caliph, could not repair the divisions among Muslims.
9. All the caliphs were assassinated.
10. Muslims divided into **Shi'ah** and **Sunni** after the death of the last caliph.
11. **Shi'ah** and **Sunni** Muslims have different ideas about who should hold authority in Islam.
12. The **Shari'ah** is the way Muslims follow and includes the **Qur'an** and **Hadith**.
13. The **Ijma** is a consensus on a matter of Islam arrived at by scholars.
14. Qiyas is the process of weighing up different perspectives from the time of the Prophet Mohammed to the present.
15. Muslims can use **Ijma** or Qiyas to answer a problem if the answer cannot be found in the **Qur'an** or **Hadith**.

Quick questions

1 Why was **Abu Bakr** chosen as the first caliph?
2 How did **Umar** convert to Islam?
3 What happened to the state of Islam under the third and fourth Caliphs?
4 How did the Caliphs die?
5 What is the difference between **Shi'ah** and **Sunni** Muslims?
6 From which sources do Muslims derive the **Shari'ah**?
7 What is the **Ijma**?
8 What is **Qiyas**?
9 Why might a Muslim use Ijma or Qiyas?

Appendix: Picture stimulus

You will have some questions which are based on pictures or drawings of either religious objects (artefacts) or religious rituals. Look at these carefully and make sure that when you read about something you can imagine what it looks like. If you aren't able to do this, look in other books to find pictures, go to the library to look particular things up, or visit your chosen faith's place of worship and see the object (or witness the ritual) yourself.

Christian artefacts

1 Lectern. This is a stand from which the Word is read by either a member of the laity or the minister. It is often decorated thus with an eagle, which is symbolic of raising the Word up to God and God raising his followers 'on eagle's wings'.

2 The pulpit. This can be found in traditional churches. It has been removed in Roman Catholic churches. It is/was used for the minister to deliver the sermon as he could be seen and heard, but it also established his position above that of the congregation.

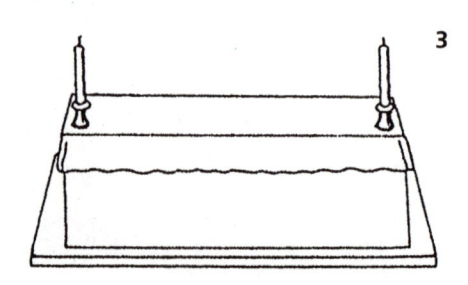

3 The altar table. Used in Christian churches to bless the bread and wine at the Communion service.

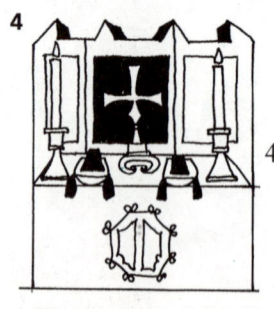

4 The high altar. This is also to be found in traditional churches and cathedrals. It is used in the Anglo-Catholic tradition to bless the bread and wine and to offer up special prayers.

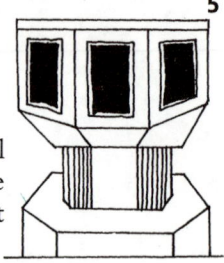

5 The baptismal font. This is found at the rear of traditional churches as a sign that new entrants to the Church are to be baptised. It is becoming more usual to baptise people at the front of the church, where they can be seen by the congregation.

Christian artefacts

6 The Paschal candle and the baptismal candle. The Paschal candle is blessed at the Easter vigil. It commemorates the idea of Christ as the beginning and the end (alpha and omega) and the Trinity. It is lit from a special fire, a fire of renewal representing the Spirit. It is carried into the church to proclaim Easter: 'The light of Christ has come into the world'. Baptismal candles are lit from this candle in the Roman Catholic tradition as each new member is called to share in the light of Christ.

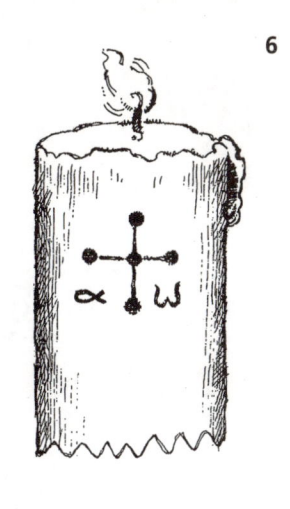

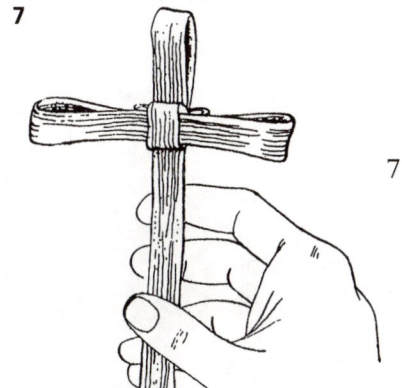

A baptism candle   A Paschal candle

7 The palm cross. On Palm Sunday Christians hold palms and sometimes form them into crosses as a symbol of Christ's entry into Jerusalem, which is greeted with joy.

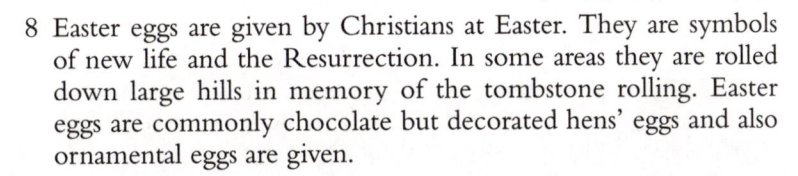

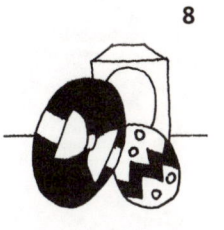

8 Easter eggs are given by Christians at Easter. They are symbols of new life and the Resurrection. In some areas they are rolled down large hills in memory of the tombstone rolling. Easter eggs are commonly chocolate but decorated hens' eggs and also ornamental eggs are given.

9 The bishop wears particularly recognisable items as signs of his authority. His cosier is a shepherd's crook, as he is shepherd to his flock in the diocese. His mitre, or pointed hat, represents the Spirit of fire.

10 Statues of the Virgin Mary (usually 'Our Lady') are to be found in Roman Catholic churches, often in a side (lady) chapel. Roman Catholics make *novenas* and say prayers which ask her to intercede on their behalf with her Son.

Appendix: Picture stimulus

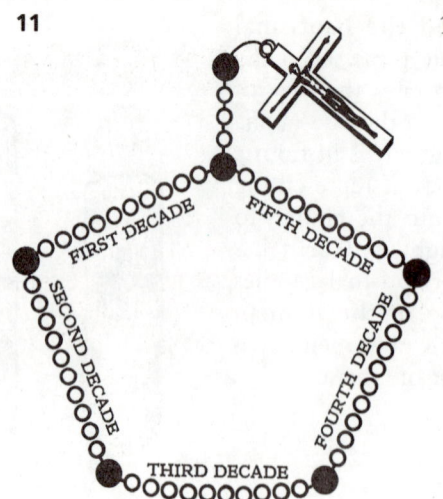

11 Rosary beads are used by Roman Catholics to meditate. A full Rosary consists of five groups of ten beads (decades) interspersed with single beads. They form a circle of prayer and are also in the form of a cross as a single strand of 1+3+1 beads leads down to a cross.
Catholics pray as they wish with these but there is an established mode of prayer.

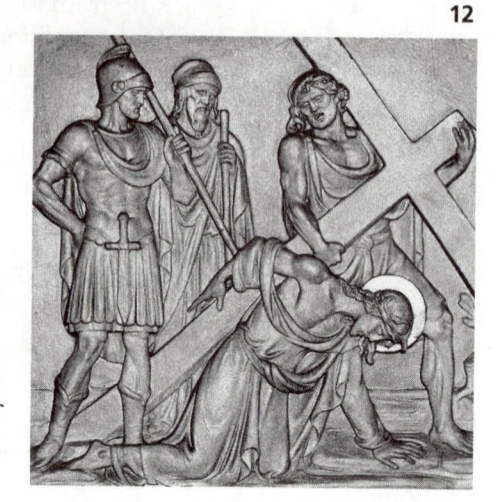

12 Around the Catholic church are 14 pictures, or carvings, showing Jesus' suffering and death. Roman Catholics use these for meditative prayer, walking around the church and praying while thinking of each stage of the passion, e.g. Jesus falling for the first time.

Jewish artefacts

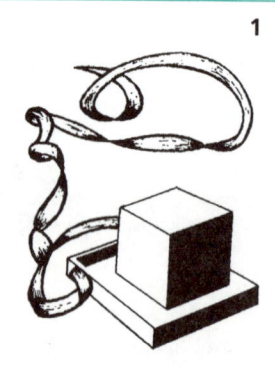

1 **Tefillin** or phylactery, which are little black leather cubes containing four pieces of paper with special verses: Exod. 13:1–10; 11–16; Deut. 6:4–9; 11:13–21. They remind Orthodox Jews to think of their faith (one is worn on the forehead) and to act on their beliefs (another is strapped to the non-dominant arm). These are worn by Orthodox Jews when saying daily prayers either at home or in the synagogue.

2 A **kippah** (cappel, yarmulke) (a small round cap) is worn by most Jewish males when the name of God is to be spoken, at meals, at prayer or when studying.

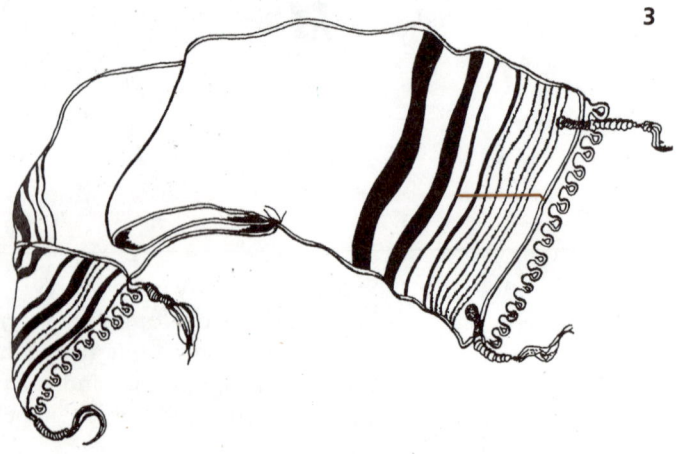

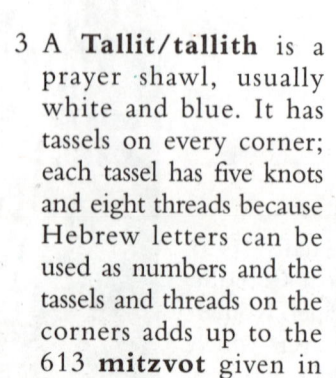

3 A **Tallit/tallith** is a prayer shawl, usually white and blue. It has tassels on every corner; each tassel has five knots and eight threads because Hebrew letters can be used as numbers and the tassels and threads on the corners adds up to the 613 **mitzvot** given in the Torah.

Jewish artefacts

4 A Chanukah candlestick. Used during the festival of Chanukah when the candles are lit for eight days.

5 A **menorah**. The seven-branched candlestick which is recognised as a symbol of Judaism.

6 **Sukkot.** A tabernacle or temporary shelter built in the garden of a Jewish home during the Sukkot festival as a reminder of the time when Jews only had tents in the wilderness.

7 A bunch of plants used during **sukkot**. They are held in the **sukkah** or synagogue. The bunch contains:
- lulav (date palm), symbolising the back – an upright life.
- Myrtle twigs (**haddassim**), symbolising the eyes – clear vision and hope.
- Willow branches (aravot), symbolising the mouth – affection and honesty.
- Citron (**etrog**), symbolising the heart – deep feelings and sincere relationships.

Appendix: Picture stimulus

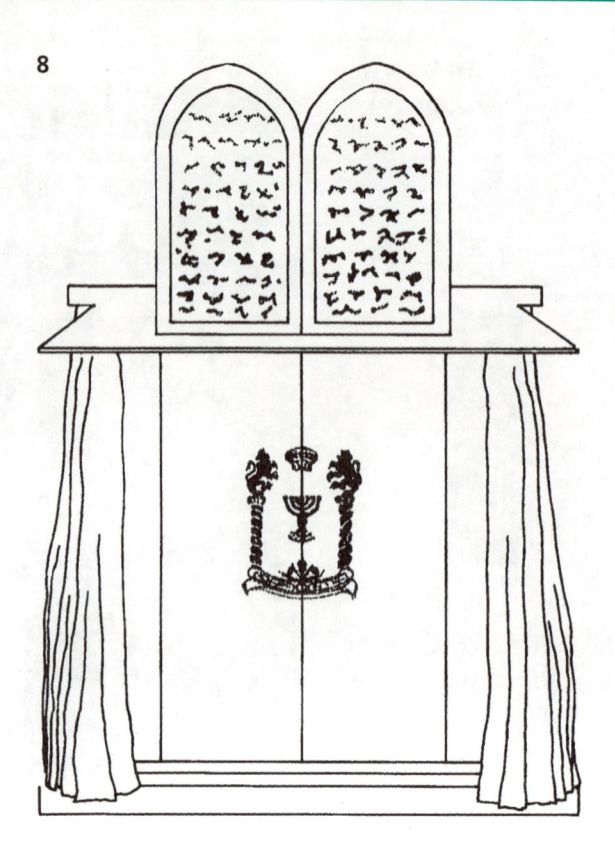

8 This is the Ark (**Aron Hakodesh**) in the synagogue which contains the **Torah** scrolls. It is the focal point and has above it the tablets on which are written the first two words of each of the Ten Commandments.

Islamic artefacts

1 The dome of a mosque. Traditional mosques have domes as symbols of the universe.

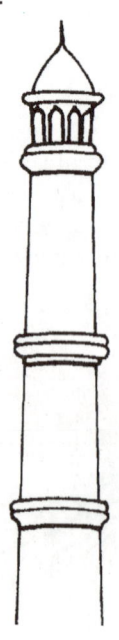

2. A minaret. Traditional mosques have a minaret at each corner of the square. They represent, together with the central dome of faith, the five pillars of Islam.

Islamic artefacts

3 The **qiblah** (direction) wall showing the direction of Mecca and shown by the **mihrab** (in this case an alcove) but this can be a decorated panel or plaque. It must be differentiated from the other walls.

4 The minbar is either a high table or (as here) a platform reached by a straight flight of steps with doors at the bottom. This is used by the **imam** so he can be seen and heard if he is giving notices. It does not elevate his position above others.

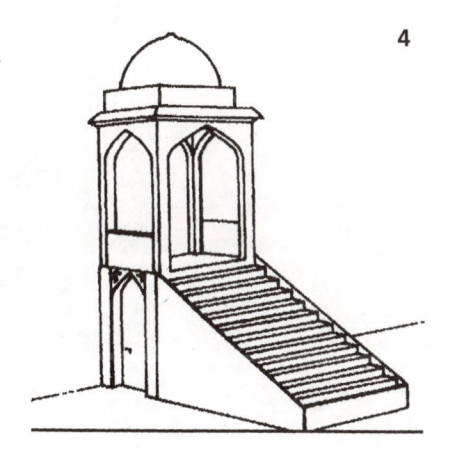

5 A panel of clocks showing the time in a variety of countries. Muslims are obliged to pray five times a day 'by the clock'.

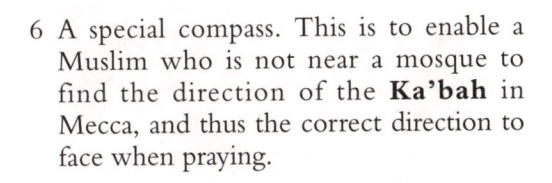

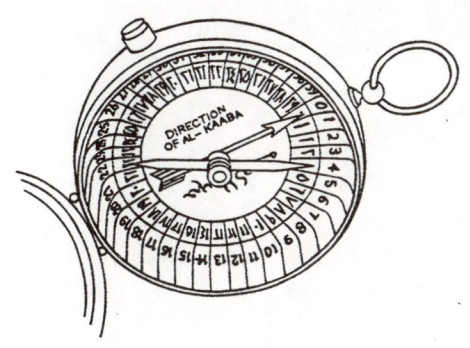

6 A special compass. This is to enable a Muslim who is not near a mosque to find the direction of the **Ka'bah** in Mecca, and thus the correct direction to face when praying.

141

Appendix: Picture stimulus

7 Prayer beads (subha) which a Muslim can use to recite the 99 beautiful names of Allah.

8 A prayer mat showing some Islamic art including a mosque and a minbar. All Muslims have these and use them in the home. There are many at the mosque. They are not strictly necessary but make it more ritualised and comfortable to perform the daily **rak'ahs**.

Questions and answers

Examination questions

Examination questions are designed to assess the extent to which you are able to demonstrate your mastery of the assessment objectives. Different boards use different structures of questions which are mainly a combination of short answers requiring perhaps one sentence and longer answers which demand a paragraph of extended prose.

It is vital that you look at how many marks are allocated to each question and write accordingly. If you write an essay when there are only two marks allocated to that question, you can only get two marks.

During the course you should become aware of the assessment objectives and be aware that you are addressing them in your answers.

The questions below are examples of the types of questions you can expect. Some of them are sample questions supplied by the boards and others are questions from past papers which are appropriate to the new syllabuses. Please note that there are many ways of answering the questions, especially the evaluation questions which are RS3 or E questions. The important thing is to support what you say with evidence or argument from an appropriate text or from practical experience.

Denominational perspectives
You may be answering questions on the Christianity papers from the perspective of a particular Christian denomination. It is sensible to indicate when you are referring to a particular denominational practice rather than what you believe to be general Christian teachings, ideas or principles.

1 Questions on Christianity

1 **Christian perspectives on personal, social and world issues.**
   Read the following passage and answer the question (a) to (d)
   In January 1991 Britain chose to be involved in a war in the Middle East (Kuwait). Some people supported this war because they thought that a moral principle was at stake. Others supported the war for the practical reason that Britain must defend its oil interests. Other people considered the war to be wrong because they believe that killing other people is never justified.
   (a) Give one Old Testament teaching which might affect the way in which Christians think about war and fighting. (2) R2
   (b) What did Jesus mean when he said, 'Put your sword back in its place, for all who draw the sword will die by the sword.' (6) R1
   (c) (i) What do you understand by the phrase 'non-violent protest'? (2) R2
       (ii) What might be an appropriate way for a Christian to respond to a situation such as the one given in the passage? (5) R2
   (d) There is no such thing as a just war. Do you agree?

   Give reasons to support your answer and show that you have thought about different points of view. (5) R3

   MEG

Examination questions

2 **Effects of Christianity on behaviour, attitudes and lifestyles. Prejudice and discrimination.**
   (a) Give one example of racial discrimination that can happen in the United Kingdom. (1) R1
   (b) A Christian might take part in a protest or demonstration against racial discrimination. Suggest two other things a Christian could do to discourage such discrimination in his/her own area. (2) R2
   (c) Some Christians take part in public demonstrations against racial discrimination. Do you think they are right to do so?
      Give a reason to support your view. (3) R3
   (d) Why are laws not able to stop racial prejudice? (2) R2

NEAB

3 The Christian life and the Gospels.

A3 GBN
27 Then Jesus and his disciples went away to the villages near Caesarea Philippi. On the way he asked them 'Tell me, who do people say I am?'
28 'Some say that you are John the Baptist,' they answered; 'others say that you are Elijah, while others say that you are one of the prophets.'
29 'What about you?' he asked them. 'Who do you say I am?'
Peter answered, 'You are the Messiah.'
30 Then Jesus ordered them, 'Do not tell anyone about me.'
31 Then Jesus began to teach his disciples: 'The Son of Man must suffer much and be rejected by the elders, the chief priests, and the teachers of the Law. He will be put to death, but three days later he will rise to life.' 32 He made this very clear to them. So Peter took him aside and began to rebuke him. 33 But Jesus turned round, looked at his disciples, and rebuked Peter. 'Get away from me, Satan,' he said. 'Your thoughts don't come from God but from man!'

NIV
27 Jesus and his disciples went on to the villages around Caesarea Philippi. On the way he asked them, 'Who do people say I am?'
28 They replied, 'Some say John the Baptist; others say Elijah; and still others, one of the prophets.'
29 'But what about you?' he asked. 'Who do you say I am?'
Peter answered, 'You are the Christ.'
30 Jesus warned them not to tell anyone about him.
31 He then began to teach them that the Son of Man must suffer many things and be rejected by the elders, chief priests and teachers of the law, and that he must be killed and after three days rise again.
32 He spoke plainly about this, and Peter took him aside and began to rebuke him.
33 But when Jesus turned and looked at his disciples, he rebuked Peter. 'Get behind me, Satan!' he said. 'You do not have in mind the things of God, but the things of men.'

RSV
27 And Jesus went on with his disciples, to the villages of Caesare'a Philippi; and on the way he asked his disciples, 'Who do men say that I am?'
28 And they told him, 'John the Baptist; and others say, Eli'jah; and others one of the prophets.' 29 And he asked them, 'But who do you say that I am?' Peter answered him, 'You are the Christ.'
30 And he charged them to tell no one about him.
31 And he began to teach them that the Son of man must suffer many things, and be rejected by the elders and the chief priests and the scribes, and be killed, and after three days rise again. 32 And he said this plainly. And Peter took him, and began to rebuke him. 33 But turning and seeing his disciples, he rebuked Peter, and said, 'Get behind me, Satan! For you are not on the side of God, but of men.'

   (a) What does the word Christ mean? (1)
   (b) Why did Jesus call himself the Son of Man? (2)
   (c) Why did some people call Jesus a prophet? (2)
   (d) Explain why Peter could not accept that Jesus would suffer and die? (2)
   (e) What did Jesus mean when he said to Peter 'Get behind me Satan'? (2)
   (f) How do the words 'Christ' and 'Son of Man' help Christians understand the importance of Jesus? (4)
   (g) Peter's answer, 'You are the Christ', shows that he had understood what Jesus had come to do.
      Do you agree? Give reasons for your answer, showing that you have thought about more than one point of view. (3)

NEAB

4 Christianity.
   (a) State three reasons which the Church gives for marriage. 3 (R1)
   (b) Give an account of the Christian marriage service. 5 (R1)
   (c) Explain how having a Christian wedding might help a couple in their married life. 7 (R2)
   (d) 'All the ceremony and dressing up hide the real meaning of a church wedding.'
      Do you agree?
      Give reasons to support your answer and show that you have thought about different points of view. 5 (R3)

MEG

1 Questions on Christianity

5 **The environment and world development.**
  (a) (i) Describe what you consider to be the biggest threat today to the natural world and its future. (4)
     (ii) Explain the teaching of one religion about responsibility for the natural world. (4)
  (b) (i) Many religious organisations are involved in the work of education and training as a means of removing ignorance and encouraging 'World Development'. Describe the different kinds of such work by one religious organisation. (4)
     (ii) Why does it do this kind of work? (4)
  (c) 'It's no good religions promising us a better world in future – we want a good life now.'
How would you reply? Give reasons for your views. (4)

ULEAC

6 **Roman Catholic specific**
  (a) Write an account of what is said and done at the Mass (Eucharist) in a Roman Catholic Church. (8)
  (b) Explain the importance for Roman Catholics of:
    (i) The Priest
    (ii) The Pope (7)
  (c) If Jesus walked into a Roman Catholic Church during Mass, do you think He would be surprised by what He would see and hear?
Give reasons for your answer. (5)

SEG 1994

7 **Denominational specific**
(a) Choose a branch of the Christian Church or denomination which you have studied and describe briefly how these Christians celebrate:
    (i) Christmas
    (ii) Easter (7)
  (b) Explain the meaning and importance for Christians of two of the following festivals: Pentecost (Whitsun); The Ascension of Christ; The Annunciation. (8)
  (c) Do you think there is any value in celebrating the same religious festivals every year? Give reasons for your opinion. (5)

SEG 1994

Short answer questions

1 (a) The service of Holy Communion is known by a number of other names. Give two of those other names.
  (b) Why do many prayers end, 'through Jesus Christ, Our Lord'?
  (c) What do bread and wine at a communion service represent?
  (d) What is the name given to the head of the Roman Catholic Church?
  (e) Which two churches joined together to form the United Reformed Church?

(all R1/2)

NEAB

2 Answer each part of this question in a single word, phrase or sentence.
(Marks shown in brackets.)
  (a) Name one Christian denomination which practises infant baptism. (1)
  (b) What is a lectern? (1)
  (c) Which festival celebrates the birth of Jesus? (1)
  (d) What does the word 'Amen' mean?
  (e) What was the name of the young woman who had a vision of the Virgin Mary at Lourdes? (1)
  (f) What is the name of the screen that divides an Orthodox Church into two parts? (1)
  (g) Name two books in the Bible that tell the story of Jesus of Nazareth? (2)
  (h) Which event in the life of Jesus is remembered during Lent? (1)
  (i) On which day does the Pope wash the feet of some Christians? (1)
  (j) According to Jesus what are the two great commandments? (2)

Examination questions

    (k) Who is said to have written most of the epistles (letters) in the new Testament? (1)
    (l) In the service of Holy Communion what represents the body and blood of Jesus? (2)

    Total (15)

SEG 1994

3 Answer each part of this question in a single word, phrase or sentence.
    (a) Which one of the synoptic Gospels contains no stories about the birth of Jesus? (1)
    (b) Who said he was ready to die because he had seen the infant Messiah? (1)
    (c) Which prophetess saw the baby Jesus in the Temple in Jerusalem? (1)
    (d) When Jesus was twelve his parents took him to Jerusalem. Name the festival they were celebrating. (1)
    (e) What did Jesus say when his parents found him in the Temple? (1)
    (f) In which town did Jesus grow up? (1)
    (g) Which one of the apostles was a tax collector? (1)
    (h) What annoyed the religious leaders about the words Jesus said when he healed the paralysed man who was lowered through the roof? (2)
    (i) What title did Simon Peter give to Jesus at Caesarea Philippi? (1)
    (j) Which one of the apostles betrayed Jesus? (1)
    (k) In which garden was Jesus arrested? (1)
    (l) Name the prisoner who was released by Pontius Pilate? (1)
    (m) Which one of the apostles denied that he knew Jesus? (1)
    (n) Name one of the women who went to the tomb of Jesus on the first day of the week? (1)

    (Total 15)

SEG 1994

4 Answer each part of this question in a single word, phrase or sentence.
    (a) Describe briefly two different ways in which humans have abused their stewardship of the earth. (2)
    (b) What is the tenth commandment? (1)
    (c) Give two descriptions of people who are 'happy' (blessed) according to the Sermon on the Mount (Matt. 5:5) (2)
    (d) Jesus described a foolish man building his house on sand. Whom did the foolish man represent? (1)
    (e) In the Sermon on the Mount, why can't the man see to take the speck out of the other man's eye? (1)
    (f) Give an example of a religious vocation. (1)
    (g) Give an example of hypocrisy from the Sermon on the Mount. (1)
    (h) What is euthanasia? (1)
    (i) What is the difference between a sin and a crime? (2)

    (Total 12)

SEG 1994

2 Questions on Judaism

1 (a) Name the site of the Jewish pilgrimage shown in the picture opposite. (1) R1
    (b) State three rituals or practices which might be performed there. (3) R1
    (c) Name one of the traditional pilgrim festivals and explain how it is linked with the site shown in the picture. (4) R1
    (d) Explain why the place shown in the picture is still so important for Jewish pilgrims. (7) R2
    (e) 'It is the home which is important for Jews, not special places. Do you agree? Give reasons to support your answer and show that you have thought about different points of view. (5) R3

MEG

The Western Wall in Jersulem

2 (a) Describe the use in Jewish worship of the Torah (Law) and the Nevi'im (Prophets) (8) R1
   (b) Explain the importance for Jews of the use of scripture in worship. (7) R2
   (c) 'Jews need to have modern versions of their holy books.' Do you agree?
       Give reasons to support your answer and show that you have thought about different points of view. (5) R3

MEG

3 Rites of passage: Marriage

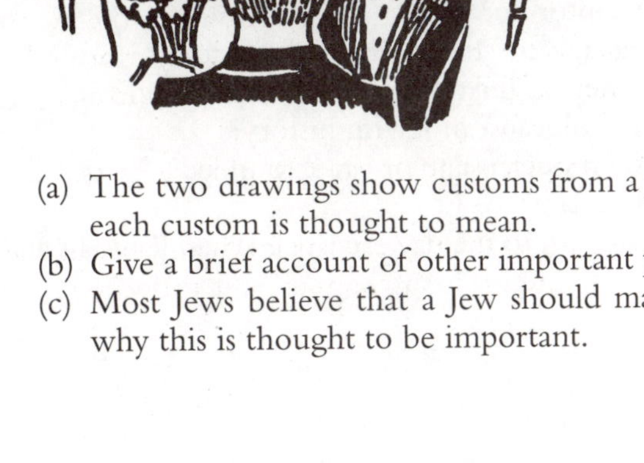

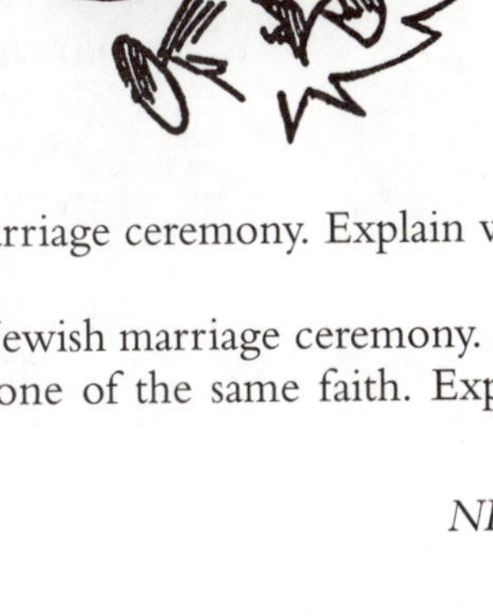

(a) The two drawings show customs from a Jewish marriage ceremony. Explain what each custom is thought to mean. (4)
(b) Give a brief account of other important parts of a Jewish marriage ceremony. (4)
(c) Most Jews believe that a Jew should marry someone of the same faith. Explain why this is thought to be important. (3)

NEAB

Examination questions

4 Festivals: Pesach (Passover)
  (a) Give a description of the events in the history of the Jewish people which are celebrated at Pesach (Passover). (10)
  (b) Choose any two of the following which are used at the Seder meal at Pesach (Passover) and explain why they are important:
    bitter herbs; matzot; haroset; wine (6)
  (c) Celebrating Pesach is very important to all Jews today. Why do you think this is so? (5)

NEAB

5 Origins, scriptures and beliefs
  (a) (i) Describe the call of Abraham and how he responded. (4)
     (ii) Explain the significance of this event for the Jewish people. (4)
  (b) The Hebrew Bible consists of Torah, Nevi'im and Ketubim. Describe with examples, some differences between them. (4)
  (c) 'Ethical monotheism' is a basic belief of Judaism. Show, by reference to the Bible, your understanding of this belief. (4)
  (d) 'The Almighty is greater than any nation or religion. The whole world is His.' How would you reply to someone who said this? Give your reasons. (4)

ULEAC

6 'Shabbat Shalom' – a Sabbath of Peace
  (a) Describe a typical Saturday morning service in an Orthodox Synagogue. (7)
  (b) Explain why Jews rest on Shabbat and how the day is kept holy in the home. (8)
  (c) How do you think people should keep a day which they regard as holy? Give examples and reasons. (5)

SEG 1994

7 (a) When is Shavuot (Weeks) and what does it celebrate? (3)
  (b) Describe the scrolls kept in the Ark in a synagogue. (5)
  (c) Use examples from festivals, daily life and worship to show that the Torah is very important to Jews. (7)
  (d) How far do you think books from ancient times can have meaning in the modern world? Give reasons to support your answer. (5)

SEG 1994

Short answer questions

1 Answer each part of this question in a single word, phrase or sentence.
  (a) Draw or describe the symbol of Judaism called the magen David, Star of David. (1)
  (b) Which person is regarded as the father of the Jewish nation? (1)
  (c) What is monotheism? (1)
  (d) Name the religious object you would find on the doorpost of a Jewish house. (1)
  (e) Briefly what are the first two of the ten commandments? (2)
  (f) Who built the first Jewish temple in Jerusalem nearly three thousand years ago? (1)
  (g) When does the Sabbath begin? (1)
  (h) What does a cantor do? (1)
  (i) In which language are the Torah scrolls written? (1)
  (j) Which movement is linked with Theodore Herzl? (1)
  (k) What was the holocaust in Jewish history? (1)
  (l) When was the modern state of Israel founded? (1)
  (m) What are kibbutzim? (1)
  (n) What name is given to the day each year when Jews fast and especially ask for God's forgiveness? (1)

(Total 15)

SEG 1994

3 Questions on Islam

1. (a) What does the word Qur'an mean and in what language is it written? (2)
   (b) The two main festivals in Islam are Eid-ul-Fitr and Eid-ul-Adha. Choose one of these festivals and then answer the questions.
   Which festival have you chosen …?
      (i) When is the festival celebrated? (1)
      (ii) Why is the festival celebrated? (2)
      (iii) Describe what happens during the festival. (3)
   (c) (i) Describe how a Muslim prepares for prayers. (6)
      (ii) Explain the difference between two types of prayer, du'a and salah. (4)
      (iii) Why do you think prayer is so important in Islam? (5)

   NEAB

2.

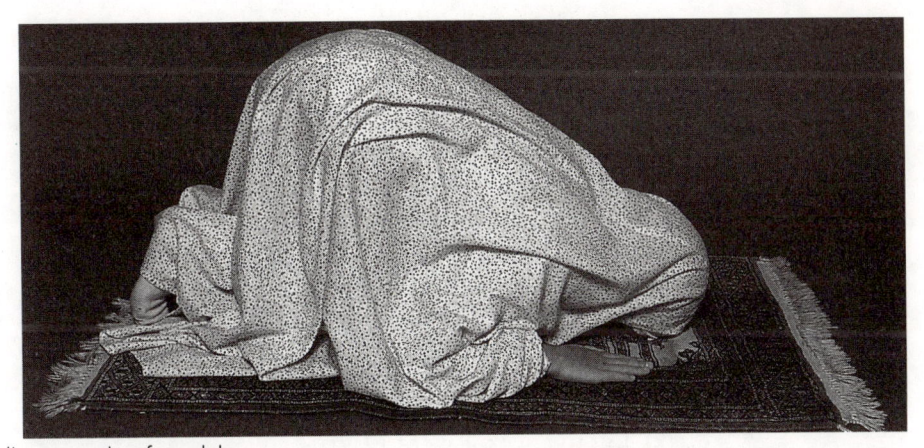

   Muslim preparing for salah

   (a) Give the name of the prayer position shown in the picture.   1 (R1)
   (b) State three other important rituals or practices of Muslim prayer.   3 (R1)
   (c) (i) Give a brief account of Friday prayers.
      (ii) Explain their importance.   4 (R2)
   (d) 'If you believe in God you do not need rituals.'
   Do you agree?
   Give reasons for your answer and show that you have thought about different points of view.   5 (R3)

3. (a) Describe four practices of a Muslim wedding ceremony.   8 (R1)
   (b) What is the importance of three of these practices?   7 (R2)
   (c) 'Without a religious ceremony, people are not really married.'
   Do you agree?
   Give reasons for your answer and show that you have thought about different points of view.   5 (R3)

   MEG

4. (a) (i) Outline examples of major and minor jihad. (4)
      (ii) Explain why many Muslims believe that major jihad is more important than minor jihad. (4)
   (b) Explain the importance of family life in Islam. (4)
   (c) Muslims treat 'The People of the Book' differently from other people. Describe ways in which they do this. (4)
   (d) 'I don't think it matters very much which religion people follow, as long as they believe in God.'
   Do you agree? Give reasons for your views.

   ULEAC

5 (a) Describe the ceremonies Muslims perform when a baby has been born. (8)
  (b) Explain the main difficulties Muslim teenagers may face when growing up in western countries such as Britain. (7)
  (c) Some Muslims want Islamic schools for their children. Do you think this would be helpful? Give reasons in support of your opinion.

SEG 1994

6 622 CE became 1 AH (the year of the Hijrah)
  (a) Explain why the Muslim calendar begins with the year of the Hijrah. (4)
  (b) Give an account of the main events in the life of Mohammed after the Hijrah. (7)
  (c) Explain the importance of the years Mohammed lived in Medina (4)
  (d) Which do you think are the most important for the Muslim faith:
    (i) The years Mohammed lived in Mecca (Makkah)?
    (ii) The years Mohammed lived in Medina?
    Give reasons for your choice. (5)

SEG 1994

Short answer questions

1 Answer each part of this question in a single word, phrase or sentence.
  (a) What is the Arabic word for God? (1)
  (b) In which country was Mohammed born? (1)
  (c) To which tribe did Mohammed belong? (1)
  (d) Name Mohammed's first wife? (1)
  (e) What is celebrated at Maulid-an-Nabi? (1)
  (f) What does the word Islam mean? (1)
  (g) What are the qibla wall and mihrab for? (1)
  (h) What is the main duty of the muezzin? (1)
  (i) What is an imam? (1)
  (j) What is hadith? (1)
  (k) List the five pillars of Islam (5)

(Total 15)

SEG 1994

4 Questions for general application

1 (a) Choose one place of worship and imagine that you are showing a visitor round it. Describe the appearance and use of the main features you would wish to point out. (7)
  (b) For any two religions choose one special feature found in the place of worship and explain the importance of each feature for the worshippers. (8)
  (c) Would a visitor learn more from a guided tour of a place of worship or from attending community worship there? Give reasons for your answer. (5)

SEG 1994

2 (a) Ceremonies which take place at birth, initiation, marriage and death are known as rites of passage.
    Explain why each of these four events is marked by a religious ceremony. (8)
  (b) Describe the initiation ceremony (not a birth ceremony) in one of the religions you have studied. (7)
  (c) 'The day I received my national insurance number in the post I felt very grown up. It was like a rite of passage.' (GCSE Student)
    How fair is it to compare this event with the initiation ceremony you have described? Give reasons for your answer. (5)

SEG 1994

5 Question structure for Standard Grade

Knowledge and understanding – Examples

Sub element 1: Demonstrating knowledge and understanding of specified sources and current practice in Christianity and one other world religion related to the key concepts of these religions.

Foundation Level
Given a visual symbol of Easter and a quotation from Luke 24, state which event this commemorates and give a reason why it is important to Christians.
Given a photograph of Muslims at prayer, state relevant facts about prayer in Islam, using some appropriate terms, and explain the key concept of submission.

General Level
Given a visual symbol of Easter and a quotation from Luke 24, explain what this event means to Christians.

Given a photograph of Muslims at prayer, state relevant facts about prayer in Islam, using appropriate terms, and explain the importance of prayer and how this relates to one of the key concepts.

Credit Level
Given a brief statement about the Resurrection, explain this key concept and consider a variety of interpretations.
Explain the concept of submission and how this is related to the nature of God, exemplified in the Muslim practice of prayer.

Sub element 2: Demonstrating knowledge and understanding of specified issues of belief and morality in relation to religion and contemporary society.

Given an extract from an article about a pro-euthanasia organisation, explain what the group believes and give a reason why some people think this belief is wrong.

Given the same extract, explain the difference between active and passive euthanasia and give reasons why some people are totally against it in any form.

Given the same extract, explain how the pro-euthanasia organisation's belief can be justified and give examples of other views on this subject, with reasons advanced for those views.

6 Writing an extended essay

The *NEAB* papers, Syllabus A & B, require students taking the higher tier (R) to write an essay which can give 20 marks. They have an extra 30 minutes in which to do this.

Examples of Essay Questions

Syllabus A Christianity Paper 2 Tier R
'It is not beliefs that are important but the way a person lives his or her life.'
Discuss this statement with reference to the Great Commandments and the Beatitudes.

Islam
How might belief in the Qur'an affect the way a Muslim might live his or her life?

Judaism
What effect has prejudice and discrimination had on the Jewish race and religion?

Syllabus B Paper 1A Christianity Tier R
'The Bible is the Word of God'

Examination questions

Discuss what Christians may mean by this statement, showing where there may be differences of interpretation. How might a belief in the Word of God affect the way a person lives?

Paper 1B
Christian Belief and Practice RC
Worshipping at home by yourself is more meaningful than worshipping with others at a church service. Discuss this with reference to the practice of at least two Christian traditions.

Paper 1C The Christian Life and the Gospel
Christians today are reminded of the last supper each time they celebrate Holy Communion. How important in the celebration of Holy Communion is the remembrance of the last supper?

Paper 2A Effects of Christianity on behaviour, attitudes and lifestyles
'It is more important to protect the unborn child than to protect the environment.'
Do you consider this statement to be a valid and Christian response to contemporary issues? Explain your answer in detail, showing that you are aware of what both issues involve.

Paper 2B Effects of Christianity RC (as above)
'A sexual relationship outside marriage can never be right'.
Do you agree? Give reasons for your answer. Show that you have thought of more than one point of view.

The essay

This book can give guidance on writing essays but it cannot write your essay for you. Writing essays is a skill which you develop through practice. There are key factors to remember.

1. Study the question carefully to be sure you know what you are being asked. Don't assume – read thoroughly. It is easy to misinterpret and a pity to write a brilliant essay about a question you haven't been asked.
2. Because of the above, hedge your bets – make your opening gambit the time when you tell the examiner what you think the question is asking. Sometimes even examiners don't realise their questions are ambiguous. Don't you be. State clearly what you are writing about.
3. Plan carefully. Essays are evaluative. Weigh up the evidence on all sides.
4. Structure your points.

Give your opinion, explain why you have it and include evidence to support it. (Evidence should include a balance of examples taken from personal experience; Scripture quotations and, where possible, specific church teachings.)

Look at the question from other perspectives. Remember, people often see things according to their upbringing, beliefs, culture and individual personalities. Understanding religions teaches you to respect others' views. Explain a perspective which differs from your own and supply evidence which supports that alternative view.

Finally draw the threads of your arguments together with a conclusion where you reiterate your interpretation of the question and your own opinion.

Suggested answer structure for first extended essay question

1. 'It is not beliefs that are important but the way a person lives his or her life.'
   Discuss this statement with reference to the Great Commandments and the Beatitudes.

   (a) Tell the examiner what the question is. The Great Commandments teach Christians to 'love God and love your neighbour as yourself'. The Beatitudes teach Christians about the abundant blessings which will fall upon those who know and show their need of God and a willingness to adopt His ways (see Matt. 5:3–12). Quote from Scripture.

   (b) What do you think? Is what you believe important? For example, Christians believe in one God; Jesus as Saviour and Lord; the messiahship of Jesus; that you should love God and love your neighbour; the teachings of the beatitudes ...

(c) Christians can believe all the above things. But what relevance does belief in the Great Commandments and the Beatitudes have if it is not lived and active – if people who profess such belief do not show how it can govern the way they live their lives?

Give examples of living Christianity using life examples such as Mother Theresa or someone of your own personal experience who puts the Gospel teachings into practice.

(d) Conclude by drawing together the threads of your arguments.

Look at the other extended essay examples given on pages 151–2 and work out how you might structure your answers. If you feel you are not being given enough practice in this skill ask your teacher to give you more titles.

Examination answers

1 Christianity: suggested answer structures

1 (a) A Christian could be affected in his thoughts about war by the Old Testament teaching in Micah that they shall beat their swords into mattocks and their spears into pruning knives and nation shall not lift up sword against nation nor ever again be trained for war.

(b) Jesus told his follower to put up his sword when he was arrested in the garden of Gethsemane. One of those present cut off the ear of a soldier. Jesus had come to show people the way of peace and reconciliation. Jesus meant that nothing can be achieved by violence, only love can conquer evil. He went on to explain that He had to be arrested to fulfil prophecy. Jesus then went on to die to redeem man from sin. This was the ultimate act of passive resistance and love, which is more powerful than violence which only leads to more violence.

(c) Non-violent protest means expressing your opposition to something in a passive way. This means writing or speaking but not taking any kind of physical action.

(d) It is almost impossible, given the conditions of modern warfare, for a war to be 'just' according to the criteria developed by Thomas Aquinas and now established as being necessary to establish justification for conflict. While it may be possible to determine a rightful authority, sufficient cause and good intention; it is very difficult to establish unequivocally that the war will discriminate between civilians and the armies or that there is proportionality and the war is not more harmful than the original problem. The latter clauses in the Just War theory are subjective and appear differently to each side. It would be possible to argue about the same war from two opposing sides, apply the criteria and be quite clear that a war was either just or unjust. A Christian could use the teachings and example of Jesus to argue that war which involves killing other people is never Just. A Christian could also argue that the cost of modern war and armaments is a gross injustice.

2 (a) Refusing to employ someone because of their race.

(b) A Christian could write to local councillors or organise events where people of different races could meet and learn about one another's way of life.

(c) Yes – because it is important to give witness against injustice and intolerance and sometimes a person has to be assertive in expressing their beliefs. Jesus stood with the oppressed and the outcasts such as tax collectors despite public ridicule. Christians should avoid becoming involved in violent demonstrations and follow a way of passive resistance to injustice.

(d) Prejudice is a thought process and the law cannot change people's thoughts. Legislation can only prevent discrimination when it can be proved. The state can legislate for an education system which helps to educate people about prejudice.

3 (a) The word Christ means 'Messiah' – anointed one.

(b) Jesus called himself 'Son Of Man' so that the disciples would understand that He was the suffering servant referred to in Isaiah. He had to stress again and again that he was not a glorious Messiah who would conquer with armies; He was the Messiah and also a mortal man who had to suffer to redeem mankind.

1 Christianity: suggested answer structures

(c) Some people called Jesus a prophet because many Jews believed he was another in the line of Old Testament prophets sent to teach people the way of God. At the Transfiguration He appears alongside Moses and Elijah.

(d) Peter could not accept that Jesus would suffer and die because he believed the Messiah would be strong and conquering. He couldn't imagine a Messiah who seemed to be contemplating an ignominious death which did not match his vision.

(e) Jesus meant that Peter was not speaking himself but was being used by evil to voice doubts about the nature of Jesus' suffering. Jesus tells Peter his thoughts are from Man not God. Jesus shows that man's rejection of suffering for good is not God's way. A true follower has to accept that it is sometimes necessary to suffer to bring good to the world.

(f) These words help Christians realise God is both fully human and fully divine. He is God and man. As the Christ Jesus is the Messiah sent to show man the way to God and eternal happiness. As the Son of Man Jesus is the one who will suffer to redeem mankind. He takes the pain of man's sin upon himself completely. Thus Christians take comfort from knowing the strength of God's love for them in giving his Son in such a special way.

(g) Peter does realise that Jesus is the Messiah because he has seen the Transfiguration and is blessed as Jesus' most perceptive disciple. He does not fully realise the type of Messiah that Jesus was. He did not appreciate how Jesus would have to suffer to fulfil his Messianic role.

4 (a) The Church (specify, e.g. of England) states that marriage is for partnership and friendship, mutual support and to provide a secure and loving environment in which to bring up children.

(b) A Christian marriage service will entail both parties stating that they are free to marry and that they are willing to marry. The bride is often symbolically 'given away' by her father or close relative. The minister speaks of the serious nature of the commitment they are making. They exchange vows: 'to have and to hold from this day forward, for better for worse, for richer for poorer, in sickness and in health, to love and to cherish, 'till death do us part'. They then exchange rings as a symbol of unbroken love and fidelity, reciting the words 'In the name of the Father and of the Son and of the Spirit.' The minister then prays 'What God has joined together, let no man put asunder.' The legality of the marriage is confirmed by the signing of the register.

(c) A Christian couple might be helped in their married life by the serious nature of the solemn vows they have made to each other. Married couples inevitably encounter difficult times when they feel pressure due to illness or unemployment, money worries and sometimes lifestyle changes for one or both partners. A commitment to the solemnity of the vows might help couples work together, remembering their promise to stay together until death ... quote marriage vows above.

(d) Give a balanced view. What is the real meaning of a Church wedding?
To make a vows in the presence of witnesses, before God and in the name of God; to bear witness to the sanctity of marriage as a holy estate instituted by Christ for the purposes aforementioned.
How does the surrounding pomp detract from this?
Does it? It doesn't have to. It can enhance the solemnity if the main purpose is held up as vital. If the main purpose is to have a big show then of course it hides the real meaning but the dressing up and ritual often help people to appreciate the momentous nature of what they are doing.

5 (a) (i) You could describe pollution, acid rain, deforestation, global warming, over-population. It is a matter of personal opinion but you must explain four main facts about your chosen area.
(ii) Christianity teaches that God created the world and gave man dominion over all living things. Man is the steward of the world and must regard himself as obliged to preserve nature which sustains life, Man must have respect for all living things (mainly Genesis).

(b) (i) Christian Aid, for example, works through setting up projects which are practical, educational and developmental. It aims to establish structures which will help communities in the short term, e.g. by providing clean water; prepare them for the long term by educating them about the need for clean water to avoid disease and allow for crop growth; and establish a pattern of self-help by perhaps, for example, showing how to dig a well and keep it working, thus breaking the dependency mentality.

(ii) Christian Aid is motivated by the teachings of Jesus to bring the good news to the poor. God's Kingdom cannot come unless believers work for it by making Jesus real through the work they do for the needy. Jesus came for the sick, not the well and is to be found among the dispossessed and hungry (compare the Beatitudes).

6 (a) In the Roman Catholic Church the Mass consists of:
- (i) Reconciliation where believers confess their sins to God and to each other and ask forgiveness and mercy.
  The reciting of the Gloria in praise of God.
- (ii) The Liturgy of the word:
  an Old Testament reading,
  a Psalm,
  a new Testament reading (read by a member of the laity),
  a Gospel reading for which all stand (read by the Priest).
- (iii) A homily or sermon by the priest, usually on the readings.
- (iv) Reciting of the Creed.
- (v) The Bidding prayers. (Read by the laity asking God's grace and mercy on several important areas of life, e.g. politics, world peace, wisdom for world leaders and for the community.
- (vi) The liturgy of the Eucharist where the bread and wine are blessed.
  The priest breaks the bread and says: 'Take this all of you and eat it. This is my body which will be given up for you.' He takes the cup of wine and says: 'Take this all of you and drink from it: This is the cup of my blood. The blood of the New Covenant. It will be shed for you and for all men so that sins may be forgiven. Do this in memory of me.'
- (vii) All say the Lord's Prayer (Our Father) and then receive Holy Communion. The Minister of the Eucharist holds up the consecrated bread/wine and says the 'Body of Christ' to which the believer replies 'Amen' and receives the bread in the hand or mouth. He or she takes the wine from the cup which is held up as the words 'Blood of Christ' are spoken and the believer replies 'Amen'.
- (viii) The believers give thanks in prayers and hymns for the gift of the Eucharist.
- (ix) The celebrant gives the parish notices and final blessings.

(b) (i) The priest is important for Roman Catholics because he is the representative of the bishop who is the Shepherd of the whole diocese and responsible for disseminating the authority of the Pope to the faithful. Only the priest has the ability to preside over the eucharistic celebration and the belief in the miracle, which occurs at every Mass and is central to Roman Catholic belief.

The priest also has an important pastoral ministry to the congregation. He ministers to the sick and dying; visits the housebound; takes a prominent part in local Catholic issues and is the figurehead of the community.

(c) It would seem from studying the Gospels, that Jesus would not be surprised at what He might see and hear at the Mass. The celebration of the sacrificial meal has evolved since the Last Supper but the words are essentially the same and Roman Catholics certainly believe that they are carrying out the instructions given at the Last Supper.

It is also unlikely that Jesus would be surprised by anything else in the Mass because each part contains something which is in keeping with the teachings of Jesus: the call to repentance and forgiveness; the statement of Belief; and the attention to the Word of God are all part of Christian life. They have merely been formalised and ritualised.

Note You will occasionally find a question which strikes you as strange but you must answer in good faith. In the above question a Roman Catholic candidate might validly point out to the examiner that Roman Catholics believe that Jesus is God, He is risen and He knows every hair on each person's head. He knows your thoughts before you do therefore, He would certainly not be surprised!

1 Christianity: suggested answer structures

7 State denomination e.g. Roman Catholic.
  (a) (i) **Christmas** – Christmas is the time to celebrate the birth of Jesus. Roman Catholics attend Mass. There is a midnight service when traditionally the model/statue of the infant Jesus is carried to a manger which has been built in the Church. The Mass is as usual but Christmas Carols are sung throughout the Christmas period. Churches often offer 'Family Masses' on Christmas morning with special care being given to make the word accessible to children. Schoolchildren usually give carol festivals with readings from the Old and New Testaments and a variety of carols. Younger children present the story of the nativity for family and friends.

  For most people the most notable aspect of Christmas is the exchange of gifts and the family gathering around a Christmas Dinner of Turkey and trimmings followed by Christmas Pudding. It is a time of feasting and jollity. Houses are decorated with tinsel, paper chains and holly and people send greetings cards to friends all over the country.

  (ii) **Easter** – This is very much an adult feast when Christians celebrate the resurrection of Jesus and the salvation of all mankind. Adult believers might celebrate by attending the vigil Mass on Holy Saturday when the priest anoints the Paschal candle and lights it from a fire proclaiming the light of Christ in the world. All Roman Catholics are obliged to receive the sacraments at Easter as an Easter Duty.

  Easter is celebrated in the home by the giving of chocolate eggs as symbols of new life. It is also the celebration of new life at springtime and symbols such as spring flowers, lambs and rabbits are associated with Easter.

  (b) **Pentecost** – this is the time when Christians remember when the Holy Spirit came upon the disciples, was visible in tongues of fire, audible in the sound of wind, and brought courage to the disciples who were then able to communicate the good news to people who spoke many languages. It is very important because the Spirit was with the disciples to give them courage once Jesus had gone to be with the Father.

  The **Ascension** is important because Christians believe that Jesus ascended to heaven to be with God. Christians believe in the Resurrection of Christ and therefore in the need for Christ to go to heaven without dying again. His ascension was visible and a sign of real hope and of His conquering of death.

  The **Annunciation** is important because God chose a young, pure girl to be the mother of His Son. She was frightened but accepted the will of God in complete submission, despite the hardship it was sure to cause her.

  (c) It is vital to celebrate the same religious festivals each year. Believers find stability and comfort in the certainty of remembering each important event annually. Many of these festivals tie in with very old ways of life and bond people from generation to generation. They give security and form to the year, helping people to plan and causing many people at particular times to focus on the spiritual dimension of their lives. Religious festivals are public holidays, which are needed periodically. They are needed more than ever in the modern world and give people a chance to relax and be with the family. They can enhance the quality of life.

Short answers

1 (a) Eucharist/Lord's Supper.
  (b) Christians pray through the Son to the Father and ask God's grace in the name of his Son and all that Jesus has done for Him.
  (c) Bread and wine represent the actions of Jesus at the last supper. They represent the body and blood of Christ. They represent Jesus as the sacrifice (depends on individual belief or course studied).
  (d) The Pope.
  (e) Congregationalist and Presbyterian.

2 (a) Church of England/Roman Catholicism.
  (b) A stand where the Bible is placed and read from during Church services in the Christian Church.
  (c) Christmas.

Examination answers

(d) 'It is agreed'.
(e) Bernadette Soubirous.
(f) Iconostasis.
(g) Mark and Luke.
(h) The forty days in the desert when He was tempted by the devil.
(i) Maundy Thursday.
(j) Love God and love your neighbour.
(k) Paul.
(l) Bread and wine.

3 (a) Mark.
(b) Simeon.
(c) Anna.
(d) Passover.
(e) 'Did you not know that I was bound to be in my Father's house?'
(f) Nazareth.
(g) Matthew (Levi).
(h) He said, 'Your sins are forgiven'. They said this was blasphemy as only God could forgive sins.
(i) Messiah.
(j) Judas Iscariot.
(k) Gethsemane.
(l) Barabbas.
(m) Peter.
(n) Mary Magdalene.

4 (a) Deforestation (Rainforests). Global warming by overuse of energy. Excessive pollution. Destruction of plants and animal species.
(b) You shall not covet your neighbour's house; his wife; his slave; his slave girl; his ox, his ass or anything which belongs to him.
(c) Those who know their need of God/those who are sorrowful/or gentle in spirit/ who hunger and thirst for right/who show mercy/pure in heart/peacemakers/ who have suffered persecution for the cause of right.
(d) The foolish man represents someone who puts his hope in the transitory things of the world and not in God.
(e) Because he has a 'log' in his own eye.
(f) To be a priest/nun or monk/brother.
(g) An example of hypocrisy is making a show of your religion and flaunting charitable giving.
(h) Killing someone because you believe their quality of life is such that death would be a release. It can be voluntary or involuntary.
(i) A sin is against the teachings of Jesus and the Church. A crime is to break the statutory law of your country.

2 Judaism: suggested answer structures

1 (a) The Western (Wailing) wall in Jerusalem.
(b) Rituals include rocking and praying; kissing the wall; pushing written prayers into the cracks.
(c) Sukkot (Feast of Tabernacles) recalls the time when Jews took offerings to the Temple and when they lived in the wilderness in tents (tabernacles). It is linked to the wall because the Jews were set to wandering the world following the destruction of the Temple in Jerusalem.
(d) The wall is important for many Jewish pilgrims who may regard Jerusalem as their holy city, because of the lack of a Jewish home; and for centuries, many have regarded the Wailing Wall (which is all that remains of the Temple destroyed in AD 70 and is on the site of the Temple built by Solomon) as a symbol of the

2 Judaism: suggested answer structures

      endurance of the Jewish people and the continuance of God's covenant with Abraham and his chosen people.

  (e) Home and Family life are extremely important to the Jewish people. Being Jewish is conveyed by birth through the mother; and the mother is essential in inculcating Jewish understanding in her children. The Jewish place of worship, the synagogue, is a meeting place. Being Jewish, however, is more about having a personal relationship with God. This is helped by living his commandments. Judaism is active, a way of life. Therefore the home is more important than holy places, but such places are an important part of Jewish understanding and its development.

2 (a) The Torah is central to worship. All understanding comes from God through the Torah. The Torah is kept in the Ark as the main focus of the synagogue. On the Sabbath, at the service and after the reading of the opening prayers and psalms, the people say the Shema and the Amidah and then face the Ark as it is opened. The Torah is carried out and is touched by the men with their tallits, which they then kiss. Members of the congregation are called to read the Torah and the place is pointed to by a special silver or ivory pointer. The Torah is held in the greatest reverence and awe. The books of the prophets are read as they give different perspectives on the understanding of God and are regarded as guidance. They are not seen as being as holy as the Torah.

  (b) The use of Scripture in worship is central to Judaism. All understanding of God is diffused through the Scriptures and essentially through the Torah which tells of God's covenant with His chosen people and their developing relationship with Him. Readings from the Tenakh unite Jewish people all over the world and in every tradition of Judaism. The Scriptures contain every instruction that God has given to the people. When the Torah is taken from the Ark these words are spoken: 'This is the law of Moses set before the children of Israel … It is the tree of life to them that grasp it.' Thus the Scriptures are all to the Jews, the essence of life.

  (c) There is no reason for the Jews to have modern versions of their holy books. Progressive or Liberal Jews hold their services in English but the Torah is always read in Hebrew. All Jews are taught the meanings of the Torah passages and spend a lifetime working out their own relationship with God in the light of His teachings. Different traditions might interpret the holy books in different ways but the essential thing about Judaism is that God doesn't change and neither does His relationship with His people.

3 (a) Marriage under the Huppah can symbolise: a new home; united in love under one roof; privacy of the couple; openness to the community; the ancient litter on which a bride was once transported.
      Smashing the glass can symbolise the destruction of the Temple; the fragility of the union, which can be shattered by infidelity; the marriage will last until the glass is again (forever); marriage is fraught with life's difficulties.

  (b) Mention blessing of the cup of wine and shared drinking; the blessing of the ring and giving of it; the vow 'By this ring you are married to me in holiness and according to the Law of Moses'; reading the Ketubah.

  (c) Jews often like to marry Jews. Jewishness is passed on through the mother. If a Jew marries a gentile the Jewishness can be lost. It is important to worship and pray together in order to develop good faith. Children are thought to benefit from a family life rich in Jewish tradition and a united giving of Jewish morality.

4 (a) Give a detailed account of the Exodus – slaves in Egypt; Moses and the burning bush; Moses returns and the Plagues of Egypt; the night of the Exodus; the Angel of Death; the First born; roast lamb; herbs; unleavened bread; sandals and girdle; smearing of blood; flight.
      Crossing the Red Sea.

  (b) *Bitter herb* = bitterness of slavery in Egypt, importance of freedom.
      Matzot = bread of affliction baked in haste before fleeing.
      Haroset = sweet mixture of apples, nuts, cinnamon = sweetness of freedom and resembles mud of bricks made by Israelites.
      Wine = Four glasses symbolise four promises. spilling drops reminiscent of plagues; symbol of happiness.

Examination answers

5 (a) (i) God called Abraham to leave his country and people and go to a country He would show. God said He would make Abraham into a great nation and bless him, Abraham did as he was asked even though he was 75 years old.
(ii) This is the beginning of Judaism when God made the Jews, descendants of Abraham, His chosen people and promised to bless the nation.

(b) The Torah is the Law and is revered by the Jews as the most important source of knowledge about God. It contains the Decalogue, the Ten Commandments, by which Jews order their lives. It is always read from on the Sabbath.
Nevi'im are the books of the Prophets which contain advice from highly regarded men about God, helping Jews understand the nature of God and develop their relationship with Him. The Prophets called people back to the true God when they lost faith. Elijah showed God's power by bringing down fire on idol-worshippers.

Ketubim concern human problems, family and social relationships. There are many examples. The book of Job is the story of a good man who suffers. Job says that the Lord gives and the Lord takes away and the name of the Lord is blessed. Suffering is a mystery and that concept is central to Jewish thought.

(c) This means belief in One God. The Jewish people have their belief in God at the centre of their lives, directing everything they do and setting a pattern for living in morality. The belief is established when Jews recite the Shema given in Deuteronomy: 'Hear O Israel the Lord Our God is One.' and in Exodus in the first commandment, 'I am the Lord your God' and 'You shall have no Gods except me.' The rules for living are, then, given. Jews must not be guided by anything else in their ethical choices, only in the commandments of the one true God.

(d) This is personal; you need to answer in the light of your understanding of faith perspectives. Jews believe in one God and certainly that God is more important than any state or nation. Religion is a word which describes a particular set of beliefs and for Jews belief in God is the most important thing and it is that which is at the heart of Jewish faith; therefore 'religion' and the Almighty could mean the same thing.

6 (a) In the Orthodox synagogue the men and women sit separately. There must be a quorum of ten males for the Torah to be read. Men wear yarmulkes and some wear the tallit as a token of obedience to the law. Some men wear phylacteries (tefillin). The Torah scroll is carried from the Ark and carried to the lectionary where the appropriate part is read. Set prayers are said from the prayer book. Readings are read from the Haftarah (prophets). Anyone in the congregation can read these. Hymns may be sung and time is allowed for private prayer. Sometimes after the Torah is read the rabbi, who is the spiritual leader of the community, may give a commentary on the reading.

It is not a very formal service and people may come and go as they please and children are free to wander.

(b) Resting on Shabbat is regarded as a law. It is one of the mishna of Moses. Jews are forbidden to work on Shabbat and, depending on the degree of Orthodoxy, this can be more or less strictly observed.

Every family welcomes in the Sabbath when the sun goes down on Friday. The mother, who is the heart of the family, aided by her daughters lights the Sabbath candles and says the blessing. The family share a special meal. The Father recites the Kaddish and everyone must wash their hands in a special way. The bread (chollah) is broken and passed around. The plaited bread is a symbol of the unity of God and man and salt is sprinkled on it to show the dignity of human labour. The family may sing songs between courses and give thanks for blessings and look to the future.

On the Sabbath morning the family attend synagogue. They do no work. They eat a meal prepared the day before and spend the day quietly. A havdalah service may be held at the end of the day with special prayers and songs. A cup of wine is drunk to symbolise the joy of the Sabbath carrying on to other days.

(c) Please give personal opinions on these questions but base them on what you know of religious belief and practice and show an appreciation of 'holiness'. A sacred day would be marked by sacred acts such as prayer, singing, sharing, giving etc ...

7 (a) Shavuot is seven weeks after Passover in the month of Sivan (May/June). It celebrates the giving of the Law.
  (b) The scrolls are the Torah scrolls and they are carefully handwritten and contain the Law of Moses, the books of Genesis, Exodus, Leviticus, Deuteronomy and Numbers. They are written in Hebrew and are regarded as the most important part of worship because they explain the faith of the Jews and their relationship with God.
  (c) The Torah is read from in the synagogue at festivals. The rite of passage into adulthood, Bar/Bat Mitvah, is marked by the young person learning to read a passage from the Torah. There is also a very important festival when the Torah is paraded around the synagogue (Simchat Torah – Rejoicing in the Torah). The Torah lays down the laws, which Jews must live, so Orthodox Jews also wear verses from the Torah in the phylacteries and nail them to the doorposts in the mezuzah as a sign of obedience to the Law.

Short answers

1 (a) The Star of David is two equilateral triangles with one superimposed upside down upon the other to form a star.
  (b) Abraham.
  (c) Belief in one God.
  (d) Mezuzah.
  (e) I am the Lord your God.
      You shall have no Gods but me.
  (f) Solomon.
  (g) Friday evening at Sunset.
  (h) He is the musical and ritual expert who will lead the singing.
  (i) Hebrew.
  (j) Zionism.
  (k) The attempted genocide perpetrated by the Third Reich in Germany, which meant the death of six million Jews in death camps in Europe.
  (l) 1948.
  (m) Communities in Israel where families live together, work and pray together, each contributing according to their ability.
  (n) Yom Kippur.

3 Islam: suggested answer structures

1 (a) Recitation/revelation.
     Arabic
  (b) (i) Eid-ul-Fitr falls on the first day of Shawwal, the tenth month.
          Eid-ul-Adha falls on the tenth day of Dhul-Hijrah, the last month.
      (ii) Eid-ul-Fitr is celebrated at the end of Ramadan, the end of the month of fasting. It celebrates the month in which the Qur'an was revealed and the end of a period of fasting, repentance, reconciliation and prayer.
           Eid-ul-Adha celebrates the end of the Hajj; Muslims give thanks to Allah for assistance in achieving the arduous pilgrimage. It is the festival of sacrifice and Muslims make a sacrifice and give to charity.
      (iii) On Festivals Muslims dress in their best clothes. They say Takbir. The Imam says Fatihah and another Qur'anic passage. He delivers a sermon accompanied by the utterance 'Allahu Akbar'.
  (c) (i) Include: Mental preparation placing Allah as mighty and self as humble; wudu/washing under pure running water, ritual = hands up to the wrist three times; mouth rinsed x 3; nostrils washed, nose blown x 3; face wiped x 3; right hand and arm up to elbow x 3; left hand and arm up to elbow x 3; wet hands run over face and neck once; ears washed once; right foot to ankle x 3; left foot to ankle x 3. Then Muslims make a statement of intent.

Examination answers

(b) The du'a is the 'Cry of the Heart' prayer; this can be said at the end of the salah; while on the knees the palms are lifted up to the chin and a private petition is offered up to Allah.

The salah is the ritualised prayer which involves a set number of rak'ahs with established words and movements at particular times of the day.

(c) Prayer is one of the five pillars of Islam. It is a duty and is enjoyable. It reminds Muslims five times a day that God is Great. Every Muslim prays with his mind, heart and body to show total submission to Allah. In praying all Muslims across the world are bonded in faith.

2 (a) Position is prostrate.

(b) Important rituals include wudu/wuzu (washing); facing Mecca; prayer mat; movement and repetition of set words.

(c) Friday prayers are obligatory at lunchtime for all men. A sermon (khutbah) is given by the imam from the pulpit (minbar). The sermon deals with problems of the day and an explanation of the Qur'an or religious practices. Muslims are called to prayer and bring in their mats and perform the daily rak'ahs.

Prayers are important as they are a duty for all. They focus each believer on the importance of prayer and worship of Allah.

(d) Rituals give people a sense of security, comfort and belonging. Habits of prayer are soothing and afford a regularity to life which helps man see a pattern. Like many habits in life, people who have them feel secure with them and need them. Many people believe in God but have not been trained to observe rituals and therefore do not need them.

3 (a) Marriage takes place at home or mosque.
Both partners must agree.
Readings from the Qur'an.
Contract Aqd nikah is written and spoken, signed, and bride and groom are given copies.
Groom gives wife mahr (dowry), which she keeps.

(b) Partners must wish to marry or the marriage is invalid.
Readings help to focus couples' ideas on the holy estate of marriage as the only status morally and legally for sexual intercourse.
Contract emphasises serious bond of marriage.
Dowry affords wife some degree of financial independence.

(c) Depends on culture and beliefs. Religious believers don't often recognise civil marriages as real marriage but those with no religious belief don't see the purpose of the religious ritual. In a religious marriage couples believe that God/Allah is part of their union.
(Give personal opinion but support with examples)

4 (a) (i) The great or major Jihad is the war within; it is the struggle to purify self which is achieved through observance of the pillars throughout life.
The lesser jihad is a war fought when all other means of resolving conflict are exhausted.

(ii) Major jihad is more important because the name Muslim means submission to God. This means learning to deny your own desires and submitting to the will of Allah. This gives direction and purpose to life and is the test of a good Muslim who has followed all the pillars.

(b) Family life is important in Islam. The Qur'an and hadith urge Muslims to treat old people with honour and respect, to raise children and treat them with justice and bring children up by example and teaching in the way of Islam.

(c) Muslims recognise that Christians and Jews also have holy books which order their lives. It is therefore acceptable for Muslims to associate with those who treat faith seriously. Muslims will discuss and mix with Christians and Jews and respect their beliefs and moral codes.

(d) This is personal and again depends on faith perspective. Always recognise that different people come from different cultures and see life differently. The idea that all non-believers are condemned to eternal fire is held by some groups but you must always balance your personal opinion with example and evidence and show knowledge of other views.

3 Islam: suggested answer structures

5 (a) The Adhan ceremony takes place as soon as possible. The baby is washed and the father whispers the call to prayer in the baby's right ear. The naming ceremony (aqiqa) is held on the seventh day. The Father names the child after reading from the Qur'an. The baby is given a family name or a name from Mohammed or Allah with the word Abd (servant of) added. The baby's head is shaved which washes away the uncleanliness of birth, oil is put on the head and money equal to the weight of the baby's hair is given to the poor. Traditionally goat or sheep are sacrificed, one for a girl and two for a boy. The meat is divided one-third to the poor and two-thirds consumed by the family. Baby boys are circumcised shortly after birth.

(b) Muslim teenagers may face a conflict of cultures in Britain. British teenagers accept alcohol and drugs as part of life. They are forbidden in Islam. It is accepted to be sexually active and have multiple partners in the British culture. It is forbidden in Islam. Girls are closely chaperoned to guard their honour in Islamic culture. In Britain, girls expect freedom. The two cultures have different dress codes. Family honour and respect are religious duties in Islam. Religious duty is not a major guiding force in the lives of most British teenagers. Daily prayer is not a habit in British culture – it is essential in Islam. Muslim teenagers could find many conflicts between the culture of their family and the culture of their British peers.

(c) Islamic schools would be a complement to the denominational Roman Catholic and Jewish schools which already exist. They would be advantageous in that they would enable Muslims to teach children in an ethos which they wished to create, an ethos which emphasised the values they teach. They would enable Muslim children to learn together, to meet each other and to be in a familiar environment.
   The disadvantage could be that Muslim children would be more isolated from the community as a whole and they might find it difficult to integrate. There may be a problem in providing a truly balanced education.

6 (a) The Muslim calendar begins with Hijrah because this was the year Mohammed left Mecca to found the first Muslim community in Medina.
(b) After the Hijrah, Mohammed lived in Medina as a leader teaching the community. The community was attacked by superior Makkan forces but Mohammed's armies triumphed. He returned to conquer Mecca in 8 AH (after Hihrah) which was 630 CE. He remained there teaching until his death, making it the capital of Islam.
(c) In Medina Mohammed showed the importance of community 'Ummah'. In Islam the community is more important than the individual. Mohammed was able to prepare his followers for the time when they would return to Mecca and the Ka'bah would be claimed for Islam. He taught his followers in Medina to pray in the direction of Mecca.
(d) The years Mohammed lived in Mecca were important for the Muslim faith because this was to become the focal point of Islam and contains the Ka'bah where Muslims make pilgrimage. The years in Medina were important to show the strength of the faith and the building of community. The two things together are equally important.

Short answers

1 (a) Allah.
  (b) Mecca (Now Saudi Arabia).
  (c) Quraish.
  (d) Khadijah.
  (e) Mohammed's birthday.
  (f) Submission to God.
  (g) To show the direction of Mecca for praying.
  (h) To call the faithful to prayer.
  (i) A man regarded as a good Muslim who acts as a leader in the community.
  (j) The sayings of the Prophet Mohammed.
  (k) Shahadah; Salah: Zakah; Saum; Hajj.
      Belief; Prayer; Giving; Fasting; Pilgrimage.

163

4 Answers to general application questions

1. (a) This is a Roman Catholic Church. By the main door is a stoop filled with Holy water. A believer blesses himself with the sign of the cross after dipping his fingers in the stoop. It is a modern church. In the entrance there are notices of parish events and Mass times. To the rear on the left is a small chapel containing a statue of Our Lady, an altar for offering Mass to small groups and the tabernacle containing the Blessed Sacrament. There is also a sanctuary lamp which is lit to indicate the presence of Jesus. There are four blocks of seating arranged in wedges, all facing the main altar which is a plain table. On the sanctuary are two lecterns, one at each side for readings from Scriptures and the Gospels. Behind the altar is a huge stained glass window bearing a representation of Jesus on the Cross. To the right of the altar is an alcove containing an organ. Towards the rear of the church on the right is a small niche containing a statue of the Sacred Heart and beyond this the entrance to the sacristy where the priest prepares for Mass. The sacristy can also be used as a small meeting room and for socialising after Sunday Mass. The Walls have plain wooden carvings showing the fourteen stations of the cross. There are a few small pedestal stands with arrangements of flowers.
(Just describe a church you know in your own words or picture one you have learnt about.)

    (b) In the Roman Catholic Church a special feature might be a special area for Confession or Penance. It can be a small room divided into two where the priest and penitent sit during the Sacrament of reconciliation. This sacrament is important as it allows Catholics to repent of sin and gain absolution, thus feeling that their relationship with God is free and clear and they have the strength of Jesus to help them try to avoid sinful behaviour.
    In the Church of England the altar table is a special feature as Eucharistic celebrations, called The Lord's Supper, are special ways of remembering the sacrifice Jesus made for all. In sharing in the sacrificial meal all Christians are called to be part of Christ's sacrifice. In some churches this special service might only occur rarely, perhaps once a month.

    (c) A visitor learns different things from a tour than from attending worship. A visitor can learn about features and rituals from a tour. From attending worship he or she can learn about prayers, hymns and the conduct of worship. Visitors of another faith will only learn a certain amount as people perceive things depending on their own perspectives. Participating in a service of one faith is only possible for a believer, otherwise a person can only be an observer.

2. (a) Major life events are marked with a religious ceremony for believers because Life is a gift from God who guides and holds every person. Initiation marks a major turning point and God is there at the difficult times. A sacrament recognises the presence of God. In the Roman Catholic tradition, Grace is conferred by Sacrament and this fills the person with the Spirit and helps him or her on the next stage of the journey.

    (b) The Roman Catholic faith has a very ritualised initiation rite in baptism. The candidate is presented by godparents or sponsors who ask for baptism. The priest makes the sign of the cross on the head to demonstrate reception into the Christian tradition. The sponsors are called to renew their own baptismal promises, rejecting Satan and professing faith in God the Father, Son and Spirit. The person's chest is anointed with oil of chrism. The candidate is baptised with water as a sign of death to sin and a new life in Jesus – the priest baptises by name in the name of the Father, Son and Spirit. A candle is lit as a sign of the life of Christ and the 'baby' is wrapped in a white garment as a sign of innocence.

    (c) Receiving such a number is a rite of passage and the public acknowledgement of adulthood or the right to work is important. The difference is that a sacrament confers Grace whereas the card only indicates that you have a place in society as a potential worker.

5 Answer structure for Standard Grade

General points about Easter
1 Resurrection is the Easter celebration.
2 Christ's Resurrection assured eternal life for mankind.
3 Easter is a time when Christians consider major themes of:
hope; new life; forgiveness; repentance; eternal life; Christ's sacrifice; the institution of the Eucharist; the re-enactment of Easter at every eucharistic celebration; the reality of a risen Christ; the possibility of physical versus symbolic Resurrection.

2 Islam Prayer
Key points on Islamic prayer are answered fully in a previous question (Islam) question 4.

3 General points about euthanasia.
Active euthanasia means actively administering death by lethal dose or other means.
Passive euthanasia means withholding treatment, not resuscitating – basically allowing death.
Pro-euthanasia groups believe people have a right to die with dignity when they choose: to be released from pain and indignity.
Opposers of euthanasia see life as a precious gift from God which must be preserved as long as humanly possible. Many religious people see euthanasia as the unlawful taking of life. Murder is against all the commandments. It is a Christian duty to care for the sick, not to kill them. On a practical level objectors may argue that sick people cannot be expected to be rational about such a subject.

Glossary

Christian glossary

Advent Coming. The period beginning on the fourth Sunday before Christmas (40 days before Christmas in the Eastern Orthodox tradition). A time of spiritual preparation for Christmas.
Apostle One who was sent out by Jesus Christ to preach the Gospel.
Ascension The event, 40 days after the Resurrection, when Jesus 'ascended into heaven' (see Luke 24 and Acts 1).
Ash Wednesday The first day of Lent. In some Churches, penitents receive the sign of the cross in ashes on their foreheads.

Baptism Rite of initiation involving immersion in, or sprinkling or pouring of, water.
Baptist (i) A member of the Baptist Church, which grew out of the Anabaptist movement during the 16th century Reformation. (ii) A Christian who practises Believer's Baptism.
Believer's Baptism The baptism of people who are old enough to understand the meaning of the rite.
Blessed Sacrament Bread and wine which have been consecrated and set aside for future use (usually in the Roman Catholic Church).

Catholic (i) Universal. (ii) Often used as an abbreviation for Roman Catholic.
Charismatic A modern movement within the Church, emphasising spiritual gifts, such as healing or speaking with tongues.
Christ The anointed one. Messiah is used in the Jewish tradition to refer to the expected leader sent by God, who will bring salvation to God's people. Jesus' followers applied this title to Him, and its Greek equivalent, Christ, is the source of the words Christian and Christianity.
Christmas Festival commemorating the birth of Jesus Christ (25 December, in most Churches).
Church (i) The whole community of Christians. (ii) The building in which Christians worship. (iii) A particular denomination.
Confession Contrition; penance. (i) One of seven sacraments observed by some Churches whose priest confidentially hears a person's confession. (ii) An admission, by a Christian, of wrong-doing. (iii) A particular official statement (or profession) of faith.
Congregationalist Member of a Christian body which believes that each local church is independent and self-governing under the authority of Christ.
Creed Summary statement of religious beliefs, often recited in worship, especially the Apostles' and Nicene Creeds.
Crucifixion Roman method of executing criminals and traitors by fastening them to a cross until they died of asphyxiation; used in the case of Jesus Christ and many who opposed the Romans.

Easter Central Christian festival which celebrates the Resurrection of Jesus Christ from the dead.
Ecumenism Movement within the Church towards co-operation and eventual unity.
Episcopacy System of Church government by bishops.
Epistle From the Greek word for letter. Several such letters or epistles, from Christian leaders to Christian Churches or individuals, are included in the New Testament.
Eucharist Thanksgiving. A service celebrating the sacrificial death and Resurrection of Jesus Christ, using elements of bread and wine (see Holy Communion).

Evangelical Group, or church, placing particular emphasis on the Gospel and the Scriptures as the sole authority in all matters of faith and conduct.
Evangelist A writer of one of the four New Testament Gospels; a preacher of the Gospel.

Font Receptacle to hold water used in baptism.
Free Churches Nonconformist denominations, free from state control (used of 20 Churches).

Good Friday The Friday in Holy Week. Commemorates the day Jesus died on the cross.
Gospel (i) Good news (of salvation in Jesus Christ). (ii) An account of Jesus' life and work.
Grace (i) The freely given and unmerited favour of God's love for humanity. (ii) Blessing. (iii) Prayer of thanks before or after meals.

Heaven The place, or state, in which souls will be united with God after death.
Hell The place, or state, in which souls will be separated from God after death.
Holy Communion Central liturgical service observed by most Churches (see Eucharist, Mass, Lord's Supper, Liturgy). Recalls the last meal of Jesus, and celebrates his sacrificial and saving death.
Holy Spirit The third person of the Holy Trinity. Active as divine presence and power in the world, and in dwelling in believers to make them like Christ and empower them to do God's will.
Holy Week The week before Easter, when Christians recall the last week of Jesus' life on Earth.

Icon/Ikon Painting or mosaic of Jesus Christ, the Virgin Mary, a saint, or a Church feast. Used as an aid to devotion, usually in the Orthodox tradition.
Iconostasis Screen, covered with icons, used in Eastern Orthodox churches to separate the sanctuary from the nave.
Incarnation The doctrine that God took human form in Jesus Christ. It is also the belief that God in Christ is active in the Church and in the world.

Jesus Christ The central figure of Christian history and devotion. The second person of the Trinity.

Lectern Stand supporting the Bible, often in the shape of an eagle.
Lent Penitential season. The 40 days leading up to Easter.
Liturgy (i) Service of worship according to a prescribed ritual such as Evensong or Eucharist. (ii) Term used in the Orthodox Church for the Eucharist.
Lord Title used for Jesus to express his divine lordship over people, time and space.
Lord's Supper Alternative term for Eucharist in some Churches (predominantly nonconformist).
Lutheran A major Protestant Church that receives its name from the 16th century German reformer, Martin Luther.

Mass Term for the Eucharist, used by the Roman Catholic and other Churches.
Maundy Thursday The Thursday in Holy Week. Commemorates the Last Supper.
Methodist A Christian who belongs to the Methodist Church which came into existence through the work of John Wesley in the 18th century.
Missal Book containing words and ceremonial directions for saying Mass.

New Testament Collection of 27 books forming the second section of the Canon of Christian Scriptures.
Nonconformist Protestant Christian bodies which became separated from the established Church of England in the 17th century.

Old Testament That part of the Canon of Christian Scriptures which the Church shares with Judaism, comprising 39 books covering the Hebrew Canon, and in the case of certain denominations, some books of the Apocrypha.
Ordination In episcopal Churches, the 'laying on of hands' on priests and deacons by a bishop. In non-episcopal Churches, the 'laying on of hands' on ministers by other representatives of the Church.
Orthodox (i) The Eastern Orthodox Church consisting of national Churches (mainly Greek or Slav), including the ancient Eastern Patriarchates. They hold the common

Glossary

Orthodox faith, and are in communion with the Patriarchate of Constantinople. (ii) Conforming to the creeds sanctioned by the ecumenical councils, e.g. Nicaea, Chalcedon.

Palm Sunday The Sunday before Easter, commemorating the entry of Jesus into Jerusalem when he was acknowledged by crowds waving palm branches.

Passion The sufferings of Jesus Christ, especially in the time leading up to his crucifixion.

Patriarch Title for principal Eastern Orthodox bishops. Also used for early Israelite leaders such as Abraham, Isaac, Jacob.

Pentecost The Greek name for the Jewish Festival of Weeks, or Shavuot, which comes seven weeks ('fifty days') after Passover. On the day of this feast, the followers of Jesus received the gift of the Holy Spirit.

Pentecostalist A Christian who belongs to a Church that emphasises certain gifts which were granted to the first believers on the Day of Pentecost (such as the power to heal the sick and speak in tongues).

Pope The Bishop of Rome, head of the Roman Catholic Church.

Presbyterian A member of a Church that is governed by elders or 'presbyters'; the national Church of Scotland.

Protestant That part of the Church which became distinct from the Roman Catholic and Orthodox Churches when their members professed (or 'protested' – hence Protestant) the centrality of the Bible and other beliefs. Members affirm that the Bible, under the guidance of the Holy Spirit, is the ultimate authority for Christian teaching.

Pulpit An elevated platform from which sermons are preached.

Purgatory In some traditions, a condition or state in which good souls receive spiritual cleansing after death, in preparation for heaven.

Quaker A member of the Religious Society of Friends, established through the work of George Fox in the 17th century.

Reconciliation (i) Sacrament of the (Roman) Catholic Church, consisting of Contrition, Confession of sins, and Absolution. (ii) The human process of reconciling Christians with one another.

Redemption Derived from the practice of paying the price of a slave's freedom; and so, the work of Jesus Christ in setting people free through His death.

Reformation A 16th century reform movement that led to the formation of Protestant Churches. It emphasised the need to recover the initial beliefs and practices of the Church.

Resurrection (i) The rising from the dead of Jesus Christ on the third day after the crucifixion. (ii) The rising from the dead of believers at the Last Day. (iii) The new, or risen, life of Christians.

Roman Catholic That part of the Church owing loyalty to the Bishop of Rome, as distinct from Orthodox and Protestant Churches.

Sacrament An outward sign of an inward blessing, as in baptism or the Eucharist.

Salvationist A member of the Salvation Army founded by William and Catherine Booth in the 19th century.

Sanctification The process by which a believer is made holy, to become like Jesus Christ.

Sin (i) Act of rebellion or disobedience against the known will of God. (ii) An assessment of the human condition as disordered and in need of transformation.

Synoptic Having a common viewpoint. It is applied to the presentation of Jesus' life in the first three gospels of Matthew, Mark and Luke in contrast with that given in the Gospel of John.

Tabernacle (i) A receptacle for the Blessed Sacrament, not immediately consumed but set aside or 'reserved' (mainly in Roman Catholic and Eastern Orthodox Churches). The presence of the consecrated elements is usually signalled by a continuously burning light. (ii) Term used by some denominations of their building.

Transubstantiation Roman Catholic doctrine concerning the Mass, defined at the Lateran Council of 1215, and confirmed at the Council of Trent in 1551. This states that in the Eucharist, at the words of consecration, the substance of the bread and wine becomes the substance of the Body and Blood of Jesus Christ, and that He is thus present on the altar.

Trinity Three persons in one God; doctrine of the three-fold nature of God – Father, Son and Holy Spirit.

United Reformed Church A Church formed by the union of English Congregationalists with the Presbyterian Church of England, and subsequently the Reformed Association of the Churches of Christ.

Vatican The residence of the Pope in Rome, and the administrative centre of the Roman Catholic Church. The chief building of the Vatican is St Peter's Basilica, built on the traditional site of St Peter's tomb.

Virgin Birth The doctrine of the miraculous conception of Jesus Christ by the Virgin Mary through the power of the Holy Spirit and without the agency of a human father.

Witness Living a life that is apparently inspired by Christian teaching. Christian witness is living out Christ's teaching.

Judaism glossary

Agadah Telling. Rabbinical teachings on moral values.
Aleinu Key prayer at the conclusion of each service.
Aliyah To go up. (i) Being called to read the Sefer Torah in the synagogue. (ii) The migration of Jews to Israel.
Amidah Standing. The standing prayer.
Aron Hakodesh Holy Ark. The focal point of the synagogue, containing Torah scrolls.
Ashkenazim Jews of Central and Eastern European origin.

Bar Mitzvah Son of Commandment. A boy's coming of age at 13 years old, usually marked by a synagogue ceremony and family celebration.
Bat Mitzvah Daughter of Commandment. As above, but for girls from 12 years old. May be marked differently between communities.
Bet din Court. There are three levels, the usual level having three judges.
Bet ha Knesset House of Assembly. Synagogue.
Brit Milah Circumcision.

Cantor Leader of reading, singing and chanting in the services of some synagogues.
Challah Enriched bread used particularly on Shabbat and during festivals.
Circumcision Religious rite of Brit Milah, performed by a qualified mohel on all Jewish boys, usually on the eighth day after birth.

Gemara Commentary on the Mishnah included in the Talmud.

Hanukkah Dedication. An eight-day festival of lights to celebrate the re-dedication of the temple following the Maccabean victory over the Greeks.
Hasidism A religious and social movement formed by Israel Baal Shem Tov (from the 18th century onwards).
Havdalah Distinction. Ceremony marking the conclusion of Shabbat.
Hebrew Ancient Semitic language; language of the Tenakh (Hebrew Scriptures) and used by Jews for prayer and study. Also, everyday language in Israel.
Huppah Canopy used for a wedding ceremony, under which the bride and groom stand.

Israel One who struggles with God. The phrase refers to the worldwide Jewish community; the land of Israel and the modern state of Israel.

Kaddish Prayer publicly recited by mourners.
Kashrut Laws relating to keeping a kosher home and lifestyle.
Kehilla Faith community.
Ketubah Document that defines rights and obligations within Jewish marriage.
Ketuvim Writings. Third section of the Tenakh.
Kibbutz Israeli collective village based on socialist principles.

Glossary

Kiddush Holy. A prayer sanctifying Shabbat and festival days, usually recited over wine.
Kidushin Marriage.
Kippah (Capel) Head covering worn during prayers, Torah study, etc. Some followers wear it constantly.
Knesset Assembly. Israeli parliament.
Kosher Fit; proper. Foods permitted by Jewish dietary laws.

Mahr Dowry.
Maimonides Rabbi Moses ben Maimon (1135–1204), a leading Jewish philosopher, medical writer and codifier of Jewish law.
Matzah A flat cracker-like bread which has been baked before it rises; used at Pesach.
Menorah Seven-branched candelabrum which was lit daily in the Temple.
Mezuzah A scroll placed on doorposts of Jewish homes, containing a section from the Torah and often enclosed in a decorative case.
Midrash Collections of various Rabbinic commentaries on the Tenakh.
Minyan Quorum of ten men, over Bar Mitzvah age, required for a service. Progressive communities may include women but do not always require a minyan.
Mishnah First writing down of the Oral Tradition. An authoritative document forming part of the Talmud, codified about 200 CE.
Mitzvah Commandment. The Torah contains 613 Mitzvot. Commonly used to describe good deeds.
Mohel Person trained to perform Brit Milah.

Ner Tamid Eternal light. The perpetual light above the Aron Hakodesh.
Nevi'im Prophets. Second section of the Tenakh.
Noahide Laws Seven laws given to Noah after the flood, which are incumbent on all humankind. These laws form the foundation for a just society.

Pesach Festival commemorating the Exodus from Egypt. One of the three biblical pilgrim festivals. Pesach is celebrated in the spring.
Pikei Avot Sayings of the Fathers. Part of the Mishnah containing ethics of Rabbinical sages.
Pogrom Organised attack on Jews, especially frequent in 19th and early 20th century Eastern Europe.
Purim Festival commemorating the rescue of Persian Jewry as told in the book of Esther.

Rabbi My teacher. An ordained Jewish teacher. Often the religious leader of a Jewish community.
Rosh Hashanah Head of the Year. Jewish New Year.

Seder Order. A home-based ceremonial meal during Pesach, at which the Exodus from Egypt is recounted using the Hagadah.
Sefer Torah Torah scroll. The five books of Moses handwritten on parchment and rolled to form a scroll.
Shabbat Day of spiritual renewal and rest commencing at sunset on Friday, terminating at nightfall on Saturday.
Shavuot Weeks. One of three pilgrim festivals. Shavuot is celebrated in the summer, seven weeks after Pesach.
Shema Major Jewish prayer affirming belief in one God. The Shema is found in the Torah.
Shiva Seven days of intense mourning following the burial of a close relation. During this period, all ordinary work is prohibited.
Shofar Ram's horn blown at the season of Rosh Hashanah.
Siddur Order. Daily prayer book.
Simchat Torah Rejoicing of the law. Festival celebrating the completion and recommencement of the cycle of the weekly Torah reading.
Sukkot One of three biblical pilgrim festivals, Sukkot (the Feast of Tabernacles) is celebrated in the Autumn.
Synagogue Building for Jewish public prayer, study and assembly.

Tallit Prayer shawl. Four-cornered garment with fringes.
Talmud Mishnah and Gemara, collected together.
Tefillin Small leather boxes containing passages from the Torah, strapped on the forehead and arm for morning prayers on weekdays.

Tenakh The collected 24 books of the Jewish Bible, comprising three sections: Torah, Nevi'im, and Ketuvim (Te;Na;Kh).

Torah Law; teaching. The Five Books of Moses.

Tzedaka (Zedakah) Righteousness. An act of charity.

Yom Kippur Day of Atonement. Fast day occurring on the tenth day after Rosh Hasshanah; a solemn day of Tefillah and Teshuva.

Zionism Political movement securing the Jewish return to the land of Israel.

Islam glossary

Abu Bakr The first Khalifah (Caliph), successor to the leadership of the Muslim community after the death of the Prophet Mohammed.

Adhan Call to prayer. From the same root, Mu'adhin (one who makes the call to prayer).

Akhirah Everlasting life after death – the hereafter.

al-Fatihah The Opener. Surah 1 of the Qur'an. Recited at least 17 times daily during the five times of Salah. Also known as 'The Essence' of the Qur'an.

Ali-al-Murtada The fourth Khaliffa (Caliph).

al-Madinah Madinatu'n-Nabi (The City of the Prophet). The name given to Yathrib after the Prophet Mohammed migrated there in 622 CE and founded the first Islamic state.

Ali Cousin and son-in-law of the Prophet Mohammed; husband of Fatimah Zahrah; father of Hassan, Hussein, and Zainab; the fourth of 'al-Khulafa ur-Rashidun' according to Sunnis, and the first successor accepted by Shi'ah Islam (Radhi-Allahu-anhum).

Allah The Islamic name for God in the Arabic language. Used in preference to the word God, this Arabic term is singular, has no plural, nor is it associated with masculine, feminine or neuter characteristics.

Angels Beings created by Allah from light. They have no free will and are completely obedient to Allah.

Arafat A plain, a few kilometres from Makkah, where pilgrims gather to worship, pray and ask for forgiveness. This takes place on the ninth day of the Islamic month of Dhul-Hijjah, the day before Id-ul-Adha.

Bilal The first Mu'adhin of Islam (see Adhan), a companion of Prophet Mohammed, formerly an Abyssinian slave (Radhi-Allahu-anhu).

Din Way of life, religion together with its practices.

Du'a Varying forms of personal prayer and supplication.

Fajr (Salat-ul-Fajr) Dawn salah which may be performed from dawn until just before sunrise.

Fard Obligatory duty according to divine law, e.g. offering salah five times a day.

Fatihah See al-Fatihah.

Fiqh Understanding. Islamic jurisprudence.

Hadith Saying; report; account. The sayings of the Prophet Mohammed, as recounted by his household, progeny and companions. These are a major source of Islamic law. Some Hadith are referred to as Hadith Qudsi (sacred Hadith) having been divinely communicated to the Prophet Mohammed.

Hafiz Someone who knows the whole Qur'an by heart.

Hajj Annual pilgrimage to Makkah, which each Muslim must undertake at least once in a lifetime if he or she has the health and wealth. A Muslim male who has completed Hajj is called Hajji, and a female, Hajjah.

Halal Any action or thing which is permitted or lawful.

Haram Anything unlawful or not permitted.

Haram Sharif The grand mosque in Makkah, which encompasses the Ka'bah, the hills of Safa and Marwah and the well of Zamzam.

Glossary

Hijab Veil. Often used to describe the head scarf or modest dress worn by women, who are required to cover everything except face and hands in the sight of anyone other than immediate family.

Hijrah Departure; exit; emigration. The emigration of the Prophet Mohammed from Makkah to Madinah in 622 CE. The Islamic calendar commences from this event.

Hira The name of a place near Makkah, where the Prophet Mohammed went for solitude and worship. It was there that he received the first revelation of the Qur'an.

Iblis The Jinn who defied Allah by refusing to bow to Adam and later became the tempter of all human beings.

Ibrahim Abraham. A Prophet of Allah to whom the 'scrolls' were given.

Id-ul-Adha Celebration of the sacrifice, commemorating the Prophet Ibrahim's willingness to sacrifice his son Isma'il for Allah. Also known as Id-ul-Kabir – the Greater Id – and Qurban Bayram (Turkish) – feast of sacrifice.

Id-ul-Fitr Celebration of breaking the fast on the day after Ramadan ends, which is also the first day of Shawal, the tenth Islamic month. Also known as Id-ul-Saghir – the Lesser Id – and Sheker Bayram (Turkish) – sugar feast.

Ijma General consensus of scholars, expressed or tacit, on matters of law and practice.

Imam Leader. A person who leads the communal prayer, or a founder of an Islamic school of jurisprudence. In Shi'ah Islam, Imam is also the title of Ali (Radhi-Allahu-anhu) and his successors.

Injil Gospel. A book given to the Prophet Isa (Jesus).

Iqamah Call to stand up for salah.

Isa Jesus. A Prophet of Allah, born of the virgin Mary.

Isha (Salat-ul-Isha) Evening salah which may be performed from just over an hour after sunset, until midnight.

Islam Peace attained through willing obedience to Allah's divine guidance.

Isma'il Ishmael. A Prophet of Allah. Son of the Prophet Ibrahim and Hajar.

Jibril Gabriel. The angel who delivered Allah's messages to His Prophets.

Jihad Personal individual struggle against evil in the way of Allah. It can also be collective defence of the Muslim community.

Jinn Being created by Allah from fire.

Jumu'ah (Salat-ul-Jumu'ah) The weekly communal salah, and attendance at the khutbah performed shortly after midday on Fridays.

Ka'bah A cube-shaped structure in the centre of the grand mosque in Makkah. The first house built for the worship of the Allah.

Khalifah (Caliph) Successor; inheritor; custodian; vice-regent (see al-Khulafa-ur-Rashidun).

Khutbah Speech. Talk delivered on special occasions such as the Jum'uah and Id prayers.

Kutubullah Belief in the books of Allah.

Laylat-ul-Qadr The Night of Power, when the first revelation of the Qur'an was made to the Prophet Mohammed. It is believed to be one of the last ten nights of Ramadan.

Madinah See al-Madinah.

Maghrib (Salat-ul-Maghrib) Sunset salah which is performed after sunset until daylight ends.

Mahdi, al-Muntazar The (rightly) guided one who is awaited and will appear towards the end of time to lead the Ummah and restore justice on Earth. The one who is promised in the Judaic, Christian and Islamic traditions.

Makkah City where the Prophet Mohammed was born, and where the Ka'bah is located.

Mihrab Niche or alcove in a mosque wall, indicating the Qiblah – the direction of Makkah, towards which all Muslims face to perform salah.

Mina Place near Makkah, where pilgrims stay on the 10th, 11th and 12th of Dhul-Hijjah and perform some of the activities of the Hajj.

Mu'adhim Caller to prayer (see Adhan). Known in English as 'muezzin'.

Mohammed (Muhammad) Praised. Name of the final prophet.

Musa Moses. A Prophet of Allah to whom the Tawrah (Torah) was given.

Muslim One who claims to have accepted Islam by professing the Shahadah.

Muzdalifah Place where pilgrims on Hajj stop for a time during the night of the day they spend at Arafat.

Islam glossary

Niyyah Intention. A legally required statement of intent, made prior to all acts of devotion such as salah, Hajj or sawm.

Qadar Allah's complete and final control over the fulfilment of events or destiny.
Qatl Murder.
Qiblah Direction which Muslims face when performing salah – towards the Ka'bah (see Mihrab).
Qur'an That which is read or recited. The Divine Book revealed to the Prophet Mohammed. Allah's final revelation to humankind.

Rak'ah A unit of salah, made up of recitation, standing, bowing and two prostrations.
Ramadan The ninth month of the Islamic calendar, during which fasting is required from just before dawn until sunset, as ordered by Allah in the Qur'an.
Riba Usury. Lending money for profit.
Rusulullah Prophethood.

Sa'y Walking and hastening between Safa and Marwah, as part of the Hajj, in remembrance of Hajar's search for water for her son Isma'il.
Sadaqah Voluntary payment or good action for charitable purposes.
Safa & Marwah Two hills in Makkah, near the Ka'bah, now included within the grand mosque (see Sa'y).
Salah Prescribed communication with, and worship of, Allah, performed under specific conditions, in the manner taught by the Prophet Mohammed, and recited in the Arabic language. The five daily times of salah are fixed by Allah.
Sariqah Theft.
Sawm Fasting from just before dawn until sunset. Abstinence is required from all food and drink (including water) as well as smoking and conjugal relations.
Shahadah Declaration of faith, which consists of the statement, 'There is no god except Allah, Mohammed is the Messenger of Allah'.
Shari'ah Islamic law based upon the Qur'an and Sunnah.
Shawwal The tenth month.
Shi'ah Followers. Muslims who believe in the Imamah, successorship of Ali (Radhi-Allahu-anhu) after the Prophet Mohammed and 11 of his most pious, knowledgeable descendants.
Shirk Association. Regarding anything as being equal or partner to Allah. Shirk is forbidden in Islam.
Sunnah Model practices, customs and traditions of the Prophet Mohammed. This is found in both Hadith and Sirah.
Sunni Muslims who believe in the successorship of Abu Bakr, Umar, Uthman and Ali (Radhi-Allahu-anhum) after the Prophet Mohammed.
Surah Division of the Qur'an (114 in all).

Takbir Saying 'Allahu Akbar!' Recited during salah, Id and other celebratory occasions.
Tawaf Walking seven times around the Ka'bah in worship of Allah. Also, a part of Hajj and Umrah.
Tawhid Belief in the Oneness of Allah – absolute monotheism as practised in Islam.
Tawrah The Torah. The book given to the Prophet Musa (Moses).

Umar ibn ul-Khattab Second Khalifah (Caliph) of Islam.
Ummah Community. World-wide community of Muslims; the nation of Islam.
Uthman The third Khalifah (Caliph) of Islam.

Wudu Ablution before salah.

Zakah Purification of wealth by payment of annual welfare due. An obligatory act of worship.
Zakat-ul-Fitr Welfare payment at the end of Ramadan.
Zamzam Name of the well adjacent to the Ka'bah in Makkah. The water first sprang in answer to Hajar's search and prayers (see Hajar and Sa'y).
Zuhr (Salat-ul-Zuhr) Salah, which can be performed after midday until afternoon.

Index

Abraham 105
Advent 32
ageism 73
Akhirah 122
Anglican church, places of worship 35
annunciation 47
apartheid system 71
Apostles' Creed 15
artefacts 136–40
Ascension 31
Ash Wednesday 31

Beatitudes 55
Bible, Christian source 18–19
birth control, Christian 61
Brandt report 88

caliphs 133–4
capital punishment, Christian 84–5
causes of poverty 88
charismatic movement, organisation 23–4
childlessness, Christian 66
Christian beliefs 15–17
Christian organisation 21–5
   charismatic movement 23
   ecumenism 23
   nature of church 24
   Orthodox church 21–2
   Protestant churches 22–3
   Roman Catholicism 21
Christian practices 26–36
   festivals and feasts 30–2
   pilgrimage 32–3
   places of worship 33–5
   rites of passage 28–30
   sacraments 28–30
   sick people 67
   worship 26–8
Christianity
   artefacts 136–8
   authority, sources of 18–20
   beliefs 15–17
   birth control 61
   childlessness 66
   church authority 98
   church and community 99
   church and state 97–8
   conflict, resolution of 78
   contemplative life 94
   corporal and capital punishment 84–5
   crime, reasons for 83
   criminals, control of 84
   dangers to planet 89–90
   decision-making 98
   employment responsibilities 94
   environmental stewardship 89–90
   family 61
   forgiveness 84, 85
   holy war 78
   individual conscience 98
   just war 78
   law and order 83–5
   leisure 93
   liberation theology 99
   lifestyle, diversity 61
   marriage 60
   medical ethics 66
   non-violent protest 79
   nuclear war 80
   organisation 21–5
   pacifism 79
   peace and conflict 77–81
   persecution 77–8
   poverty 89–90
   practices 26–36
   professions 94
   relationship with state 97–9
   relationships 59–61
   relationships between sexes 59
   religion and society 97
   religious law and state law 83
   responses to world poverty 89–90
   right to work 93
   social issues 66–8
   unemployment 94
   violent protest 80
   vocation and career 93
   war, cost of 80
   war and persecution, reasons 77
   work, concept of 93
   work and leisure 93–4
church authority, Christian 98
class prejudice 72
Communion 29
Communion of Saints 17
community, Christianity 99
confirmation 30
conflict 78
   see also peace and conflict
contemplative life, Christian 94
contemporary issues, recommended passages 103–4
corporal punishment, Christian 84–5
crime, Christian reasons for 83
criminals, Christian control of 84
cultures, Judaism 113–14

dangers to the planet 89–90
death
   Islamic 69
   Jewish 68
decision-making, Christianity 98

Index

disability prejudice 73
discipleship, Luke's Gospel 51
discrimination 73–5

ecumenism, organisation 23
employment, Christian responsibilities 94
environment 88–92
    Christian stewardship 89–90
    Islam 91
    Judaism 90–1
    man as vice-regent 91
    Zakah 91
    Zedakah 90–1
Epiphany 32
Exodus 105–6

family 61, 63, 64
feast days *see* festivals
festivals
    Advent 32
    Ascension 31
    Ash Wednesday 31
    Christian 30–2
    Epiphany 32
    Harvest 32
    Holy week 31
    Islamic 130
    Judaism 115–16
    Pentecost 32
    Shrove Tuesday 31
five pillars, Islamic practice 127–30
forgiveness 84, 85
Free church, worship 28
funeral rites 30

gender prejudice 71
Gospels 37–58
    Luke's Gospel 47–53
    Mark's Gospel 39–46
    Matthew's Gospel 53–5
    miracles of Jesus 56–7
    person of Jesus 37–8

Hadith, Qur'an 123–4
Harvest Festival 32
Holy Orders 30
holy war 78
Holy week 31
human rights 80
humanitarian work, Judaism 100

individual conscience, Christian 98
inequality, reasons for 88
infancy narrative 47, 53
Islam
    artefacts 140–2
    authority, sources of 123–6
    beliefs 121–2
    environment 91
    family 64
    infertility 69
    law and order

    marital breakdown 63–4
    medical ethics 68–9
    old age and death 69
    organisation 133–5
    peace and conflict 81–2
    poverty 91
    practices 127–32
    prophet Mohammed 124–5
    Qur'an 123–4
    relationship with state 100–1
    relationships between sexes 63
    sick people, treatment of 69
    social issues 68–9
    work and leisure 95
Islamic beliefs 121–2
Islamic organisation 133–5
Islamic practices 127–32
    festivals 130
    five pillars 127–30
    rites of passage 131

Jacob called Israel 105
Jesus
    arrest and death 45–6, 52
    commandments of 16
    incarnation of 16
    miracles 39–41, 48–9, 53, 56–7
    parables 41–3, 49–50, 53–4
    person of 37–8
    resurrection of 16–17
        Luke's Gospel 52–3
        Mark's Gospel 46
        Matthew's Gospel 54
    in temple 48
    temptations of
        Luke's Gospel 48
        Matthew's Gospel 53
    trial of, 45–6, 52
Jewish beliefs 105–7
John the Baptist 47, 48
Judaism 108–12
    artefacts 138–40
    authority, sources of 110–11
    beliefs 105–7
    cultures 113–14
    environment 90–1
    family 63
    festivals 115–16
    humanitarian work 100
    kashrut 117–18
    Ketubim 109
    law and order 85
    Maimonides 110
    marital breakdown 62
    marriage 62–3
    medical ethics 68
    Midrash 110
    Mishnah 109–10
    Nevi'im 109
    Noahide code 108–9
    old age and death 68
    peace and conflict 81

Index

pilgrimage 117
poverty 90–1
practice and organisation 113–20
relationship with state 100
relationships 61–3
rites of passage 117
sick people, treatment of 68
social issues 68
suffering 68
synagogue in community 100
synagogues 118
Talmud 109
Tenakh 108
Torah 108
traditions 113
work and leisure 95
worship 114–15

kashrut 117–18
Ketubim 109
Koran *see* Qur'an

law and order 83–7
   Christianity 83–5
   Islam 85–6
   Judaism 85
   religious law 83
   state law 83
leisure 93, 95
   see also work and leisure
liberation theology, Christianity 99
lifestyle, diversity 61
Lord's supper 45, 52
Luke's Gospel 47–53
   annunciation 47
   arrest, trial and death of Jesus 52
   birth of John the Baptist 47
   discipleship 51
   episodes of conflict 51
   infancy narrative 47
   Jesus in temple 48
   John the Baptist 48
   Lord's supper 52
   miracles 48
   nativity 47–8
   parables 49–50
   Passover meal 51
   presentation 48
   resurrection of Jesus 52–3
   shepherds 48
   stewardship 51
   temptations of Jesus 48
   visitation 47

Maimonides 110
marital breakdown 60, 62, 63–4
Mark's Gospel 39–46
   arrest, trial and death of Jesus 45–6
   discipleship 43–5
   episodes of conflict 43
   Lord's supper 45
   miracles 39–41

   parables 41–3
   Passover meal 45
   resurrection of Jesus 46
marriage 30
   Christian 60
   Jewish 62
martyrdom 79
Matthew's Gospel 53–5
   authority 54
   Beatitudes 55
   beliefs 54
   community 55
   infancy narrative 53
   justice 55
   lifestyle and social practices 55
   miracles 53
   morality 55
   parables 53–4
   resurrection of Jesus 54
   temptations of Jesus 53
   worship 54
Mecca, conquest of 125
medical ethics
   Christian 66
   Islamic 68–9
   Jewish 68
Messianic Age 106–7
miracles
   Gospels 56–7
   Luke's Gospel 48–9
   Mark's Gospel 39–41
   Matthew's Gospel 53
Mishnah 109–10
Mohammed *see* prophet Mohammed

nativity 47
Nevi'im 109
Nicene Creed 15
Noahide code 108–9
Nonconformist church 35
nuclear war 80

old age
   Islamic 69
   Jewish
Orthodox church
   organisation 21–2
   places of worship 33
   worship 26

pacifism 79
parables
   Luke' Gospel 49–50
   Mark's Gospel 41–3
   Matthew's Gospel 53–4
Passover meal
   Luke's Gospel 51
   Mark's Gospel 45
peace, Christian views of 81
peace and conflict 77–82
   Christianity 77–81
   Islam 81–2

Index

Judaism 81
Pentecost 32
persecution 77–8
pilgrimage
    Christian 32–3
    Jewish 117
places of worship
    Christian 33, 34, 35
    Islam 127–9
    Judaism 118
poverty 88–92
    causes of 88–9
    Christian responses to 89–90
    Islam 91
    Judaism 90–1
    Zakah 91
    Zedakah 90–1
prejudice 70–3
prejudice and discrimination 70–6
professions, Christian 94
prophet Mohammed 124–5
    conquest of Mecca 125
protest
    non-violent 79
    violent 80
Protestant churches
    organisation 22–3
    worship 26–7

Qur'an 123–4
    Hadith 123–4
    Surah 123

racial prejudice 71
reconciliation 29, 84
relationships 59–65
    between sexes 59, 63
    Christian 59–61
    Islamic 63–4
    Jewish 61–3
religion, relationship with state 97–104
    Christian 97–9
    Islam 100–1
    Judaism 100
religious law, Christian 83
religious prejudice 72–3
resurrection of Jesus 16, 54
    Luke's Gospel 52–3
    Mark's Gospel 45
rites of passage
    Christian 28–30
    Islamic 131
    Judaism 117
Roman Catholicism
    organisation 21
    places of worship 34
    worship 26–7
Rusulullah 121–2

sacraments 28–30
    baptism 28–9
    Communion 29

confession 29
confirmation 30
funeral rites 30
Holy Orders 30
marriage 30
penance 29
reconciliation 29
sick people 30
Shari'ah 134
shepherds 48
Shrove Tuesday 31
sick people
    Christian treatment 67
    Islamic treatment 69
    Jewish treatment 68
    sacraments 30
social issues 66–9
sources of authority
    Bible 18–19
    Christian 18–20
    Islam 123–6
    Jewish 110–11
    personal experience 19
state, relationship with religion 97–104
state law 83
Surah, Qur'an 123
synagogues 100, 118

Talmud 109
Tawhid 121
temptations *see* Jesus, temptations of
Tenakh 108
third world poverty 88
Torah 105, 108
traditions, Judaism 113
Trinity 16

unemployment, Christianity 94–4

vocation and career, Christian 93–4

war 77, 78, 80
    see also peace and conflict
women, gender prejudice 71
work, concept of 93
work and leisure 93–6
    Christianity 93–4
    Islam 95
    Judaism 95
worship
    Catholic tradition 26–7
    Free church tradition 28
    Islam 127–30
    Judaism 114–15
    Matthew's Gospel 54
    Orthodox tradition 26
    places of 33–5
    Protestant tradition 27–8

Zakah, poverty and environment 91
Zedakah, poverty and environment 90–1